AF600354

THE CUSTODY OF THE HOLY EUCHARIST

A Historical Synopsis and Commentary

THE CATHOLIC UNIVERSITY OF AMERICA
CANON LAW STUDIES
No. 292

The Custody of the Holy Eucharist

A Historical Synopsis and Commentary

A DISSERTATION

SUBMITTED TO THE FACULTY OF THE SCHOOL OF CANON LAW
OF THE CATHOLIC UNIVERSITY OF AMERICA IN PARTIAL
FULFILLMENT OF THE REQUIREMENTS FOR THE DEGREE
OF DOCTOR OF CANON LAW

BY

REV. DANIEL RAYMOND CAHILL, A.B., J.C.L.
PRIEST OF THE ARCHDIOCESE OF SAN FRANCISCO

THE CATHOLIC UNIVERSITY OF AMERICA PRESS
WASHINGTON, D. C.
1950

NIHIL OBSTAT:

Clement V. Bastnagel, J.U.D.
Censor Deputatus
Washingtonii, D. C., die 19 augusti, 1949.

IMPRIMATUR:

✠ John Joseph Mitty
Archiepiscopus Sancti Francisci
Sancti Francisci, die 29 augusti, 1949.

Murray & Heister
Washington, D. C.

Printed by
Times and News Publishing Co.
Gettysburg, Pa., U. S. A.

TO MY MOTHER
AND
IN MEMORY OF
MY FATHER

TABLE OF CONTENTS

PART ONE

HISTORICAL SYNOPSIS

TABLE OF CONTENTS (Continued)

PART TWO

CANONICAL COMMENTARY

TABLE OF CONTENTS (Continued)

TABLE OF CONTENTS (Continued)

TABLE OF CONTENTS (Continued)

TABLE OF CONTENTS (Continued)

TABLE OF CONTENTS (Continued)

FOREWORD

The title of this dissertation is: "The Custody of the Holy Eucharist." The word "custody" will in the following pages be limited to the meaning of "guardianship" or "protection." Thus such topics as the ornamentation of the tabernacle, the places where the Blessed Sacrament can be reserved, or other cognate concepts shall not be of primary relevance. In fact, these topics will be ignored in the historical synopsis, and will be treated mainly for the sole purpose of background in the canonical commentary. Furthermore, there will be a limitation of treatment in respect to the Holy Eucharist itself. Only those questions which pertain to the Holy Eucharist under the aspect of Its reservation will be treated. Thus such topics as the care of the Sacred Host during the time of Mass, the rules in regard to the "Forty Hours Devotion," or other related subjects, will not be treated. Finally, in view of the fact that a later dissertation prepares to deal with the penalties for negligence and abuse of the Blessed Sacrament, this dissertation will treat of penalties only in passing.

In the organization of Part One, the historical synopsis, the first chapter follows a chronological order, and the second a topical order. The sparsity of legislation on all points before the Council of Trent, and the abundance of legislation on all points after the Council of Trent, plainly warrant such an arrangement.

The Council of Trent (1545-1563), it will be noted, has been made a landmark in the division of chapters in the historical synopsis. This at first glance may appear to be an improper dividing point. Certainly the Council of Trent through its own proper enactments and decrees evinced little development for the current law regarding the custody of the Holy Eucharist. However, in view of the fact that the Council of Trent prepared the way for the publishing of the *Roman Ritual,* it stands as a major factor in the development of modern legislation on the proper custody of the Holy Eucharist.

Part Two, the canonical commentary, is in scope limited to a treatment of eight canons, namely, canons 1265 to 1272 inclusive. In the treatment of these eight canons the chapters follow, not the numerical sequence that is found in the Code of Canon Law, but rather a topical arrangement that has been created by the present writer.

By far the most important of these eight canons as here treated in the canonical commentary is canon 1269. Some of the other canons receive but little treatment in this work in that they form, more or less, only a background for the development of the main theme, the protection of the Blessed Eucharist reserved. Canon 1269, however, most directly concerns the protection of the Blessed Eucharist reserved, and therefore constitutes the focal point of the entire dissertation.

The present writer wishes to express his sincere gratitude to His Excellency, the Most Reverend John J. Mitty, D.D., Archbishop of San Francisco, for the opportunity to pursue graduate studies in Canon Law at the Catholic University of America; to the members of the Faculty of the School of Canon Law for their kind assistance and their helpful direction; and to all others who have contributed towards the completion of this dissertation.

PART ONE

Historical Synopsis

CHAPTER I

THE CUSTODY OF THE HOLY EUCHARIST BEFORE THE COUNCIL OF TRENT

ARTICLE I. PRE-GRATIAN HISTORY

Despite the fact that the Blessed Eucharist in Its state of reservation contains the true Body and Blood of Christ, the early history of the Church reflects many examples of abuse and lack of care. At times the Sacred Species were used as a healing agent to be applied to ailing parts of the body;[1] at times It was buried with the dead;[2] at times It was used in the place of relics under the altar stone.[3] No doubt such practices arose from good motives. However, from the I Council of Tours (461), it can be inferred that other practices were not so well-intentioned. Those in charge of the Blessed Eucharist were so careless in respect to the place of reservation, or with regard to the actual receptacle of the Sacred Hosts, that as a result mice consumed the Body and Blood of Christ. Again, those in charge lacked vigilance to such an extent as to allow sacrilegious hands to seize the Sacred Hosts for evil purposes.[4]

---

[1] St. Gregory Nazianzen, *In Laudem Sororis Suae Gorgoniae*—Migne, *Patrologiae Cursus Completus, Series Graeca* (161 vols. in 164, Parisiis, 1856-1866), XXXV, 810 (hereafter cited *MPG*); St. Augustine, *Contra Iulianum*, III, n. 162—Migne, *Patrologiae Cursus Completus, Series Latina* (221 vols., Parisiis, 1844-1864), XLV, 1315 (hereafter cited *MPL*); Muratori, *Liturgia Romana Vetus* (2 vols., Venetiis, 1748), I, 282 (hereafter cited Muratori); Smith-Cheetham, "Reservation of the Eucharist," *A Dictionary of Christian Antiquities* (2 vols., London, 1880), II, 1786.

[2] III Council of Carthage (397), cap. 6—Bruns, *Canones Apostolorum et Conciliorum Veterum Selecti* (2 vols., Berolini, 1839), I, 123 (hereafter cited Bruns); Council of the Novatians (ca. 400), n. 18—Mansi, *Sacrorum Conciliorum Nova et Amplissima Collectio* (53 vols. in 60, Parisiis, 1901-1927), III, 719 (hereafter cited Mansi); Muratori, I, 283.

[3] Muratori, I, 283.

[4] I Council of Tours, cap. 4—Mansi, VII, 950.

Furthermore, the penalties that were enacted in the councils of the sixth and seventh centuries[5] and in other sources of this period[6] point to a general lack of care for the Holy Eucharist. Penalties which ran the gamut between the mildness of a few weeks of fasting and the severity of perpetual excommunication were inflicted for such offences as the dropping or the losing of consecrated Hosts, the vomiting of Them because of drunkenness or voracity, the dire neglect which allowed Them to be consumed by worms, and the wanton act of casting Them away for lack of faith that They contained the Divine Presence.

Although such abuses were from time to time being perpetrated against the Blessed Sacrament, the Church was in many ways continually insisting on the great care that should be shown towards this Sacrament. The repeated prohibitions of the various councils against private reservation, and the anathematizing of those who dared to receive the Sacred Species and not consume Them;[7] the insistence that it was the rôle of the priest to take care of the sick, and probably therefore his rôle primarily to act as guardian of the Blessed Eucharist;[8] the constant prohibition that those below the office of deacon should not touch the sacred vessels, or enter the place where the Blessed Sacrament was reserved;[9] the many

---

[5] I Council of Orleans (511), cap. 5—Mansi, VIII, 365; IV Council of Arles (524), cap. 6—Mansi, VIII, 628; XI Council of Toledo (675), cap. 11—Bruns, I, 314; III Council of Braga (675)—Bruns, II, 98-99.

[6] The Gallican Sacramentary—Mabillon, *Museum Italicum* (2 vols., Parisiis, 1687-1689), I, 393-394 (hereafter cited Mabillon); Excerpts from a Penitential (748) of Ecgbert, Archbishop of York (735-766)—Mansi, XII, 455; *Canones Ecberti de Remediis Peccatorum*, c. 13—Mansi, XII, 496.

[7] Council of Saragossa (380), sent. 3—Bruns, II, 13; I Council of Toledo (400), cap. 14—Bruns, I, 205; Council of Rouen (650), cap. 2—Mansi, V, 1199; VII Council of Toledo (646), c. 2—Mansi, X, 777.

[8] VII Council of Toledo (646), c. 2—Mansi, X, 777; *Excerpts (748) of Ecgbert, Archbishop of York*, n. 22—Mansi, XII, 415; *Capitula (850) of Rudolph, Archbishop of Bourges*, cap. 6—Mansi, XIV, 947; *Capitula Walteri* in the synod of Bouillon (858), cap. 8—Mansi, XV, 506.

[9] I Council of Orleans (511), cap. 4—Mansi, VIII, 364; II Council of Braga (572), cc. 41, 42—Bruns, II, 52; XVII Council of Toledo (694), sent. 19—Mansi, XII, 106; *Epitome Canonum (773)* of Pope Hadrian I (772-795) to Charlemagne, c. 21—Mansi, XII, 867.

regulations concerning the existence and the quality of the pyx;[10] the instructions concerning sick-calls, when the Blessed Sacrament was carried in public;[11] the constant demand to renew the Sacred Hosts frequently[12]—all these facts are abundant proof of the Church's consummate care for the Blessed Eucharist in these early centuries previous to the time of Gratian.

ARTICLE II. LEGISLATION IN GRATIAN

Around the middle of the twelfth century, a Camoldolese monk, Gratian, Master of Theology in the University of Bologna, published a collection of canons which superseded all the collections of earlier times and which became the classical text studied and commented upon in the schools. Although this work never was approved officially, and therefore always remained a private collection, nevertheless it enjoyed great authority and reflected especially the canonical legislation in use during that period.

In this *Decree* of Gratian there are many references to the proper care of the Blessed Eucharist. These references were not always of a direct character, but from all of them inferences could be drawn as to the attitude of the Church at that period in respect to the proper custody of the Blessed Eucharist.

One canon, borrowed in all probability from the second canon of the Council of Rouen (650), discountenanced the practice whereby priests allowed lay people, men or women, to carry the Blessed Eucharist to the sick.[13] From this it can be concluded that ordinarily it was the office of the priest to take Holy Communion to the sick, and therefore no doubt it was principally his rôle to take care of the Blessed Sacrament.[14]

---

[10] I Council of Tours (461), cap. 4—Mansi, VII, 950; *Capitula (858) of Hincmar, Archbishop of Rheims,* cap. 8—Mansi, XV, 480.

[11] *Synodal Statutes of Rheims* (630)—Mansi, X, 599.

[12] I Council of Tours (461), cap. 4—Mansi, VII, 950; I Council of Orleans (511), cap. 4—Mansi, VIII, 364; Council of Bourges (1031), c. 2—Mansi, XIX, 503.

[13] C. 29, D. II, *de cons.* Cf. also Bruns, II, 268.

[14] For the rôle of the deacon and the layman in time of necessity, cf. *Glossa Ordinaria,* ad c. 29, D. II, *de cons.,* s. v. *per semetipsum;* c. 18, D. XCIII; *Glossa Ordinaria,* ad c. 18, D. XCIII.

The same conclusion can possibly be drawn from another canon in Gratian, originally the twenty-first of the Council of Laodicea (348-381), which commanded that even subdeacons should not touch the sacred vessels, or enter the *sacrarium* or *secretarium*, which the Greeks called the *diaconium*.[15] According to Rufinus (+1190), however, this prohibition against entering the *sacrarium* held only during the time of Mass and at other solemn services.[16]

With the use of the word *sacrarium*, reference no doubt was being made to the most prevalently employed place for the reservation of the Blessed Sacrament in the days of antiquity.[17] This place was quite commonly called the *sacrarium*, but it was also known as the *secretarium*, the *oblationarium*, the *paratorium*, the *diaconium*, and the *episcopium*. By whatever name it was called, however, the *sacrarium* was a small edifice attached to the church, and thus constituted a rather safe place for the Blessed Sacrament, inasmuch as it was generally shut off on all sides except for one narrow opening, a strongly built door that faced the main body of the church.[18] Although one cannot find any explicit evidence that this early *sacrarium* was kept locked or barred, nevertheless that was most probably done, especially since other things in the church which were of far less importance were kept locked, barred, or sealed for their protection.[19]

Under such circumstances the *sacrarium* would have served just

---

[15] C. 26, D. XXIII.

[16] *Summa Decretorum* (ed. H. Singer, Paderborn, 1902), pp. 55-56. This comment of Rufinus stood fully confirmed in the light of the text incorporated in c. 30, D. II, *de cons.*

[17] Conc. Trident., sess. XIII, *de Eucharistia,* c. 6—Schroeder, *Canons and Decrees of the Council of Trent* (St. Louis: Herder, 1941), p. 77; I Council of Nicaea (325), c. 13—*Codicis Iuris Canonici Fontes,* cura Emi Petri Card. Gasparri editi (9 vols., Romae [postea Civitate Vaticana]: Typis Polyglottis Vaticanis, 1923-1939. [Vols. VII-IX, ed. cura et studio Emi Iustiniani Card. Serédi]), n. 1 (hereafter cited *Fontes*). Cf. also c. 6, C. XXVI, q. 6; I Council of Orleans (511), cap. 4—Mansi, VII, 364; II Council of Braga (572), cc. 41, 42—Mansi, IX, 855; XVII Council of Toledo (695), sent. 19—Mansi, XII, 106.

[18] Corblet, *Histoire Dogmatique, Liturgique et Archéologique du Sacrament de l'Eucharistie* (2 vols., Paris, 1886), I, 549-550 (hereafter cited as Corblet).

[19] *Capitula (858) of Hincmar, Archbishop of Rheims,* c. 9—Mansi, XII, 480.

as effectively for a careful custody as the *armarium,* which as a place of reservation remains to be discussed later, and much more effectively than the two other means employed at an earlier time, for sometimes, though very rarely, the Holy Eucharist was placed on the altar or reposed in a vessel suspended above the altar.[20] The protective value inherent in the placing of the Holy Eucharist on the altar depended largely on where the altar was located, as also on the type of vessel or receptacle that may have been used. Since evidence of a strongly built and immovable receptacle on the altar is detectible at only a much later time, it appears that the *sacrarium* constituted the preferred place of reservation.

Again, the Blessed Sacrament was reserved at times by being included in a vessel suspended above the altar. A Eucharistic receptacle in the form of a tower, of a dove, or of a cup, was supported over the altar by means of a chain which was attached ordinarily to the cross or the baldachin.[21] The use of this method proved effective indeed in safeguarding the Blessed Eucharist against profanation through approach by mice, a continual worry of the early Church.[22] Nevertheless it proved less effective than the *sacrarium* in safeguarding the Blessed Eucharist against profanation by men. Too many factors had to be postulated, such as the employing of an exceedingly strong chain, the use of an unbreakable receptacle, and so forth, if this method was to furnish equal security with the method that resorted to the use of a *sacrarium.*

In the *Decree* of Gratian there was incorporated one other canon that is worthy of special attention in any treatment of the custody of the Blessed Eucharist. This canon, taken from the I Council of Orleans (511), stated the obligation of careful guardianship of

---

[20] St. Gregory Nazianzen, *In Laudem Sororis Suae Gorgoniae—MPL,* XLV, 1315; Synod of Verona (432)—Mansi, XVIII, 369 E; Homily of Pope Leo IV, n. 8—Mansi, XIV, 891; Gasparri, *Tractatus Canonicus de Sanctissima Eucharistia* (2 vols., Parisiis, 1897), II, 257 (hereafter cited Gasparri).

[21] Corblet, I, 554, 556; II, 295-298. Cf. also the II Council of Tours (567), c. 2—Mansi, IX, 798.

[22] I Council of Tours (461), c. 4—Mansi, VII, 950; I Council of Orleans (511), cap. 5—Mansi, VIII, 765.

the Blessed Sacrament in a negative way, inasmuch as it prescribed punishments for those who were guilty of neglect. The canon reads as follows:

> *Qui bene non custodierit sacrificium et mus vel aliud aliquod animal illud comederit, XL dies poeniteat. Qui autem perdiderit illud in ecclesia, aut pars eius ceciderit, et inventa non fuerit, XXX dies poeniteat.*[23]

This canon was merely part of a much longer list of penalties which had been prescribed in chapter five of the I Council of Orleans for those who showed lack of care for the Blessed Eucharist.[24]

ARTICLE III. THE SYNODAL CONSTITUTIONS OF ODO, ARCHBISHOP OF PARIS (1196-1208)

To employ a whole article in consideration of a piece of local legislation could at first sight appear unwarranted. However, for several reasons it seems duly warranted to give separate and special attention to the *Synodal Constitutions* which Odo, the archbishop of Paris, compiled around the year 1197.[25] For one thing, these constitutions exhibited their author as a bishop consumed with zeal for the proper custody of the Blessed Eucharist. Again, of all legislation in the first twelve centuries, it was by far the clearest in giving expression to the proper care that was due the Blessed Sacrament. Finally, it mentioned various conditions and circumstances with reference to the question of reservation, and these were very much akin to those which at the present day relate to the same question.

The opening chapter on the Blessed Eucharist[26] more or less summed up the general tone of the constitutions:

> *Summa reverentia et honor maximus sacris altaribus*

[23] C. 94, D. II, *de cons.* Cf. also c. 28, D. II, *de cons.;* c. 17, C. XII, q. 2.

[24] Mansi, VIII, 365. Cf. also IV Council of Arles (524), c. 6—Mansi, VIII, 628; *Penitential (748) of Ecgbert, Archbishop of York*—Mansi, XII, 455: *Canones Ecberti de Remediis Peccatorum,* c. 13—Mansi, XII, 496.

[25] Mansi, XXII, 675-683.

[26] *Capitula de Sacramento Altaris,* c. 1—Mansi, XXII, 677.

exhibeatur, et maxime ubi sacrosanctum Corpus Domini reservatur et Missa celebratur.

From this statement it is clear that the altar was used as a place of reservation in Paris at the end of the twelfth century. The custom of reservation on the altar first originated in the ninth century in France. In the tenth century this practice spread to a certain extent in the Germanic parts of France, and in the diocese of Verona, Italy, but it flourished especially in France proper. In the twelfth and thirteenth centuries, almost all mention of reservation on the altar was restricted to these localities. Certainly, however, some parts of England had this practice in the thirteenth century, and again some parts of Spain adopted this practice in the fifteenth century.[27]

In another section of his *Synodal Constitutions,* Bishop Odo complained that the priests were negligent in obeying his former precepts, which had made it mandatory to use an ivory pyx, and to employ a tabernacle for the Body of the Lord.[28] Most likely he was speaking of a tabernacle very much similar to that of the present day. At about that time, or shortly afterwards, tabernacles appeared in the form of small chests, made of wood or of metal, and covered with a tent of silk. They were usually movable, and ordinarily were placed on the left side of the altar.[29] Perhaps the tabernacle that Bishop Odo called for was one of the first of this type. Still from the wording of the text as previously quoted one may have sufficient warrant to assume that the tabernacle was contemplated, not as movable, but as fixedly set on the altar itself.

The word "tabernacle" was by no means a new expression in the time of Bishop Odo. The term first came into ecclesiastical use during the course of the early Middle Ages. It then was applied to different Eucharistic receptacles and fixtures. It was the name given at times to the Eucharistic dove, the ciborium, the osten-

---

[27] Köster, *De Custodia Sanctissimae Eucharistiae* (Romae: Catholic Book Agency, 1940), pp. 66-68 (hereafter cited Köster).

Ioannes Teutonicus (+1245) also identified the altar as a place of reservation—*Glossa Ordinaria,* ad c. 26, D. XXIII, s.v. *sacrarium.*

[28] *Praecepta Communia,* n. 35—Mansi, XXII, 683.

[29] Corblet, I, 560-561.

sorium, or the architectural canopy, which is still called "tabernacle-work" by the English. At times it was the term applied even to the baldachin, from which the Eucharistic dove was suspended. However, the first kind of repository which, the while it was designated as a "tabernacle," resembled also in some way the tabernacle of the present day was the Eucharistic *armarium.* These *armaria,* of very ancient origin, generally were dug into the wall, or into a pillar of the choir. They were strong containers, inasmuch as they generally were made of marble or of stone, and were shut off by means of strong rectangular doors. But there existed also other kinds of *armaria,* which were movable pieces of furniture, but at the same time of a similar strong construction. No doubt this latter type of *armarium* developed into the tabernacle of Bishop Odo's time in Paris.[30]

From the sixth chapter of Odo's *Synodal Constitutions* one can draw the conclusion that the tabernacle as specified by him at that time was locked with a key.[31] Although this may have been the first demand in ecclesiastical legislation for the use of keys in caring for the Blessed Eucharist, no doubt in times previous various methods of locking up and sealing the Blessed Sacrament were practiced. When one considers the demand in councils that such things as the Baptismal font and the Holy Oils should be sealed, barred, or locked up in some manner,[32] one feels constrained *a fortiori* to conclude that the Blessed Sacrament was also guarded under lock in some way. The fact that no mention of such a practice was made in the councils may simply indicate that there was much less, if any, abuse relative to the duty of keeping the Blessed Eucharist under lock than with reference to the mandatory locking up of the Holy Oils and the Baptismal Font.

Many of the other chapters in these *Synodal Constitutions* also reflected the zeal of Bishop Odo for the reverence that was due the Eucharist. Among other things he demanded great cleanliness

[30] Corblet, I, 550-569.

[31] *Capitula de Sacramento Altaris,* c. 6: "In pulchriore parte altaris cum summa diligentia et honestate sub clave sacrosanctum Corpus Domini custodiatur."—Mansi, XXII, 678.

[32] *Capitula (858) of Hincmar, Archbishop of Rheims,* c. 9—Mansi, XII, 480; *Synodal Statutes of Odo, Capitula de Baptismo,* c. 3—Mansi, XXII, 677.

near the place of reservation, assiduous care in connection with a sick call, and a zealous custody of even the unconsecrated hosts.[33]

ARTICLE IV. LEGISLATION IN THE DECRETALS OF POPE GREGORY IX

In the early part of the thirteenth century, Pope Gregory IX (1227-1241) commissioned his chaplain, St. Raymond of Pennafort (1175-1275), a Dominican priest, to prepare a new collection of decretals to replace all others. This work, when finished, was approved by Pope Gregory IX in the Bull *Rex Pacificus* of September 5, 1234.[34] Thereafter these decretals had the force of universal law. Therefore the regulations contained therein concerning the Blessed Eucharist were by no means a matter of choice, but rather a matter of general obligation for the whole church.

The first incorporated decretal in the Collection of Gregory IX under the title which dealt directly with the Blessed Sacrament had some years previously become a matter of general legislation. St. Raymond of Pennafort assumed this legislation from the IV General Council of the Lateran (1215), over which a predecessor of Gregory IX, namely Pope Innocent III (1198-1216), had presided.[35] That Council had enacted the following universal law:

> *Statuimus, ut in cunctis ecclesiis chrisma et Eucharistia sub fideli custodia, clavibus adhibitis, conserventur, ne possit ad illa temeraria manus extendi ad aliqua horribilia vel nefaria exercenda. Si vero is, ad quem spectat custodia, ea incaute reliquerit, tribus mensibus ab officio suspendatur, et, si per eius incuriam aliquid nefandum inde contigerit, graviori subiaceat ultioni.*[36]

Since the foregoing canon was the enactment of a general Council, and since later it was incorporated in the official body

---

[33] *Capitula de Sacramento Altaris,* cc. 2, 5, 6—Mansi, XXII, 677-678; *Praecepta Communia,* n. 39—Mansi, XXII, 683.

[34] Potthast, *Regesta Pontificum Romanorum inde ab anno post Christum natum MCXCVIII ad annum MCCCIV* (2 vols., Berolini, 1874-1875), I, n. 9694 (hereafter cited Potthast).

[35] Can. 20—Mansi, XXII, 1007.

[36] C. 1. X, *de custodia Eucharistiae, chrismatis, et aliorum sacramentorum,* III, 44.

of the Church's universal laws, the following conclusions resulted: 1) The use of the keys for the due safeguarding of the Blessed Eucharist was no longer a matter of custom or of local legislation, but a matter of universal law, and 2) since suspension from office was enacted as the penalty for negligence towards the Blessed Sacrament, it was evident that the clerical status which was postulated in the enacted penalty similarly pointed to clerics as the ones who by the universal law were constituted as the custodians of the Holy Eucharist.

The early commentators offered many interesting notes on this canon. The *Glossa Ordinaria* in interpreting the phrase *sub fideli custodia*[37] referred to the Decretal *Sane* of Pope Honorius III (1216-1227)[38] as an expression of the careful study that was due the Holy Eucharist. In addition the *Glossa Ordinaria* cited some texts from Gratian[39] to indicate the comprehensive extent of the called for custody: the Eucharist was never to be carried to the sick by lay people, and by a deacon only in a time of necessity.[40]

In his commentary on the word *manus,* Hostiensis (+1271) made mention of the many and unspeakable sacrileges committed in his own day by the fortune-tellers. At that time such sacrileges were a matter of almost daily experience, and thus not infrequently became the subject-matter of confession.[41]

The early commentators were especially prolific in their treatment of the last part of the Decretal *Statuimus,* the part namely which dealt with the penalties for the neglect of the Blessed Sacrament. The one in charge—the sacristan according to Ioannes Andreae (+1348)[42]—was to be suspended from the exercise of

[37] Ad c. 1, X, *de custodia Eucharistiae, chrismatis, et aliorum sacramentorum,* III, 44, s.v. *sub fideli custodia.*

[38] C. 10, *de celebratione missarum, et sacramento Eucharistiae, et divinis officiis,* III, 41.

[39] C. 19, D. II, *de cons.;* c. 18, D. XCIII; c. 13, D. XCIII.

[40] *Glossa Ordinaria, loc. cit.* Cf. also Hostiensis (Henricus de Segusio), *Commentaria in Quinque Decretalium Libros* (5 vols., Venetiis, 1581), lib. III, III, tit. XLIV, c. 1, s.v. *sub fideli custodia* (hereafter cited Hostiensis).

[41] Hostiensis, *ibid.,* s.v. *manus.* Cf. also Ioannes Andreae, *In Quinque Decretalium Libros Novella Commentaria* (5 vols., Venetiis, 1581), lib. III, tit. XLIV, c. 1. s.v. *manus* (hereafter cited Ioannes Andreae).

[42] *Ibid.,* s.v. *spectat.*

his office for three months in the event that he had neglected to put the Blessed Sacrament under lock and key. It made no difference at all whether his lack of care resulted from sheer stupidity or from culpable negligence. Regardless of the non-occurrence of any act of sacrilege, and regardless even of the absence of any formal guilt on the part of the cleric, he became subject to the infliction of this set punishment.[43]

However, if an act of sacrilege did ensue, then there was to be inflicted upon the sacristan some additional punishment, the nature of which remained to be determined within the discretion of the sentencing judge. No such additional punishment was to be meted out to the sacristan if his carelessness was simply the result of his stupidity. Before any added punishment could be inflicted, the case had to be one in which the negligence connoted at the same time the presence of a mortal sin.[44]

It could be that the sacristan had no way of foreseeing the sacrilege which resulted. Could he then be made subject to this second punishment? The *Glossa Ordinaria*[45] argued that the sacristan who was gravely negligent in his care for the Eucharist could be held responsible for the sacrileges that followed, even though these sacrileges were unforeseen. In support of this contention the *Glossa Ordinaria* cited some canons from Gratian,[46] and furthermore appealed to an axiom which had been adopted from the Roman Law: *"Qui occasionem damni dat, damnum dedisse videtur."*[47]

Panormitanus (1386-1453)[48] appealed to the same axiom for his

---

[43] Hostiensis, *ibid.*, s.v. *incaute, suspendatur, graviori.*

[44] Hostiensis, *ibid.*, s.v. *graviori, incuriam.*

[45] Ad c. 1, X, *de custodia Eucharistiae, chrismatis, et aliorum sacramentorum*, III, 44, s.v. *graviori.* Cf. also Hostiensis, lib. III, tit. XLIV, c. 1, s.v. *subiaceat.*

[46] C. 3, C. XXXI, q. 5; c. 22, C. I, q. 1; c. 9, C. XXXV, q. 1.

[47] In the *Corpus Iuris Civilis* the corresponding passage reads as follows: ". . . nam et quo occasionem praestat, damnum fecisse videtur. . . ."—D. (9, 2) 30.

[48] *Commentaria in Quinque Libros Decretalium* (5 vols. in 7, Venetiis, 1588), lib. III, tit. XLIV, c. 1. s.v. *si vero* (hereafter cited Panormitanus). Cf. also Ioannes Andreae, lib. III, tit. XLIV, c. 1, s.v. *contigerit.*

argument, and even invoked the application of the *Lex Aquilia*[49] in order to prove that a sacristan *praeter voluntatem* could be responsible for an unforeseen sacrilege. However, he limited the application of this doctrine in such a manner as to relate it exclusively to the external forum. In the internal forum a gravely negligent sacristan who did not foresee the subsequent sacrilege was not to be held responsible for that ensuing crime.[50]

Another important decretal of relevant import in the present discussion was the letter which Pope Honorius III sent to the bishops and prelates of Sweden in the year 1219.[51] The most relevant part of this decretal is as follows:

> *Ne propter incuriam sacerdotum divina indignatio gravius exardescat, districte praecipiendo mandamus, quatenus a sacerdotibus Eucharistia in loco singulari, mundo et signato semper honorifice collocata, devote ac fideliter conservetur. . . .*[52]

In the particular part of the decretal here quoted, two interesting items are to be noted. First, according to Panormitanus,[53] the phrase *in loco singulari* pointed to the requirement that the Blessed Eucharist be kept in a place which was exclusively set aside for the purpose. Secondly, Panormitanus,[54] Hostiensis[55] and the *Glossa Ordinaria*[56] emphasized in various ways that the Blessed Eucharist was to be kept in a vessel or receptacle that could be securely locked.

The rest of the decretal adverted to some other interesting points that referred to the proper custody of the Blessed Sacrament. In view of the great care that was exercised in the Old Testament with reference to the golden vessel which contained the manna,

---

[49] D. (9, 2) 45.

[50] Panormitanus, *loc. cit.* Cf. also Ioannes Andreae, *loc. cit.*

[51] C. 10, X, *de celebratione Missarum, et sacramento Eucharistiae, et divinis officiis,* III, 41.

[52] Potthast, n. 6166.

[53] Lib. III, tit. XLI, c. 10, s.v. *singulari.*

[54] *Ibid.*, s.v. *signato.*

[55] Lib. III, tit. XLI, c. 10, s.v. *collocata.*

[56] Ad c. 10, X, *de celebratione Missarum, et sacramento Eucharistiae, et divinis officiis,* III, 41, s.v. *fideliter conservetur.*

which was a mere symbol and prefiguration of the Body of Christ, Pope Honorius III reflected his deep distress over the great lack of care evinced by many priests regarding the custody of the real Body of Christ. His expressions and words indicated that there were some serious abuses prevailing at the time. He indicated that this display of negligence was current despite the fact that strong canonical sanctions had been invoked against it in the past. He thereupon furnished particular instructions for the due care of the Blessed Sacrament when It had to be carried to the sick. Finally, he enjoined upon the bishops and the prelates of Sweden that they be not dilatory in punishing all transgressors who disobeyed his command. He did not formulate any set punishment, but rather left the specification of the penalty within the prudence and discretion of the ecclesiastical judges.

Particular attention should be given to the fact that Pope Honorius III demanded punishment for the *priests* who were guilty of negligence. This seems to point to two possible situations in those places where the sacristan had the care of the Blessed Sacrament.[57] Either the sacristan, or the custodian—one and the same according to Hostiensis[58]—was himself constituted in priestly orders, or else acted under the surveillance of one in priestly orders. The existence of the latter practice seems confirmed in the light of the text of certain other decretals.[59] The sacristan was entrusted with the guardianship of the church utensils, of the treasures, and also of the Blessed Eucharist. In the care of the Holy Eucharist he was subject to the archpriest, whose duty it was to instruct the sacristan concerning the proper mode of reservation. So it easily can be conceived that in those churches where a sacristan in minor orders had the care of the Blessed Sacrament, he acted under the guidance of another person, an overseer, namely a priest.

Although the two decretals that have been considered here made no specific mention of the word "tabernacle," nevertheless the demands as therein established could best be fulfilled by means of the

---

[57] Ioannes Andreae, lib. III, tit, XLIV, c. 1, s.v. *spectat.*

[58] *Summa Aurea* (Lugduni, 1568), p. 64.

[59] Cf. c. 1, X, *de officio custodis,* I, 27; c. 1, X, *de officio sacristae,* I, 26; c. 3, X, *de officio Archipresbyteri,* I, 24.

construction of an immovable tabernacle united with the altar itself, built with structural strength, and kept in a locked condition. No doubt the requirements as then made actually did pave the way for the present-day tabernacle. The Blessed Eucharist was to be put in a place reserved exclusively for It. This pointed to the need of but a small receptacle. The Blessed Sacrament was to be preserved in a clean place. This indicated the need of an enclosed receptacle. The Blessed Sacrament was to be kept under lock for the sake of frustrating all attempts of sacrilege. This called for the construction of a strong and immovable receptacle, inasmuch as it would have been futile to maintain a locked receptacle that could readily have been smashed open, or that could easily have been carried away. Finally, the Blessed Sacrament was to be kept in a place that commanded honor, respect and reverence. This suggested that the Blessed Sacrament be reserved on the altar.

ARTICLE V. PRE-TRIDENTINE LEGISLATION

From the death of Pope Gregory IX until the time of the celebration of the Council of Trent (1545-1563) there was little juridical development in the legislation on the custody of the Blessed Eucharist. The universal law remained the same, and particular laws contributed little by way of additional or new enactments. The doctrine of the commentators of the *Corpus Iuris Canonici* reflected of course some degree of jurisprudential development. This is apparent from the teaching of such decretalists as Hostiensis (+1271), Ioannes Andreae (+1348) and Panormitanus (+1453), whose interpretations of the law in question were given some consideration in the previous article.[60] Their comments were of value not only for an interpretation of the decretals themselves, but also as an indication of how the law was understood in their own times.

In the centuries immediately preceding the celebration of the Council of Trent there seems to have been more legislation on

[60] Cf. Kurtscheid-Wilches, *Historia Iuris Canonici,* Tom. I, *Historia Fontium et Scientiae Iuris Canonici* (Romae: Officium Libri Catholici, 1943), 259-267, concerning these decretalists and their influence in shaping the current interpretation of the decretal laws.

punishments for negligence and abuse relative to the Blessed Eucharist than on any other phase regarding Its proper custody. First of all, many councils repeated or summarized the twentieth canon of the IV General Council of Lateran.[61] The Council of Florence (1517), a council confirmed by Pope Leo X (1513-1521), made reference to those canons in the *Decree* of Gratian which singled out the penalties consequent upon the lack of care for the Blessed Eucharist.[62] Other sources of law during this period demanded that those who were guilty of abuse of the Blessed Sacrament be visited with various sanctions such as a fine, imprisonment, loss of benefice, suspension, and even excommunication in the more serious cases.[63]

Legislation, however, on other points relative to the custody of the Holy Eucharist were not lacking. Thus the Statutes as enacted for the Province of Canterbury[64] demanded that the pyx which was used for the reservation of the Lord's Body was not only to be made of gold, of silver, or of ivory, but was also to be lined on the inside with a clean white piece of linen. Again, various conciliar enactments demanded a frequent renewal of the Sacred Hosts.[65]

Finally, during the pre-Tridentine period the decretals of Popes

[61] A statute of John Peckham, Archbishop of Canterbury (1279-1292), taken from the *Provinciale Anglicanum* (ed. ca. 1509, and comprising the statutes of fourteen Archbishops of Canterbury from 1222 to 1415)—Mansi, XXXI, 367-368; Council of Freising (1440), c. 18—Mansi, XXII, 14; Council of Salzburg (1490)—Mansi, XXXII, 509 C; Council of Magdeburg (1489)—Mansi, XXXII, 467 C; Constitutions of Province of York (1518), n. 14—Mansi, XXXV, 200.

[62] The Council of Florence, cc. 25, 33, 39—Mansi, XXXV, 316.

[63] Pope Clement V (1305-1314) in the Council of Vienne (1311-1312)—C. 1, *de celebratione Missarum, et aliis divinis officiis,* III, 14, in Clem.; Council of Florence (1517), c. 4—Mansi, XXXV, 235; Pope Hadrian VI (1522-1523), ep. *Dudum,* 20 iul. 1522, 3—*Fontes,* n. 78.

[64] A statute of John Peckham (1279-1292), taken from the *Provinciale Anglicanum*—Mansi, XXXI, 424; cf. also Council of Münster (1279), c. 11—Mansi, XXIV, 315.

[65] Council of Münster (1279), c. 13—Mansi, XXIV, 315; Council of Freising (1440), c. 18—Mansi, XXXII, 14; Statute of John Peckham as taken from the *Provinciale Anglicanum*—Mansi, XXXI, 424. Cf. also Innocentius IV, ep. *Sub catholicae,* § 3, n. 9—*Fontes,* n. 34.

Innocent III and Honorius III which received specific mention in the previous article probably exercised a considerable influence in the development of the tabernacle. In the thirteenth century the use of a tabernacle built as a little chest of wood or of metal, and covered with a tent of silk, became fairly common. More often than not such a tabernacle could be moved from place to place. In fact, it was only during the course of the fifteenth century that the tabernacle in the majority of cases became a locally fixed receptacle which was furnished with a lock, and which was constructed in the center of the altar in the form of a small temple that provided a closet for the storing of the consecrated elements.[66]

However, during the late Middle Ages other methods of reservation still continued in use. Still much in evidence was the ornamental receptacle which hung suspended above the altar.[67] Furthermore, *armaria* of all types, that is to say, chests, coffers, safes, treasuries and depositories, continued to be built separated from the altar. They were constructed with elaborate ornamentation, and not infrequently constituted a structure of monumental size.[68]

---

[66] Corblet, I, 560-561; Ayrinhac, *The Administrative Legislation in the New Code of Canon Law* (New York: Longmans, Green & Co., 1930), p. 140 (hereafter cited Ayrinhac).

[67] Corblet, I, 551-554.

[68] Corblet, I, 561-569.

CHAPTER II

The Custody of the Blessed Eucharist After the Council of Trent

Article I. The Guardian of the Blessed Sacrament

During the post-Tridentine period it is apparent that one of the first requisites for the reservation of the Blessed Sacrament was the presence of a guardian, who day and night was charged with the careful custody of the Real Presence. In 1593 the Sacred Congregation of Rites allowed the reservation of the Holy Eucharist in an *ecclesia simplex* under several conditions, one of which was the following: *"Dummodo ecclesia . . . nunc habeat beneficiatum perpetuum qui eius curam gerat, et Sacramentum possit caute custodiri, et ibi lampas perpetuo accensa habeatur."*[1] Again, in 1881, the same Congregation issued a very clear instruction to the Bishop of Alton, Illinois: "*. . . ut provideat quatenus in quavis ecclesia, ubi SSmum Sacramentum retinetur, nunquam desit custos, qui prope eam commoretur, prouti ab ecclesiasticis praescriptionibus sancitum est.*"[2]

Ordinarily the office of guardian devolved upon a priest. The *Caeremoniale Episcoporum* (1600) entrusted the custody of the Blessed Eucharist to the sacristan, "*. . . qui in sacerdotali ordine sit constitutus. . . .*"[3] The *Rituale Romanum* (1614) mentioned the pastor as the one who was required to fulfill its instructions concerning the care of the Blessed Sacrament.[4]

---

[1] *Bavariae*, 23 mart. 1593—*Fontes*, n. 5163.

[2] *Altonen.*, 17 febr. 1881—*Fontes*, n. 6127.

[3] *Caeremoniale Episcoporum, Benedicti Papae XIV Jussu Editum et Auctum* (Mechliniae, 1867), lib. I, c. VI, nn. 1-2 (hereafter cited *Caeremoniale Episcoporum*). In this passage, as in others which will be cited, reference was made to the *Caeremoniale Episcoporum Clementis VIII primum, nunc denuo Innocentii Papae Auctoritate Recognitum* (Romae: Ex Typographia Rev. Camerae Apostolicae, 1651).

[4] *Rituale Romanum Pauli V Pontificis Maximus jussu editum et a Benedicto XIV auctum et castigatum, cui novissima accedit Benedictionum et In-*

The frequent demand that a pastor, a rector, or a chaplain should retain the key of the tabernacle was another indication that the priest was the ordinary guardian. This custody of the key by a priest shall be fully treated in a later article.

Again, the obligation of the priest to reside at or near the place of reservation, as also his obligation to celebrate Mass daily at the altar of the Blessed Sacrament, was an additional indication that he was the ordinary guardian.[5]

In the latter part of the nineteenth century, however, there was a relaxation in the demand that a priest should always be the guardian of the Blessed Eucharist. In 1850 the Provincial Council of Rouen, which in accordance with the general rule forbade the reservation of the Blessed Sacrament in filial churches at which no priest was resident, nevertheless made an exception for the Lenten season.[6] Furthermore, the Sacred Congregation of Rites, through its use of the word *custos* in its Instruction to the Bishop of Alton in 1881, indicated a departure from the stricter norm according to which in bygone days the residence of a priest at or near the church was a prerequisite for the reservation of the Blessed Sacrament in that church.[7] Unlike the earlier sources that pertained to the subject of the Eucharistic guardian, this rescript of the Sacred Congregation did not use the words *sacerdos,* or

---

structionum Appendix (Tornaci, Nerviorum, 1896), tit. IV, c. 1, *de sanctissimo Eucharistiae sacramento,* n. 2 (hereafter cited *Rituale Rom.*). In this passage, as in others which will be cited, reference was made to the *Rituale Romanun Pauli V. Pont. Max. Iussu Editum* (Romae: Typis et Sumptibus Philippi de Rubeis, 1652).

[5] S.R.C., *Firmana,* 16 mart. 1833—*Decreta Authentica Congregationis Sacrorum Rituum* (5 vols. et 2 appendices, Romae: Ex Typographia Polyglotta, 1898-1927), n. 2700 (hereafter cited *D.A.*) ; S.R.C., *Papien.,* 23 nov. 1880, ad III—*D.A.,* n. 3525; S.R.C., *Baionen.,* 14 maii 1889—*D.A.,* n. 3706; S.C.C., *Fulden.,* 17 febr. 1883—*Acta Sanctae Sedis* (41 vols., Romae, 1865-1908), XV (1883), 528 (hereafter cited *ASS*) ; Provincial Council of Vienna (1858), tit. III, cap. IV—*Acta et Decreta Sacrorum Conciliorum Recentiorum, Collectio Lacensis* (7 vols., Friburgi Brisgoviae, 1870-1892), V, 163 (hereafter cited *Coll. Lac.*) ; Provincial Council of Prague (1860)—*Coll. Lac.,* V, 499.

[6] Decretum, XVI, n. 10—*Coll. Lac.,* IV, n. 529.

[7] *Altonen.,* 17 febr. 1881—*Fontes,* n. 6127.

parochus, or *perpetuus beneficiatus,* but simply the quite generic word *custos.*

Indeed, certain grants and concessions as made in the nineteenth century substantiate the fact that a relaxation of the strict norm of the previous centuries was under way. Thus in 1833 Pope Gregory XVI (1831-1846) granted to the Daughters of Charity of St. Vincent de Paul an indult whereby no resident chaplain was required, and whereby the key of the tabernacle was left in charge of the sister sacristan. This indult was granted in favor of a house of the institute, and in effect made the sister sacristan the guardian of the Blessed Sacrament at any of the houses where a chaplain was not in residence.[8]

Furthermore, in 1833 the Bishop of Fulda presented a problem to the Sacred Congregation of the Council for a solution.[9] The Blessed Sacrament was reserved in certain chapels where the priest could be present for Holy Mass only twice a month. During his absence the Blessed Eucharist could be duly safeguarded by trustworthy lay people.[10] What was to be done? The Sacred Congregation allowed the reservation in such chapels, even though no priest could be in residence, provided that Mass was said at least once a week.

Lastly, in 1889 the Bishop of Bayonne inquired of the Sacred Congregation of Rites about the number of times the celebration of Mass was required in private oratories when the Blessed Sacrament was reserved there.[11] The Sacred Congregation reiterated the norm regarding the celebration of daily Mass, but mentioned that the Holy See was accustomed to grant an apostolic indult for the reservation of the Blessed Sacrament if Mass was offered at least once each week. Certainly in connection with such a grant

---

[8] Litt. ap., *Caritatis viscera,* 14 maii 1833—*Ius Pontificium de Propaganda Fide* (ed. R. de Martinis, *Pars Prima,* 7 vols., Romae, 1888-1897; *Pars Secunda,* 1 vol., Romae, 1909), *Pars Prima,* V, 76-77 (hereafter cited *Ius Pont.*). Cf. also, S.R.C., *Oriolen.,* 8 maii 1886, ad III—*D.A.,* n. 3662.

[9] *Fulden.,* 17 febr. 1883—*ASS,* XV (1883), 528.

[10] S.R.C., *Fulden.,* 17 febr. 1883: "Procul dubio Sacramentum per ludimagistrum, sacristam vel alios viros fideles caute custodiri potest, et lampas perpetuo accensa haberi."—*ASS,* XV (1883), 528.

[11] *Baionen.,* 14 maii 1889—*D.A.,* n. 3706.

the Holy See did not demand the residence of a priest at or near the church or chapel in which the reservation of the Blessed Sacrament was made permissible.

Another factor that confirms the increasing relaxation of the strict demand for a priest as guardian of the Blessed Sacrament was the comparative silence of the Holy See in respect to the divergent practices that were arising in houses of women religious. Many convents reserved the Blessed Sacrament in the absence of priests to act as Its guardians. Yet the Holy See did not insist on the abolition of these customs, in view, no doubt, of the scarcity of priests. Many convents of nuns were without resident chaplains.[12] Many sisters' communities likewise enjoyed an apostolic indult for the reservation of the Blessed Sacrament in their chapels or oratories when they were without the benefit of a resident chaplain.[13]

Furthermore, it is clear that in some places sisters without the possession of an apostolic indult were appropriating the privilege of the reservation of the Blessed Sacrament in the chapels of their convents.[14] The maintenance of this practice on their part would in strict accordance with the law have heightened the demand of resident priests at their chapels even beyond the need which already existed. In view of these circumstances then, the only solution whereby these nuns and sisters could within the law retain the reservation of the Blessed Sacrament at their chapels was a relaxation on the part of the Holy See of the stricter demand that had obtained for centuries.

ARTICLE II. THE TABERNACLE

The reservation of the Blessed Eucharist in a tabernacle which was similar to that of the present day became the general practice on the continent of Europe in the fifteenth century. In 1614 the *Roman Ritual* demanded the use of such a tabernacle. To clear up any doubt that the word *"tabernacle"* was to be understood

---

[12] Köster, p. 154.

[13] Gasparri, II, 267.

[14] Petition of the Fathers of the IX Provincial Council of Baltimore (1859) to the Holy Father—*Coll. Lac.*, III, 179-180.

in the very sense that now attaches to that word, and therefore was not to be construed as an *armarium* which was separated from the altar, the Ritual demanded that the tabernacle be set either on the main altar or some other altar.[15] So there is no doubt that from that time onward the tabernacle as such was always to be inseparably connected with the altar. One decree after another of the Sacred Congregation of Rites mentioned this factor with relation to the tabernacle.[16]

It was likewise in the post-Tridentine period that the tabernacle came to be set in the middle of the altar[17] and came to be constructed in a manner that made it immovable from the altar.[18]

In spite of the demands that the tabernacle rest upon the middle of the altar and be inseparable from it, nevertheless the older methods of preserving the Blessed Sacrament did not cease everywhere at once. There is evidence that in 1659 a certain church in

---

[15] "Curare porro debet [parochus], ut perpetuo aliquot particulae consecratae eo numero, qui usui infirmorum et aliorum fidelium communioni satis esse possit, conserventur in pyxide ex solida decentique materia, eaque munda, et suo operculo bene clausa, albo velo cooperta, et quantum res feret, ornato in tabernaculo clave obserato. Hoc autem tabernaculum . . . in altari maiori vel in alio, quod venerationi et cultui tanti Sacramenti commodius ac decentius videatur, sit collocatum. . . ."—*Rituale Rom.*, tit. IV, c. 1, *de sanctissimo Eucharistiae sacramento,* nn. 5-6.

[16] *Sarnen.*, 17 iul. 1688—*D.A.*, n. 1796; *Augustae Praetoriae,* 21 iul. 1696, ad 3—*D.A.*, n. 1946; *Sanctis Iacobi de Cile,* 14 mart. 1861, ad XIII—*D.A.*, n. 3104; *Urgellen.*, 5 dec. 1868, ad II—*D.A.*, n. 3192; *Gandaven.*, 18 maii 1878, ad I, II—*D.A.*, n. 3449; *Cuneen.*, 2 iunii 1883, ad VI—*D.A.*, n. 3576.

[17] Benedictus XIV, const. *Accepimus,* 16 april. 1746, n. 7—*Fontes,* n. 368; S.R.C., 23 aug. 1863—Gasparri, II, 257; De Herdt, *Sacrae Liturgiae Praxis* (4. ed., 3 vols., Lovanii, 1863), III, 247 (hereafter cited De Herdt).

[18] *Acta Ecclesiae Mediolanensis, a Sancto Carolo Cardinali S. Praxedis Archiep. Mediolan. Condita, Frederici Cardinalis Borromaei Archiepiscopi Mediolan iussu undique diligentius collecta, et edita* (2 vols., Lugduni, 1682-1683. Tom. I, 1682; Tom. II, 1683), I, pars IV, *Instructiones de Sacramento Sanctissimae Eucharistiae,* p. 424 (hereafter cited *Acta Ecclesiae Mediolan.*); *Acta Ecclesiae Mediolan.*, I, pars IV, *Instructiones Fabricae Ecclesiasticae,* p. 472; S.R.C., *Sarnen.*, 10 iul. 1688—*D.A.*, n. 1796; Giraldi, *Animadversiones et additamenta ex posterioribus Summorum Pontificum constitutionibus et Sacrarum Congregationum decretis desumptis ad Aug. Barbosa De officio et potestate parochi descriptio* (Romae, 1774), pars II, c. XX, c. XX, n. 27 (hereafter cited Giraldi).

Bologna retained the practice of the Eucharistic vessel suspended above the altar.[19] In 1688 the Synod of Paderborn still sanctioned the *armarium*.[20] During the eighteenth century it was still the custom in many cathedrals of France to preserve the Holy Eucharist in an ornamental vessel which was suspended above the altar. Likewise in the nineteenth century the so-called Sacrament Houses were still maintained in use in many places.[21] In fact, even at the turn of the century large *armaria* were still in use in many parts of Germany.[22]

Certainly in those places where through immemorial custom such methods had never been discontinued, they could be tolerated and actually were tolerated by ecclesiastical authority.[23] Thus, for example, the Sacred Congregation of Rites tolerated the continuance of the custom for a group of Colettine Nuns in the archdiocese of Cambrai. In accord with that custom the Blessed Sacrament was reserved perpetually in an ostensorium visible in the wall of the chapel both from the choir and from the sanctuary.[24] However, under no circumstances whatsoever was a reintroduction of the *armarium* or of the hanging Eucharistic vessel to be permitted. The Sacred Congregation of Rites very definitely reprobated any such practice in the letter which it sent to the Bishops of Belgium in the name of the Holy Father on August 21, 1863.[25]

ARTICLE III. THE CONSTRUCTION OF THE TABERNACLE

The material to be used in the construction of the tabernacle was not determined by the *Roman Ritual*. However, under date of October 20, 1575, the Sacred Congregation of Bishops and

---

[19] S.R.C., *Bononien.*, 22 nov. 1659—*D.A.*, n. 1132.

[20] Köster, p. 136.

[21] Braun, "Tabernacle,"—*The Catholic Encyclopedia,* XIV, 424. Cf. also Corblet, I, 554.

[22] Van der Stappen, *Sacra Liturgia* (5 vols., Vol. IV, 3. ed., Mechliniae, 1912), IV, 112 (hereafter cited Van der Stappen).

[23] Vermeersch-Creusen, *Epitome Iuris Canonici* (6. ed., 3 vols., Mechliniae-Romae: H. Dessain, 1937-1945; Vol. II, 1940), II, 418 (hereafter cited Vermeersch-Creusen).

[24] *Cameracen.*, 11 dec. 1885, ad I—*Fontes,* n. 6170.

[25] Van der Stappen, IV, 112.

Regulars issued the following decree: "*Tabernaculum regulariter debet esse ligneum, extra deauratum, intus vero aliquo panno serico decenter contectum.*"[26]

However, in view of the practice both before and after the issuance of this decree, it can be said that the Sacred Congregation in question merely meant to set a minimum requirement. St. Charles Borromeo, in his *Instructiones Fabricae Ecclesiasticae,* definitely advised, whenever possible, the use of silver, of brass, or of marble.[27] Furthermore, the Provincial Councils of Aachen (1585),[28] Avignon (1725),[29] and Benevento (1693),[30] although they prescribed wood as a minimum, nevertheless desired the use of more precious materials. Finally, on different occasions there were sent to the Sacred Congregation of Rites doubts and questions in which mention was made of many materials more precious than wood, and yet not once was the use of such materials forbidden or reprobated.[31]

The use either of metal, or of stone, or of wood was certainly determinable at the discretion and through the prescriptions of the ordinary.[32] Thus in the month of March, 1898, the Sacred Congregation of Rites praised an inventor for his efforts in initiating new methods of security for the tabernacle, but declared that his efforts awaited the approbation of the ordinary in order to be put into effect.[33] From this it can be certainly concluded that in the pre-Code law the ordinary acted lawfully no matter what material he prescribed, provided that his choice took into consideration at least the protective value of wood.

However, if wood was used, the structural work was to be skillfully done, or, in other words, the structure was to be artistically

[26] Mühlbauer, *Decreta Authentica Congregationis Sacrorum Rituum* (4 vols., Monachii-Parisiis-Neo-Eboraci, 1863-1867), III, pars II, 365, s.v. *tabernaculum* (hereafter cited Mühlbauer).

[27] *Acta Ecclesiae Mediolan.,* I, pars IV, p. 472.

[28] Mansi, XXXIV, b. 947.

[29] Tit. XXVIII, c. II—*Coll. Lac.,* 528.

[30] Tit. XXXVII, c. III—*Coll. Lac.,* I, 72.

[31] *Auxitana,* 7 aug. 1880—*D.A.,* n. 3520; *Toletana,* 20 sept. 1806, ad II—*Fontes,* n. 5826.

[32] Gasparri, II, 264.

[33] *D.A.,* n. 3987.

built by a professional.[84] The various parts were to be fittingly and firmly put together.[85]

On the contrary, if metal was used, then some provision was to be made for overcoming the added occasions for dampness and moisture. St. Charles Borromeo, in his province of Milan, demanded that metal tabernacles should be fitted on the inside with poplar, or with some other type of wood, in order to offset the danger of quick corruption of the Sacred Species.[86]

There was a further demand that the tabernacle should be well-enclosed.[87] Thus, for example, not even the smallest opening could be tolerated.[88] It is true that for the sake of beauty the doors of the tabernacle were at times constructed or fabricated with perforations. To counteract the danger of such a practice, however, the Provincial Council of Prague (1860) ordered that such tabernacle doors be covered on the inside to keep away the approach of flies and of insects.[89]

The presence of a rear door in the tabernacle apparently did not offend against the demand for a well-enclosed receptacle. St. Charles Borromeo, in his *Instructiones Fabricae Ecclesiasticae,* demanded such rear doors, especially in the larger churches where the choir was behind the altar. Such a second door facilitated the distribution of Holy Communion, and also obviated all interruptions in the divine services on the occasion of a sudden request for

---

[84] S.R.C., *Ordinis Minorum Capuccinorum S. Francisci,* 7 dec. 1883, ad XIII: ". . . tabernaculum affabre elaboratum. . . ."—*Fontes,* n. 6192; Provincial Council of Avignon (1725), tit. XXVIII, c. II: ". . . saltem ex ligno affabre elaborata compacta sint. . . ."—*Coll. Lac.,* I, 528. Cf. also Provincial Council of Ravenna (1855), pars II, cap. IV, n. II—*Coll. Lac.,* VI, 155; I Provincial Council of New Granada (1868), tit. IV, cap. IV—*Coll. Lac.,* VI, 505.

[85] ". . . apte beneque inter se compactum. . . ."—*Acta Ecclesiae Mediolan.,* I, pars IV, *Instructiones Fabricae Ecclesiasticae,* p. 472.

[86] *Acta Ecclesiae Mediolan.,* I, pars IV, *Instructiones Fabricae Ecclesiasticae,* p. 472.

[87] Provincial Council of Benevento (1693), tit. XXXVI, c. III—*Coll. Lac.,* 72; S.R.C., *Vallisoletana,* 30 mart. 1886, ad I—*Fontes,* n. 6173; Provincial Council of New Granada (1868), tit. IV—*Coll. Lac.,* VI, 505.

[88] Giraldi, pars II, c. XX, n. 27.

[89] Mühlbauer, III, pars II, 366, s.v. *tabernaculum.*

Holy Viaticum. Since in later times the Sacred Congregation of Rites never forbade such a practice, it is apparent that the use of a rear door was not considered inconsonant with the proper security for the tabernacle.[40]

The major concern and interest of the Church in pre-Code law revolved around the factor of security for the tabernacle.[41] Regardless of the material used, as long as the tabernacle enjoyed structural strength, was immovable, and remained well-enclosed, the Church was satisfied. As long as due protection was afforded against possible profanation by thieves, against likely disturbance by insects, and against the process of a quick corruption in consequence of heavy moisture, the ordinary could safely act according to his own discretion and judgment in the specification of the material to be used for the construction of the tabernacle.

ARTICLE IV. THE CUSTODY OF THE TABERNACLE KEY

It is apparent that during the post-Tridentine period the key of the tabernacle was not to be left carelessly unguarded, whether in the sacristy, or in the door of the tabernacle, or in any other place.[42] Thus, in 1724 the Sacred Congregation of Bishops and Regulars, at the mandate of Pope Innocent XIII (1721-1724), demanded that all ordinaries were to take care that those who were charged with the custody of the tabernacle should either keep the keys personally, or else put them in a place made safe under lock and key.[43]

Certainly the key to the tabernacle was not to be retained either

---

[40] *Acta Ecclesiae Mediolan.*, I, pars IV, p. 472.

[41] Excerpt from Provincial Council of Cologne (1860)—Mühlbauer, III, pars II, 363, s.v. *tabernaculum;* excerpt from Provincial Council of Prague (1860)—Mühlbauer, III, pars II, 363, s.v. *tabernaculum;* S.R.C., *Dubium quoad varios modos asservandi in Tabernaculo sacram Pixidem,* 18 mart. 1898—*D.A.*, n. 3987.

[42] S.R.C., 22 sept. 1593—André-Condis-Wagner, *Dictionnaire de Droit Canonique* (5. ed., 4 vols., Paris, 1901), III, 580 (hereafter cited André-Wagner) ; S.C. Ep. et Reg., *Faventina,* 25 mart. 1591—*Fontes,* n. 1442.

[43] André-Wagner, III, 580-581. Cf. also S.C. Ep. et Reg., ep. encycl., 9 febr. 1751—*Fontes,* n. 1868.

by lay persons, or by sisters,[44] or even by cloistered nuns.[45] In answering doubts concerning the custody of the key for the repository of Holy Thursday, the Sacred Congregation of Rites on numerous occasions forbade the consignment of the key to a lay confraternity, to the governor, to a secular judge, to a patron, or to any other person, regardless of his dignity or his position, any and all customs notwithstanding.[46] Thus, for example, the Archbishop of Corfù demanded the observance of an immemorial custom, which entrusted the key of the repository to the lay head of a Sodality of the Blessed Sacrament. The Canons of the Cathedral Church objected, and the Prefect of the Sacred Congregation sustained their objection: *"Iuxta alias [alia?] decreta clavem, in casu, nulli esse omnino tradendam."*[47]

Certainly the ordinary custodian of the tabernacle key was to be a priest.[48] The Sacred Congregation of Rites, in its numerous demands that on Holy Thursday the key should be given to the one designated as the celebrant for the Mass of the Presanctified, certainly indicated that such was to be the practice on all occasions.[49] According to the II Plenary Council of Baltimore (1866), the key of the permanent tabernacle was to be entrusted to the priest who had the care of the church or of the chapel concerned.[50]

---

[44] S.R.C., *Atrebaten.*, 13 sept. 1866—Reiffenstuel, *Ius Canonicum Universum* (5 vols. in 7, Venetiis, 1735), lib. III, tit. 44, n. 1, adnotatio XLIV; Provincial Council of Prague (1860), tit. V, cap. IV—*Coll. Lac.*, V, 534; Provincial Council of Cologne (1860), tit. II, c. XXX—*Coll. Lac.*, V, 374.

[45] S.R.C., *Societatis Iesu*, 11 maii 1878, ad VI—*Fontes*, n. 3448; S.C. Ep. et Reg., *Vallisoletana*, 12 mart. 1705—*Fontes*, n. 1822.

[46] Pacen., 30 ian. 1610—André-Wagner, III, 582; *Compostellana*, 29 ian. 1682—André-Wagner, III, 582; *Civitaten.*, 6 dec. 1631—*Fontes*, n. 5341; *Hispalense*, 22 nov. 1636—*Fontes*, n. 5363; *Tiburtina*, 7 dec. 1737—*Fontes*, n. 5774.

[47] S.R.C., *Corcyren.*, 22 maii 1841, ad I—*Fontes*, n. 5910.

[48] S.R.C., 22 sept. 1593—André-Wagner, III, 580; Provincial Council of Vienna (1858)—Mühlbauer, III, pars II, 365, s.v. *tabernaclum;* Provincial Council of Halifax (1857), decr. XII, n. 1—*Coll. Lac.*, III, 741; I Provincial Council of Westminster (1852), decr. XVIII, n. 7—*Coll. Lac.*, III, 931; *Acta Ecclesiae Mediolan.*, I, pars IV, *Instructiones de Sacramento Sanctissimae Eucharistiae*, p. 424; Giraldi, pars IV, c. XX, n. 27.

[49] See footnote 46.

[50] N. 266—*Coll. Lac.*, III, 468.

In non-parochial churches, oratories, or chapels, the key was to be entrusted to the chaplain or to the rector.[51] In parochial churches, according to a decree of the Sacred Congregation of the Council in 1689, it was the exclusive right of the pastor, in spite of any contrary custom, to care for the tabernacle key.[52] Yet in 1770 the Sacred Congregation of Rites allowed the chaplain of a Confraternity of the Blessed Sacrament which had been established at a particular church to have equal rights with the pastor in the guardianship of the key.[53]

Although these were the general rules of the post-Tridentine period as enacted with respect to the custody of the tabernacle key, nevertheless certain modifications remain to be considered. In 1669 the Provincial Council of Naples demanded that the key should be retained by the pastor in the parochial churches, and in the other churches by one who was at least *in sacris*.[54] In 1860 the Provincial Council of Cologne permitted no one less than a subdeacon to guard the key.[55] From these two councils it is apparent that at times, by way of exception, clerics in major orders were entrusted with the key of the tabernacle.

Again, in individual provinces, as in many of Spain, there existed general and immemorial customs, whereby lay men of proven worth retained the custody of the key. According to Schmalzgrueber (1663-1735), such customs could be tolerated.[56] However, the Sacred Congregation of Rites forbade the continuance of such an immemorial custom in respect to the guarding of the repository for Holy Thursday.[57]

---

[51] S.C. Ep. et Reg., *Vallisoletana*, 12 mart. 1705—*Fontes*, n. 1822; S.C. Ep. et Reg., ep. encycl., 9 febr. 1751—*Fontes*, n. 1868; S.C.C., *Neapolitana*, 14 nov. 1693—André-Wagner, III, 580; Provincial Council of Utrecht (1865), tit. IV. cap. IV—*Coll. Lac.*, V, 819; I Prov. Council of New Granada (1868), tit. IV, cap. IV—*Coll. Lac.*, VI, 505; Schmalzgrueber, *Jus Ecclesiasticum Universum* (5 vols. in 12, Romae, 1843-1845), lib. III, tit. 44, n. 28 (hereafter cited Schmalzgrueber).

[52] *Ausculana*, 25 iun. 1689—André-Wagner, III, 580.

[53] *Eugubina*, 7 aug. 1717, ad 16—*D.A.*, n. 2243.

[54] Tit. III, cap. IV, n. 14—*Coll. Lac.*, I, 194.

[55] Tit. II, c. XXX—*Coll. Lac.*, V, 374.

[56] *Jus Ecclesiasticum Universum*, lib. II, tit. 44, n. 28-29.

[57] *Corcyren.*, 22 maii 1841—*Fontes*, n. 5910.

Again, in the nineteenth century there seems to have been a generous relaxation with reference to the custody of the tabernacle key. By virtue of apostolic indults in individual cases, the key was often entrusted to women religious and lay people.[58] Even in the absence of any such indult there nevertheless existed in many places the practice of leaving the key in the sacristy to be cared for by people other than priests. In private homes which by papal privilege contained domestic oratories wherein the Blessed Sacrament was legitimately reserved it was quite often the family itself, rather than the chaplain, that exercised all guardianship over the tabernacle key.[59] Only immemorial custom could have legitimated such a practice.

However, even in churches the pastor or rector often kept the tabernacle key within a locked compartment in the sacristy. The key to this compartment was then left with a lay sacristan for the time that the pastor or rector was absent. Also, towards the end of the nineteenth century, nuns and religious of simple vows, even apart from any apostolic indult, retained the key themselves perpetually. Relative to these last two cases Gasparri (1852-1934) maintained that necessity legitimated such a practice. Until it was forbidden by the Congregation of Rites, so he continued, the practice could be tolerated.[60]

In conclusion, it should be remarked that the Church was severe in penalizing those who were careless in the guardianship of the tabernacle key. In 1724 the Sacred Congregation of Bishops and Regulars, at the command of Pope Innocent XIII (1721-1724), issued a letter to the ordinaries on the question of penalties. From then on, if anyone broke into the tabernacle, either because it was left open, or because the key was left in the door or in any other place where it could be easily obtained, the one in charge was to be punished in accord with the Decretal *Statuimus* of Pope Innocent III. Furthermore, the guilty custodian was to be condemned to prison, was to have other discretionary penalties inflicted upon

---

[58] Gregorius XVI, ap. litt. *Caritatis viscera,* 14 maii 1833—*Ius Pont.,* Pars Prima, V, 76-77; SC.C., *Fulden,* 17 febr. 1883—*ASS,* XV (1883), 528.

[59] Gasparri, II, 267.

[60] *Tractatus Canonicus de Sanctissima Eucharistia,* II, 267.

him, and was forever to be deprived of the office of sacristan. As long as there was negligence, even though no actual theft ensued, the Decretal *Statuimus* was to be followed to the letter. Finally, these penalties were to be inflicted upon the one in charge, even though some other priest had left the door of the tabernacle open, or had dealt carelessly with the key, for it was the duty of the custodian to see that everything was in proper order at the conclusion of any service which had required the use of the key.[61]

As a result of the Constitution *Apostolicae Sedis* of Pope Pius IX (1846-1878), which revised the penal law regarding *latae sententiae* censures, these penalties no longer continued as applicable penal law after the year 1869. After that time the ordinary could indeed punish a past delict of this type, or he could also enact *latae sententiae* censures for negligent custodians.[62]

ARTICLE V. THE PYX

In 1614 the *Roman Ritual* demanded that the Sacred Species in whatever number they were needed for the sick or as Communion for the faithful were to be reserved in a pyx.[63] No exceptions to this rule were allowed. On different occasions the Sacred Congregation of Rites forbade other practices.[64] Thus in 1881, when the Bishop of Alton, Illinois, asked whether the priests of his diocese could leave the Blessed Sacrament wrapped in plain corporals rather than stored in precious vessels which attracted thieves, the Sacred Congregation of Rites answered: *"Non expedire; et curet*

[61] Ep. encycl., ian. 1724—André-Wagner, III, 580-581. Cf. also S.C. Ep. et Reg., ep. encycl., 9 febr. 1751—*Fontes*, n. 1868.

[62] Gasparri, II, 267.

[63] "Curare porro debet [parochus], ut perpetuo aliquot particulae consecratae eo numero, qui usui infirmorum et aliorum fidelium communioni satis esse possit, conserventur in pyxide ex solida decentique materia, eaque munda, et suo operculo bene clausa, albo velo cooperta, et quantum res feret, ornato in tabernaculo clave obserato."—*Rituale Rom.*, tit. IV, c. 1, *de sanctissimo Eucharistiae sacramento*, n. 5.

[64] *Civitatis Conchen.*, 13 aug. 1667, ad 2—*Fontes*, n. 5564; *Portugaliae*, 11 iun. 1904—*Collectanea S. Congregationis de Propaganda Fide* (2 vols., Romae: Typographia Polyglotta S. C. de Propaganda Fide, 1907), n. 2196 (hereafter cited *Collectanea*).

Episcopus ut Sacra Eucharistia cautius custodiatur."[65] So also the Sacred Congregation for the Propagation of the Faith, which allowed the Blessed Sacrament to be carried occultly in times of persecutions, nevertheless always demanded the use of a small pyx.[66]

Despite these regulations that the Sacred Species should always be placed in a pyx, or in a ciborium, there nevertheless arose the practice of leaving the Sacred Host for exposition at all times in the ostensorium. In other words, in large tabernacles the ostensorium itself was placed within the tabernacle. Inasmuch as the *Roman Ritual*, when it demanded the use of the pyx, merely spoke of the Sacred Hosts which were to serve as Communion for the sick and for the rest of the faithful, and omitted all mention of exposition, such a practice was deemed legitimate.[67]

Furthermore, in the nineteenth century there arose in many churches and oratories of France the practice of placing the Sacred Host that was used for exposition "*intra duo crystalla apte cohaerentia, eamque in Tabernaculo reponendi absque ulla capsa seu custodia.*" When the Sacred Congregation of Rites was questioned whether such a practice was lawful, it answered: *Affirmative; dummodo sacra Hostia in dictis crystallis bene sit clausa atque crystalla non tangat, iuxta Decreta alias edita.*"[68]

Again, the *Roman Ritual* demanded that the pyx be made of solid and well-suited material.[69] At different times a variety of ideas existed as to what constituted a pyx of solid and well-suited material. During the early part of the post-Tridentine period, that is, prior to the appearance of the *Roman Ritual*, certainly such materials as alabaster, aluminum, wood, bronze, copper, gold, crystal, silver, ivory, marble, platinum and glass were used.[70] However, in 1600 the *Caeremoniale Episcoporum* demanded, as

---

[65] *Altonen.*, 17 febr. 1881—*Fontes*, n. 6127.

[66] Litt. encycl., 25 febr. 1859, ad 3—*Fontes*, n. 4846. Cf. also Benedictus XIV, ep. encycl. *Inter omnigenas*, 2 febr. 1744, § 23—*Fontes*, n. 339.

[67] De Herdt, III, 251.

[68] *Dubium seu Galliarum*, 14 ian. 1898—*ASS*, XXX (1898), 473; *D.A.*, n. 3974.

[69] Tit. IV, c. 1, *de sanctissimo Eucharistiae Sacramento*, n. 5.

[70] Corblet, II, 288.

a general rule, pyxes of gold, or at least pyxes of silver which were gold-plated on the inside.[71]

This demand of the *Caeremoniale Episcoporum* was accordingly recognized as indicating the ordinary norm regarding the material to be used in the construction of pyxes.[72] By way of exception other materials, such as copper, could still be used.[73] The exceptional use of other materials, however, was not unrestricted. Thus the Sacred Congregation of Rites forbade the use of glass, even though its use might serve as a deterrent to robbery by thieves.[74] Furthermore, Schmalzgrueber[75] outlawed the use of wooden pyxes in view of the danger of breakage, and of stone pyxes because of their ponderous weight and also in view of their absorption of moisture. Finally, Gasparri[76] disapproved the use of wood or of compressed cardboard on the score of their lack of substantial solidity, and of bronze and of ivory on the score of their lack of due fitness and propriety.

Again, the *Roman Ritual* demanded that the pyx be well-enclosed by its cover.[77] This cover, according to the Provincial Council of Naples (1699), was to be at least gold-plated.[78] According to the *Instructiones Variae* of St. Charles Borromeo, this cover was to be such that it could be removed without difficulty. No doubt he had in mind the danger of spilling the Sacred Species if one had to struggle with the removal of a cover that fit too snugly. He also suggested that the cover for the pyx be attached by some sort of clasp. Thus there would be obviated all danger of possible profanation of the Sacred Species in the event that the pyx fell accidentally to the ground.[79] It appears certain that reference was

---

[71] Lib. II, c. 30, n. 31.

[72] Schmalzgrueber, lib. III, tit. 44, n. 11; Zitelli, *Apparatus Iuris Ecclesiastici* (2. ed., Romae, 1895), p. 292 (hereafter cited Zitelli). Cf. also the Provincial Council of Benevento (1693), tit. XXXVII, c. 2—*Coll. Lac.*, I, 72; the I Provincial Council of New Granada (1868), cap. IV—*Coll. Lac.*, VI, 505.

[73] S.R.C., *Sancti Hippolyti*, 21 aug. 1867, ad VI—*D.A.*, n. 3162; Gasparri, II, 270; Zitelli, p. 292.

[74] *Mindonien.*, 30 ian. 1880—*Fontes*, n. 6123.

[75] *Jus Ecclesiasticum Universum*, lib. III, tit. 44, n. 11.

[76] *Tractatus Canonicus de Sanctissima Eucharistia*, II, 271.

[77] Tit. IV, c. 1, *de sanctissimo Eucharistiae Sacramento*, n. 5.

[78] Tit. III, c. IV, n. 12—*Coll. Lac.*, I, 183.

[79] *Acta Ecclesiae Mediolan.*, I, pars IV, 703.

here made to the small pyx which had to be employed on Communion calls to the sick.

Finally, the *Roman Ritual,* as another precautionary measure for the proper safeguarding of the Sacred Species, demanded that the pyx with its Sacred Contents should always be kept in a locked tabernacle.[80]

ARTICLE VI. THE RENEWAL OF THE SACRED SPECIES

The *Roman Ritual* merely[81] demanded that the Sacred Species be renewed frequently. On several occasions during this post-Tridentine period, however, the Sacred Congregation of Rites[82] insisted upon the observance of the norm of the *Caeremoniale Episcoporum,*[83] which prescribed that the Sacred Species should be renewed at least once a week.

Although this norm of the *Caeremoniale Episcoporum* became the norm for the universal discipline of the Latin Church,[84] nevertheless it was never inflexibly urged by the Holy See.[85] Thus some provincial councils simply repeated the prescription which was incorporated in the *Roman Ritual.*[86] Other provincial councils specifically allowed the renewal to be postponed until the fifteenth day.[87] Other provincial councils even allowed the renewal to be postponed for one month.[88]

---

[80] Tit. IV, c. 1, *de Sanctissimo Eucharistiae Sacramento,* n. 5.

[81] Tit. IV, c. 1, *de sanctissimo Eucharistiae Sacramento,* n. 7.

[82] *Conchen.,* 3 sept. 1672, ad 3—Gardellini, *Decreta Authentica Congregationis Sacrorum Rituum* (cura H. Capalti, 4 vols., Romae, 1856-1858), n. 2602 (hereafter cited Gardellini); *Sanctorien.,* 12 sept. 1884, ad II—*Fontes,* n. 6161.

[83] Lib. I, c. VI, n. 2.

[84] Van der Stappen, IV, 138.

[85] Köster, p. 167.

[86] I Provincial Council of Westminister (1852), decr. XVIII, n. 7—*Coll. Lac.,* III, 931; II Council of the Colonies of England, Holland, and Denmark (1867), sect. I, art. III, n. 2—*Coll. Lac.,* III, 1112-1113.

[87] Provincial Council of Embrun (1727), c. X, n. IV—*Coll. Lac.,* I, 629; Council of Strigonia (1858), tit. V, 5, 2—*Coll. Lac.,* V, 46; Provincial Council of Prague (1860), tit. V, c. VII—*Coll. Lac.,* V, 542; Provincial Council of Kalocsa (1863), tit. III, cap. IV—*Coll. Lac.,* V, 647.

[88] Provincial Council of Vienna (1858)—*Coll. Lac.,* V, n. 163; Provincial Council of Utrecht (1865)—*Coll. Lac.,* V, n. 920.

Those councils which allowed a renewal of the sacred particles to be effected every fifteenth day, or every other week, seemed to have much justification in this enactment.[89] Thus, for example, Pope Clement VIII (1592-1605) in an Instruction to the Italo-Greeks of Southern Italy,[90] and Pope Benedict XIV (1740-1758) in a Constitution to the same group,[91] and also in a later Encyclical to the missionaries in the Orient,[92] demanded a renewal of the Sacred Species every eight or at least every fifteen days.

However, among the pre-Code authors and decretalists, Schmalzgrueber (1663-1735),[93] Giraldi (1692-1775),[94] Ferraris (+ ca. 1763),[95] Santi (1830-1885),[96] and Wernz (1842-1914)[97] demanded that the regulation of the *Caeremoniale Episcoporum* should be followed. Gasparri[98] made the same demand, but also made allowance for an exceptional norm if special circumstances necessitated a postponement until the fifteenth day. Gardellini (1757-1829)[99] in his notes on a decree of the Sacred Congregation of Rites to the diocese of Ghent on December 16, 1826, made the following observation: "*Quod si ad quindecim dies protrahatur renovatio, non id reprobandum, culpaeque vertendum, quia hoc intra breve tempus haud formido quod sacrae species corrumpantur.*" Zitelli (+1887)[100] taught that the Sacred Species should be

---

[89] Cf. *Acta Ecclesiae Mediolan.*, I, pars IV, *Instructiones de Sacramento Sanctissimae Eucharistiae,* p. 424; S.C. Ep. et Reg., *Ravennaten.*, 5 aug. 1573—*Fontes,* n. 1308.

[90] Instr. *Sanctissimus,* 31 aug. 1595, n. 2—*Fontes,* n. 179.

[91] Const. *Etsi pastoralis,* 26 maii 1742, VI, n. II—*Fontes,* n. 328.

[92] Ep. encycl. *Allatae sunt,* 26 iul. 1755—*Fontes,* n. 434.

[93] *Jus Ecclesiasticum Universum,* lib. III, tit. 44, n. 11.

[94] *Animadversiones et additamenta ex posterioribus Summorum Pontificum constitutionibus et Sacrarum Congregationum decretis desumpta ad Aug. Barbosa, De officio et potestate parochi descriptio,* pars II, c. XX, n. 27.

[95] *Prompta Bibliotheca Canonica, Iuridica, Moralis, Theologica, necnon Ascetica, Polemica, Rubristica, Historica* (9 vols., Romae, 1885-1889), III, 751, s.v. *Eucharistia.*

[96] *Praelectiones Iuris Canonici* (5 vols. in 1, Ratisbonae-Neo-Eboraci-Cincinnatii, 1886), lib. III, tit. 44, n. 2.

[97] *Ius Decretalium* (6 vols., Romae, 1898-1904; Vol. V, 3. ed., Prati, 1914), III, 556, footnote n. 219.

[98] *Tractatus Canonicus de Sanctissima Eucharistia,* II, 274.

[99] *Decreta Authentica Congregationis Sacrorum Rituum,* n. 4623.

[100] *Apparatus Iuris Ecclesiastici,* p. 292.

renewed no later than every eight days in a warm climate, and no later than every fifteen days in a cold climate. Van der Stappen[101] allowed the renewal to be made every fifteen days on condition that the presence of dampness or moisture did not necessitate a more frequent renewal. Finally, Many (+1922)[102] discreetly declared that it was difficult in view of the possible divergent circumstances to set a general rule, so that the renewal should be made either once every week, or once every two weeks. In such a matter legitimate custom and diocesan statute could well be followed as indicating an acceptable norm.

According to the *Roman Ritual,* not only were the Sacred Species to be renewed frequently, but also the hosts for consecration were to be baked recently.[103] In 1826 the Sacred Congregation of Rites declared that the custom which obtained in the diocese of Ghent, namely of using hosts which had been baked three or six months before, was to be eliminated.[104] St. Charles Borromeo (1538-1584) set the allowance of the time-limit between the baking of the hosts and their subsequent consecration at twenty days.[105] The Plenary Council of Latin America (1899) adopted this norm of St. Charles Borromeo.[106] Gasparri[107] and Wernz[108] also agreed to this norm. Furthermore, Gasparri noted that those who made use of the fifteen-day period of renewal should then use hosts which were made no earlier than fifteen days before the consecration. In other words, the combined lapse of time between the baking of the hosts and their renewal was not to exceed the duration of a month.[109]

Another point to be considered in connection with the renewal of the Sacred Hosts was the practice of placing newly consecrated

---

[101] *Sacra Liturgia,* IV, 138.

[102] *Praelectiones Canonicae de Missa* (Parisiis, 1903), p. 290.

[103] Tit. IV, c. I, *de sanctissimo Eucharistiae Sacramento,* n. 7.

[104] *Gandaven.,* 16 dec. 1826—*D.A.*, n. 2650.

[105] *Acta Ecclesiae Mediolan.*, I, pars I, IV Provinciale Concilium Mediolanense (1576), p. 110.

[106] *Acta et Decreta Concilii Plenarii Americae Latinae* (2 vols., Romae, 1900), I, n. 347.

[107] *Tractatus Canonicus de Sanctissimae Eucharistiae,* II, 276.

[108] *Ius Decretalium,* III, 552.

[109] *Op. cit.,* II, 276.

Hosts in the same ciborium with Hosts consecrated a week or so before. As early as the publication of the *Caeremoniale Episcoporum* this practice was forbidden. The *Caeremoniale* declared that the Sacred Hosts were to be changed as well as renewed.[110] Furthermore, the *Roman Ritual* declared very explicitly: ". . . *et ubi eas [hostias seu particulas] consecraverit, veteres primo distribuat, vel sumat.*"[111]

Lastly, if in spite of all precautions the Sacred Species became corrupt, then according to Gasparri the incorrupt particles or portions of them were to be separated from the rest and consumed. Those, however, which had become corrupt or putrid were to be burnt, and the ashes were then to be disposed of in the sacrarium.[112]

ARTICLE VII. THE CUSTODY OF THE BLESSED SACRAMENT OUTSIDE THE CHURCH

During the post-Tridentine period the ancient practices of receiving and of reserving the Blessed Sacrament apparently revived to a certain extent, for the Holy See on several occasions found it necessary to again condemn such practices.[113] At times, however, the practice of reserving the Blessed Sacrament in private homes was warranted through the grant of apostolic indults. Thus the Holy Father allowed Mary, Queen of Scots (+1587), to retain the Blessed Eucharist in her prison cell for the purpose of Viaticum on the occasion of her execution.[114] Furthermore, missionaries were by means of special faculties allowed at times to keep the Blessed Sacrament in their homes, in other decent places,[115] and even in the bedroom of a sick person.[116] Such an

---

[110] ". . . mutetur et renovetur. . . ."—*Caeremoniale Episcoporum,* lib. I, c. VI, n. 2.

[111] Tit. IV, c. I, *de sanctissimo Eucharistiae Sacramento,* n. 7.

[112] *Op. cit.,* II, 276.

[113] S.C.C., 2 oct. 1677—Anonymous, "*De la Frequente Communion,*"—*Analecta Juris Pontificii* (Romae, 1855-1869; Parisiis, 1872-1891), VII (1869), 817-818; Benedictus XIV, const. *Etsi pastoralis,* 26 maii 1742, § VI, n. VII—*Fontes,* n. 328. Cf. also, Köster, p. 105.

[114] Schmalzgrueber, lib. III, tit. 44, n. 4.

[115] S.R.C., *Vicariatus Apostolici de Dania,* 10 febr. 1871—*Fontes,* n. 6035.

[116] S.C. de Prop. Fide, *Tunkin. Occident.,* 22 sept. 1850—*Collectanea,* n. 1052; *Fontes,* n. 4832.

indult was customarily granted when there was danger from heretics and infidels,[117] when the only church in the locality was a non-Catholic one, or when the Catholic church building did not offer security, as, for example, when it lacked doors and windows.[118]

In some places, even apart from any indult, the Blessed Sacrament was transferred at night from the church to some safe place, for example, the safe in the sacristy or in the priest's house. According to some pre-Code canonists,[119] such a practice, which was introduced in different dioceses and approved by the local ordinaries, could be tolerated because of the danger of sacrilegious thefts. That the Holy See was in sympathy with such a view is apparent from the fact that several provincial councils during this period contained statutes to the effect that such a practice could be lawfully continued.[120]

Also during the post-Tridentine period the occasions on which a priest could lawfully transfer the Blessed Sacrament outside the church were very limited. In 1638 the Sacred Congregation of rites declared:

> *Delationem SS. Sacramenti extra ecclesiam non esse permissam, nisi occasione solemnis Processionis in Festo et per octavam Corporis Christi, nec non occasione infirmorum, et orationis quadraginta horarum iuxta Sac. Canonum Decreta.*[121]

Thus, according to the norms of this decree of the Sacred Con-

---

[117] Ordinarily, according to Schmalzgrueber, the Blessed Sacrament was not to be reserved in times of persecution. "Hinc in locis sub dominio infidelium vel haereticorum ne exponatur periculo irreverentiae tantum sacramentum, illud non retinetur in ecclesia, aut domi, sed tantum olea sacra apud parochus, ut retulit practicari in dioecesi Tribiniensi sub Turcarum ditione Episcopus Macharensis et Tribiniensis in relatione facta occasione visitationis sacrorum liminum die 11 sept. 1706."—Lib. III, tit. 44, n. 4.

[118] S.C. de Prop. Fide (*C.P. -Iaffnae*), 23 aug. 1852, n. 2—*Fontes,* n. 4835.

[119] Gasparri, II, 263; Many, p. 285.

[120] I Provincial Council of Australia (1884), decr. XI—*Coll. Lac.,* III, 1048-1049; III Provincial Council of Tuam (1858), cap. XV, n. 1—*Coll. Lac.,* III, 886.

[121] *Sulmonen.,* 12 iun. 1638—*D.A.,* n. 648.

gregation, the following practices, which were current at various times during this period, were not to be tolerated: 1. The practice of priests whereby they allowed sick people, who could not swallow, to look at, adore, and kiss the Sacred Host;[122] 2. the practice of missionaries whereby they carried the Blessed Sacrament on long journeys for the purpose of communicating themselves, or carried the Blessed Sacrament on their persons from morning to night in view of the possibility of meeting a sick person;[123] 3. the practice of priests whereby they carried the Blessed Sacrament in public in order to stop a fire or in order to calm a storm.[124]

The Roman Pontiffs, such as Pope Innocent XI (1691-1700) and Pope Alexander VIII (1689-1691), were severe in penalizing those who violated the above mentioned regulations about the private reservation of the Blessed Sacrament and the unlawful carrying of the Blessed Sacrament on a journey.[125] Any unauthorized retention, transfer, or carrying away of the Blessed Sacrament gave rise at least to a suspicion of heresy. Therefore all

---

[122] Benedictus XIV, const. *Cum ut recte nosti,* 27 iul. 1755, n. 12—*Fontes,* n. 435. Cf. also, *Rituale Rom.,* tit. IV, c. 4 *de Communione Infirmorum,* n. 5.

[123] S.C. de Prop. Fide, litt. encycl. 25 febr. 1859—*Fontes,* n. 4846. Cf. also, S.C. de Prop. Fide, instr. (*ad Vic. Ap. Indiar. Orient.*), 8 sept. 1869, n. 30—*Fontes,* n. 4876; S.R.C., *Vicariatus Apostolici de Dania,* 10 febr. 1871, ad I—*Fontes,* n. 6035.

In its encyclical letter of February 25, 1859 the Sacred Congregation for the Propagation of the Faith referred with approval to the teachings of two authors. The first, Vericelli (+1656), taught that it was forbidden by universal custom and by the decrees of many councils to carry the Blessed Sacrament secretly on a journey, except to bring Communion to the sick in those places where there was danger from infidels, and provided that the journey did not exceed a day's travel. The second, Thomas a Iesu (+1627), considered as allowable the practice of missionaries who under the same kind of circumstances, when they were face to face with imminent danger of death, secretly carried Holy Viaticum along with them.

[124] Benedictus XIV, const. *Cum ut recte nosti,* 27 iul. 1755, nn. 1, 4, 13, 14, 15—*Fontes,* n. 435.

In this same constitution Pope Benedict XIV forbade the use of the Sacred Species in the ritual of exorcism.

[125] Innocentius XI, const. *Ad nostri apostolatus,* 12 mart. 1677, 1, n. 2—*Fontes,* n. 250; Alexander VIII, const. *Cum alias,* 22 dec. 1690—*Fontes,* n. 255; Benedictus XIV, const. *Ab augustissimo,* 5 mart. 1744—*Fontes,* n. 340.

guilty persons were to be investigated by the Holy Office of the Inquisition, and punished in proportion to the gravity of their crimes. Unless it was apparent that the act was not perpetrated for an evil purpose, then even at the first offence those who were over the age of twenty-one were to be handed over to the secular authorities for condign punishment.[126]

[126] Cf. Schmalzgrueber, lib. III, tit. 44, n. 9.

PART TWO

Canonical Commentary

CHAPTER III

The Place of Reservation

ARTICLE I. THE CONDITIONS REQUIRED FOR THE RESERVATION OF THE BLESSED SACRAMENT

Can. 1265, § 1. *Sanctissima Eucharistia, dummodo adsit qui eius curam habeat et regulariter sacerdos semel saltem in hebdomada Missam in sacro loco celebret:*

1°. *Custodiri debet in ecclesia cathedrali, in ecclesia principe Abbatiae vel Praelaturae nullius, Vicariatus et Praefecturae Apostolicae, in qualibet ecclesia paroeciali vel quasi-paroeciali et in ecclesia adnexa domui religiosorum exemptorum sive virorum sive mulierum;*

2°. *Custodiri potest, de licentia Ordinarii loci, in ecclesia collegiata et in oratorio principali sive publico sive semi-publico tum domus piae aut religiosae, tum collegii ecclesiastici quod a clericis saecularibus vel a religiosis regatur.*

Can. 1266. *Ecclesiae in quibus sanctissima Eucharistia asservatur, praesertim paroeciales, quotidie per aliquot saltem horas fidelibus pateant.*

The Most Blessed Eucharist may under the following conditions be reserved in the sacred places designated by the law:

1. There must be a guardian.
2. A priest must say Mass regularly at least once a week.
3. Churches, especially parochial churches, in which the Blessed Sacrament is reserved, must be open to the faithful every day for at least a few hours.

Section I. ". . . dummodo adsit qui eius curam habeat. . . ."

The obligation to have a guardian of the Blessed Sacrament is at all times a grave obligation. On occasion the Holy See, in view of an extant deficiency in the number of normally requisite priests, has dispensed particular pastors and rectors from their obligation to say Mass once a week, but never has the Holy See made any similar concession relative to the requisite continued guardianship of the Holy Eucharist.[1]

That fact serves as an indication of the importance of the guardian of the Blessed Eucharist. Indeed, so many points are to be considered in respect to the guardian that the present writer has determined to deal more fully with this subject in a later chapter.

Section II. ". . . regulariter sacerdos semel saltem in hebdomada Missam in sacro loco celebret."

The obligation to say Holy Mass at least once a week in a place where the Blessed Eucharist is reserved must be regarded as a duty which in and of itself is binding *sub gravi.*[2] The canon uses the word *regulariter.* As a rule, then, the pastor or rector of the place of reservation cannot to the exclusion of a serious violation of the law omit the celebration of Holy Mass for more than one week.

This rule, however, is not absolute in character. For a reasonable cause Holy Mass can be delayed for ten or fifteen days.[3] Provided a just cause is present, such delays seem permissible as often as four or five times a year. Furthermore, in the presence of a grave and extraordinary cause such omissions appear justified even as often as ten times a year.[4] In such circumstances, of course, there

---

[1] S.C. de Sacramentis, *Instructio de Sanctissima Eucharistia sedulo Custodienda* (hereafter cited *Instruction*), 26 maii 1938, n. 3—*Acta Apostolicae Sedis, Commentarium Officiale* (Romae, 1909-1929); Civitate Vaticana, 1929—), XXX (1938), 199 (hereafter cited *AAS*); Cappello, *Tractatus Canonico-Moralis de Sacramentis* (3 vols. in 6, Vol. I, 4. ed., Romae: Marietti, 1945), I, 283 (hereafter cited Cappello); Pauwels, "*Annotationes ad Instructionem de Eucharistiae Custodia,*"—*Periodica de Religiosis et Missionariis,* Brugis, 1905-1919; from 1920: *Periodica de Re Canonica et Morali utilia praesertim Religiosis et Missionariis,* Brugis, 1920-1927; from 1927: *Periodica de Re Morali, Canonica, Liturgica,* Brugis (1927-1936) et Romae (1937—), XXVII (1938), 387 (hereafter cited *Periodica*).

[2] *Instruction,* n. 3—*AAS,* XXX (1938), 199; Cappello, I, 283.

[3] Cappello, I, 283.

[4] Berutti, *Institutiones Iuris Canonici* (6 vols. in 7, Vol. IV, *De Rebus,* Taurini-Romae: Marietti, 1940), IV, 245 (hereafter cited Berutti).

still remains the need of complying with the prescription of canon 1272, which concerns the renewal of the Sacred Species.

Section III. ". . . *quotidie per aliquot saltem horas fidelibus pateant* [*ecclesiae*]."

The rectors of churches in which the Blessed Sacrament is reserved, and especially parochial churches, are in the usual course of things obliged *sub gravi* to keep these churches open for the faithful during at least a few hours every day. The purpose of this prescription of canon 1266 is very evident from the primary reason which underlies the very act of reserving the Blessed Eucharist, namely, the adoration of the Eucharistic Christ. The obligation is so strict that only in consequence of an apostolic indult may such a church lack an outside door.[5] Generally the existence of such an outside door is made an explicit *conditio sine qua non* in the indults through which the privilege of the reservation of the Blessed Sacrament is granted.[6]

Although canon 1266 makes explicit mention only of churches, nevertheless in virtue of canon 1191, § 1, the same principle holds for public oratories.[7]

ARTICLE II. THE PLACES WHERE THE BLESSED SACRAMENT MUST BE KEPT

> Can. 1265, § 1, 1°. *Custodiri debet* [*Sanctissima Eucharistia*] *in ecclesia cathedrali, in ecclesia principe Abbatiae vel Praelaturae nullius, Vicariatus et Praefecturae Apostolicae, in qualibet ecclesia paroeciali vel quasi-paroeciali et in ecclesia adnexa domui religiosorum exemptorum sive virorum sive mulierum.*

Provided that the conditions imposed by the law are observed, the Blessed Sacrament must be kept in the cathedral church, in the main church of an abbacy or prelacy *nullius,* of a vicariate or prefecture apostolic, in every parochial or quasi-parochial church,

---

[5] S.R.C., *Baionen.*, 14 maii 1899—*D.A.*, n. 3706.

[6] Cappello, I, 287; S.R.C., *Compostellana,* 15 nov. 1890—*D.A.*, n. 3739.

[7] Cappello, I, 287.

and in the church which is attached to a house of exempt religious whether of men or of women.

Section I. Reservation in Cathedral Churches

In the pre-Code law extremely few were the cathedrals in which the Blessed Sacrament was not reserved. This situation prompted a number of authors to look upon the reservation of the Blessed Sacrament in cathedral churches as an obligation. Nevertheless, as a matter of fact, only such cathedrals which had the care of souls attached to them were so obligated.[8]

With the advent of the Code, however, there did arise an ordinarily grave obligation for all cathedrals, and for all churches which the law regards as equivalent to cathedrals, to reserve the Blessed Sacrament. The reason for this obligation is that cathedrals, and also the churches which in an abbacy or prelacy *nullius,* or in a vicariate or prefecture apostolic take the place of cathedral churches, are looked upon as parish churches serving the entire respective territories.[9]

Section II. Reservation in Parish Churches

The Code of Canon Law merely repeats the earlier law when it declares that parish churches must reserve the Blessed Sacrament.[10] The Code admits no exception. Whether the parish is a territorial parish, a national parish, or a purely personal parish for certain families or for certain persons, the pastor is strictly obliged to reserve the Blessed Sacrament in the parochial church.[11] According to the common opinion of the canonists this obligation is in and of itself a most grave obligation, since it is universally acknowledged that the divine law itself necessitates the administering of Holy Viaticum to the faithful. Neither contrary custom nor the fact of an equal convenience in that the Blessed Sacrament is reserved in a nearby church can excuse the pastor from the

[8] Cappello, I, 281; Köster, p. 192.

[9] Augustine, *A Commentary on the New Code of Canon Law* (8 vols., Vol. VI, 2 ed., St. Louis: Herder, 1923), VI, 215 (hereafter cited Augustine).

[10] Köster, p. 192.

[11] Köster, p. 194.

invariable duty of reserving the Blessed Sacrament in the parochial church.[12]

Some authors[13] contend that the expression "... *in qualibet ecclesia paroeciali* ..." includes all churches in which the care of souls is exercised. According to their opinion, therefore, the pastor is obliged to reserve the Blessed Eucharist in a filial or a subsidiary church in which the care of souls is exercised. Their contention, however, receives no support from the earlier law, and the decisions of the Holy See which they cite in support of their conclusion in no way prove that the Blessed Sacrament must be reserved in such subsidiary churches.[14]

At times a lack of funds sufficient to insure a proper and decent custody may be urged as an excuse from the obligation to reserve the Blessed Eucharist in a parochial church. According to Cappello[15] and Köster,[16] in such an eventuality the local ordinary can transfer the seat of the parish to another church in agreement with the permissive norm enacted in canon 1187. However, canon 1187 speaks of a church which "in no way" can be used for divine worship. Certainly the ineptitude of a church for the reservation of the Blessed Sacrament does not disqualify that church for use in other acts of divine worship. Furthermore, the Sacred Congregation of the Council in a decree of August 17, 1697,[17] declared that the inability of a parish church to reserve the Blessed Sacrament was not a sufficient excuse for the transferral of the seat of a parish to another church.

A less drastic means of solving the financial problem connected with the decent and proper custody of the Blessed Eucharist is the one mentioned by the same Congregation of the Council in 1604.[18] The Sacred Congregation judged it expedient in a certain territory where there were several indigent parishes that all of them should co-operate in supporting one parish church which

---

[12] Cappello, I, 281-282.

[13] Coronata, II, 164; Vermeersch-Creusen, II, 412.

[14] Köster, p. 193.

[15] *Tractatus Canonico-Moralis de Sacramentis,* I, 282.

[16] *De Custodia Sanctissimae Eucharistiae,* p. 194.

[17] Gasparri, II, 249.

[18] *Spoletana,* 12 aug. 1604—Schmalzgrueber, lib. III, tit. 44, n. 27.

would reserve the Blessed Sacrament for the convenience of the rest of the parochial churches. In virtue of this authoritatively suggested procedure for such a case of emergency there seems to be no reason for regarding it as unfeasible if today a pastor of an indigent church contributed what he could to a nearby church with the understanding that on the occasion of sick-calls he could make use of the Blessed Sacrament there reserved. The pastor, however, should not regard this working agreement as a permanent fulfillment of his obligation to reserve the Blessed Sacrament in the parochial church. The Sacred Congregation of the Council in its decree of August 17, 1697, it must be noted, regarded such a procedure as only a temporary measure to care for a transient need. Pastors were allowed to make use of such a procedure only while other arrangements more in keeping with the strict letter of the law were pending.[19] Furthermore, in view of the possible clash of opinions that could arise over such a working agreement, it would be far better for the pastor of the indigent church to economize in every way possible before resorting to this unusual disposition of the case. For the sake of economy the pastor could seek the faculty of using an electric light before the tabernacle instead of a lamp kept burning with expensive olive oil or beeswax.[20]

Another excuse that may be urged as freeing the pastor from this most serious obligation is the fact that the church is in need of repair, or the fact that the church is one used in common with non-Catholics. In such situations Coronata,[21] Cappello[22] and Augustine (1872-1943)[23] allow the application of an Instruction as issued by the Sacred Congregation for the Propagation of the

[19] Gasparri, II, 249; Cavanaugh, *The Reservation of the Blessed Sacrament,* The Catholic University of America Canon Law Studies, n. 40 (Washington, D. C.: The Catholic University of America, 1927), p. 23 (hereafter cited Cavanaugh).

[20] Cappello, I, 282.

[21] *Institutiones Iuris Canonici ad Usum Utriusque Cleri et Scholarum* (2. ed., 5 vols., Taurini: Marietti, 1939-1947), II, 164 (hereafter cited Coronata).

[22] *Tractatus Canonic-Moralis de Sacramentis,* I, 282.

[23] *A Commentary on Canon Law,* VI, 216. Cf. also Many, *Praelectiones de Missa* (Parisiis, 1903), p. 275 (hereafter cited Many; Gasparri, II, 249-250.

Faith on August 23, 1852.[24] In this Instruction the Sacred Congregation adverted to such situations and expressed the wish that the pastor then reserve the Blessed Sacrament in his own house, or in the house of another Catholic priest, if no other *locus proprius* was available.

The above mentioned authors make no mention of the need of an apostolic indult nor of the need of the approval of the local ordinary.

So today, according to the opinion of these authors, if a pastor realized that the windows and the doors of his church were in need of repair to insure the proper custody of the Eucharist, he could of his own accord transfer the reservation of the Blessed Sacrament to another safe place belonging to the parish, or even to his own parish house. The same would be true if the sole available church were a hall, a community church, or a movie theater shared in common with non-Catholics for divine services. Köster[25] objects to such a method of private reservation of the Blessed Sacrament. He claims that the several decisions given by the Sacred Congregation for the Propagation of the Faith concerning this matter were particular decisions and did not create

---

[24] (C.P. -*Iaffnae*), n. 2—*Fontes,* n. 4835. The following doubt was proposed to the Sacred Congregation:

> Quando missionarius non potest decenter servare Eucharistiam quia in ecclesia non sunt nec ianuae nec fenestrae, quaeritur utrum possit vel debeat servare Eucharistiam, sint infirmi vel non.

The Sacred Congregation answered as follows:

> Detur Instructio data ad Helvetios 3 augusti 1803.—*En Instructio:* "Ad impedire qualunque irriverenza della cose sagre, la S. C. non ha giudicato opportuno che dai catolici si ritenga nella sagrestia commune ai protestanti l'Olio santo, il S. Crisma, e la SS. Eucaristia; ma vuole che siano conservate in luogo del tutto separato dagli acattolici, e quando altro non ve ne sia proprio, si conservino piuttosto con tutta la possibil decenza nella casa del parroco, o di altro cattolico sacerdote."

[25] *De Custodia Sanctissimae Eucharistiae,* pp. 189-190. On this point see also Wernz-Vidal, *Ius Canonicum ad Codicis Normam Exactum* (7 vols. in 8, Romae: Apud Aedes Universitatis Gregorianae: Vol. IV, *De Rebus,* Pars I, 1934), IV, Pars 1, 538, footnote 22 (hereafter cited Wernz-Vidal); Cavanaugh, p. 24.

Wernz-Vidal apparently considered the Instruction of the Sacred Propagation of the Faith as a special faculty for missioners. Cavanaugh admits the use of this Instruction only in mission territories.

common law. Furthermore, he claims that the missionaries in their faculties from the Holy See have been accorded the privilege of such a method of reservation.

The present writer does not see the applicability of Köster's first objection. Certainly the particular decisions of the Sacred Congregation for the Propagation of the Faith do not create common law. However, the particular decisions of the Sacred Congregation can at times be used as a commentary on the present law. Many decisions of the Sacred Congregation for the Propagation of the Faith implied nothing more than an explanatory interpretation of the common law. From the wording of the disputed text, that of August 23, 1852, it seems that the Sacred Congregation was merely in an urgent case interpreting the common law according to its normal practice. There was no question of a restrictive or of an extensive interpretation. Nor did the Sacred Congregation use words with an implication of command or dispensation. The mood of the text was the optative rather than the imperative. Finally, the fact that the reply was given by way of an "Instruction" seemed in itself indicative of merely an explanatory interpretation. In accord with the ruling of canon 6, 2°, the text as borrowed from an earlier Instruction given on August 3, 1803, has merit not only in its nature of a commentary on the pre-Code law, but also by way of reflecting the impact of the present law, which has continued unchanged from the past.

On the other hand, the present writer agrees very much with Köster's second objection. In the recently prepared new formulas of the faculties which are customarily granted to mission ordinaries, faculty 15 of the *Formula Maior* reads thus: *"Permittendi, si sit periculum sacrilegii, ut Sanctissimum Sacramentum pro infirmis sine lumine in loco tamen decenti retineri possit."*[26]

In consequence of the fact that such a faculty is granted to missionary ordinaries it seems that the opinion of Cappello, Coronata, and Augustine, relative to the present day application of the Instruction of the Sacred Congregation for the Propagation of the Faith of August 23, 1852, is altogether too liberal. The

[26] Winslow, *A Commentary on the Apostolic Faculties* (New York: Field Afar Press, 1946), p. 59 (hereafter cited Winslow).

Holy See apparently does not approve such a present day application of this Instruction inasmuch as it explicitly grants missionary ordinaries powers of dispensation in cases when the circumstances as contemplated by the Instruction prevail.

It is true that in this faculty no explicit mention is made of a church in need of repair, or of a church used in common with non-Catholics for divine services. Can it then be argued that in these two particular instances of a *"periculum sacrilegii"* there is no need of an apostolic dispensation? It seems more likely that the Sacred Congregation for the Propagation of the Faith wisely chose the phrase *"periculum sacrilegii"* in order to dispense with the need of compiling an extensive complete list of the conditions that would *de facto* constitute a source of danger to the Blessed Sacrament.

So the present writer thinks that there is a need of an apostolic indult for a pastor of these times to reserve the Blessed Sacrament privately when his church is in need of repair or when his church is one that is used in common with non-Catholics.

However, these adverse circumstances may be of a very temporary nature. In such a case an individual pastor should consult the local ordinary. The local ordinary should then discuss with the pastor the feasibility of obtaining the Blessed Sacrament, when It is needed, from a parish of the neighboring territory.[27] If such a parish church is so far distant that it would take an undue amount of time to reach it, then the local ordinary in virtue of canon 81 can dispense from the common law and allow a private reservation of the Blessed Sacrament in the house of the pastor.[28] There is no doubt that a danger of grave harm would exist if the Blessed Sacrament were not available for the use of the sick during the period of time necessary for recourse to the Holy See.

Moreover, under adverse circumstances of this nature the pastor on his own authority could presume to reserve the Blessed Sacrament in his own house if he cannot contact the local ordinary in time sufficient for the forestalling of grave harm.[29]

---

[27] Cf. S.C.C., *Spoletana,* 12 aug. 1664—Schmalzgrueber, lib. III, tit. 44, n. 27.

[28] Coronata, II, 166; Cappello, I, 288.

[29] Köster, p. 190.

Section III. Reservation in Churches of Exempt Religious

The obligation to reserve the Blessed Sacrament in churches which are attached to the houses of exempt religious is of itself a grave obligation, inasmuch as such a church takes the place of the parish church for the members of the institute. In the pre-Code law regulars were permitted, not obliged, to reserve the Blessed Eucharist.[30] Now not only the churches of regulars, but those of all exempt religious, with no distinction between clerical and lay religious, between men and women, between a *domus formata* and a *domus non-formata,* must reserve the Blessed Eucharist. In all such cases, however, as in the pre-Code law, the canonical erection of the religious house is a prerequisite for the existence of this obligation.[31]

ARTICLE III. THE PLACES WHERE THE BLESSED SACRAMENT MAY BE KEPT WITH THE PERMISSION OF THE LOCAL ORDINARY

> Can. 1265, § 1, 2°. *Custodiri potest Sanctissima [Eucharistia], de licentia Ordinarii loci, in ecclesia collegiata et in oratorio principali sive publico sive semipublico tum domus piae aut religiosae, tum collegii ecclesiastici quod a clericis saecularibus vel a religiosis regatur.*
>
> Can. 1265, § 2. *Ut in aliis ecclesiis seu oratoriis custodiri possit, necessarium est indultum apostolicum: loci Ordinarius hanc licentiam concedere potest tantummodo ecclesiae aut oratori publico ex iusta causa et per modum actus.*

With the permission of the local ordinary, the Blessed Eucharist may be reserved in a collegiate church, and in the principal oratory, whether it be public or semi-public, of a pious or religious house, and of an ecclesiastical college conducted either by secular clerics or by religious. Formerly this privilege could be enjoyed solely in virtue of an apostolic indult, but according to the present Code of Canon Law this privilege can now be enjoyed with the

---

[30] Köster, p. 194.

[31] Vermeersch-Creusen, II, 412; Beste, *Introductio in Codicem* (3. ed., Collegeville, Minn.: St. John's Abbey Press, 1946), p. 636 (hereafter cited Beste).

sole consent of the local ordinary. This consent may be either written or oral, explicit or implicit, or even presumed.[32]

In order that the Blessed Eucharist may be reserved in other churches or oratories, an apostolic indult is necessary. The local ordinary can grant such a permission only to a church or to a public oratory for a just cause and *per modum actus.*

Section I. Domus Pia

A *domus pia* is a house which has for its purpose the fostering of religious worship or the exercise of Christian charity in some way. Hospitals, orphanages, homes for the aged, nursing homes, nurseries, summer camps, and all schools and colleges where work is done for the advance of the Catholic training of youth, can be included under the general heading of *domus piae.*[33] Such institutions need not have been erected by ecclesiastical authority.[34]

Furthermore, if strict attention is paid to the very words of canon 1265, § 1, 2°, such institutions need not be dependent upon ecclesiastical authority. In other words, such institutions need not be recognized as Catholic institutions. In fact, the only ecclesiastical control which is necessary in order that the local ordinary may allow the reservation of the Blessed Eucharist in the principal oratory, public or semi-public, of these institutions is that a chaplain attends to the spiritual needs of the residents.[35]

Augustine[36] maintained on the contrary that such charitable institutions must be under ecclesiastical government. In substantiation for this doctrine he pointed to canon 1489. This canon, however, simply acknowledges for the local ordinary the right to erect such an institution, and by means of his decree to constitute it as an ecclesiastical moral person.

Blat[37] suggests an additional characteristic for an institution if

---

[32] Ayrinhac, p. 134; Augustine, VI, 215.

[33] Cappello, I, 287; Coronata, II, 165; Vermeersch-Creusen, II, 412.

[34] Cappello, I, 287; Beste, p. 637.

[35] Vermeersch-Creusen, II, 412; Wernz-Vidal, IV, Pars I, 538, footnote 20; Cavanaugh, p. 29.

[36] *A Commentary on the New Code of Canon Law,* VI, 215.

[37] *Commentarium Textus Codicis Iuris Canonici* (6 vols., Vol. IV, Romae, 1923), IV, 161 (hereafter cited Blat).

it is to exist as a *domus pia*. He implies that institutions which professedly foster works of charity are such for the reason that at least in part they receive inmates free of charge. Such gratuitous service does indeed stamp the institution as a "pious house," and charitable institutions should accordingly be willing to render their service even if it cannot always be compensated financially.

Section II. Domus Religiosa

The local ordinary may grant permission for the reservation of the Blessed Sacrament in the main oratory, either public or semi-public, of a religious house. It makes no difference whether this house belongs to a lay or a clerical institute, whether it is composed of men or of women, whether it is exempt or non-exempt. There is only the one requirement, namely, that it be a religious house. Under this heading Coronata[38] includes retreat houses and the houses of men or women who live in common without the profession of vows, for example, the Daughters of Charity of St. Vincent de Paul. Both of these, however, should rather be listed under the heading of *domus piae*.[39]

Only if a retreat house is conducted by some religious institute can it be called a religious house. The retreatants themselves can surely not be regarded as belonging to the membership of religious. Neither do those who live in common without the profession of vows fulfill the qualifications for the religious state as mentioned in canon 487. Furthermore, it can be added as a further point of refutation that in such institutes the men and women do not enjoy the privileges of religious apart from a direct concession made in virtue of an apostolic indult.[40]

Section III. Collegium Ecclesiasticum

The local ordinary may grant permission for the reservation of the Blessed Sacrament in the main oratory, public or semi-

---

[38] *Institutiones Iuris Canonici ad Usum Utriusque Cleri et Scholarum,* II, 165. See also Vermeersch-Creusen, II, 412.

[39] Cappello, I, 287.

[40] Can. 680.

public, of an ecclesiastical college conducted either by the secular clergy or by religious. Any school which functions as a Catholic school may be included under the heading of an "ecclesiastical college." It is not postulated, however, that such schools be erected or supported by ecclesiastical authority.[41]

Many authors list such institutions as seminaries, juniorates, scholasticates, and novitiates under the heading of an "ecclèsiastical college."[42] In fact, they restrict the meaning of an ecclesiastical college to a house of residence in which students are trained either for the clerical or for the religious life, the house itself being subject to control by the Church.

This strict interpretation hardly seems in keeping with the text of canon 1265, § 1, 2°. If the name of ecclesiastical college were applicable only to such places as novitiates, juniorates, seminaries, and scholasticates, then there would not have been any need for the more specificative phrase in the law, *"quod a clericis saecularibus vel a religiosis regatur."*

Section IV. Curata Ecclesia

There is still another case in which the local ordinary habitually may grant permission for the reservation of the Blessed Sacrament. His possession of this additional power was confirmed by the Pontifical Interpretation Commission on May 20, 1923, in answer to a question concerning a fuller understanding of the law enacted in canon 1265.[43]

In this answer it was stated that in view of an existing immemorial custom the local ordinary can grant permission to reserve the Blessed Sacrament *in curatis ecclesiis,* although strictly they are not parish churches, but rather subsidiary churches in which a *cura animarum* is exercised.[44]

---

[41] Köster, p. 206; Blat, IV, 161; De Meester, *Juris Canonici et Juris Canonico-Civilis* Compendium (nova ed., 3 toms. in 4 vols., Brugis: Desclée, 1921-1928; Vol. III, Pars I, 1926), Pars I, 161; Cappello, I, 288.

[42] Bouscaren-Ellis, *Canon Law* (Milwaukee: The Bruce Publishing Company, 1946), p. 651 (hereafter cited Bouscaren-Ellis); Vermeersch-Creusen, II, 412; Coronata, II, 165.

[43] *AAS,* XVI (1924), 115.

[44] Wernz-Vidal, IV, Pars I, 537, footnote 18.

It appears that the Code Commission was referring to filial or mission churches located within the boundaries of the parish church.[45] In the pre-Code law such churches, inasmuch as they were regarded as connoting a territorial projection of the juridical reality of the parochial church, enjoyed through custom the right of reserving the Blessed Sacrament. In 1923 the Pontifical Interpretation Commission set its approval upon the continued licit application of this pre-Code custom. So today in very extensive parishes filial or mission churches may be built for the convenience of the laity to attend Sunday Mass. For example, some parishes have chapels located within their territory to take care of the additional crowds at the summer resorts.

There is, of course, no strict obligation to reserve the Blessed Sacrament in such churches or oratories. However, to serve the needs of the people, and to forestall all possible irreverences to the Blessed Sacrament in the event of a sick-call which would take the priest a distance of many miles, the local ordinary may grant permission for the reservation of the Blessed Sacrament in such churches. For the granting of such a permission it is assumed that these mission churches have curates, clerics, or else some trusted lay people to act as guardians of the Blessed Sacrament.

Section V. "Per modum actus"

With reference to all churches other than those already enumerated, such as domestic and infirmary chapels, wayside and rural chapels, oratories of confraternities and sodalities, shrines and pilgrimage churches which are not at the same time parochial churches, an apostolic indult is necessary for the reservation of the Blessed Sacrament. However, *per modum actus,* if a just cause exists, the local ordinary can grant permission for the reservation of the Blessed Sacrament even in sacred places such as these, provided that the sacred place in question is at least a church or a public oratory.

The phrase *per modum actus* implies the presence of some need in a special case or under circumstances that deviate from the

---

[45] Gasparri, II, 250; Cavanaugh, p. 24.

usual course of things. The permission thus granted can extend only for that period of time during which the particular need continues or the unusual circumstances obtain. Thus *per modum actus* the local ordinary can allow the reservation of the Blessed Sacrament during the period of a triduum, of a novena, or of a mission. But the granted permission is not restricted in its continuance to a day or two.[46] The use of the permission can be extended longer, but not beyond a period of time which is plainly recognized as evincing simply a transient need. When, once this need has been served, a similar need again arises at the same church or public oratory, then a new permission *per modum actus* can be granted. The law contains no prohibition against a repeated granting of the permission. The grant, however, may not be made in such a manner as to connote a standing permission; the use of the permission, for whatever time it continues, must plainly reflect a merely transitory provision in the case.[47]

Scholion: Some authors claim that bishops and cardinals do not need an apostolic indult in order to reserve the Blessed Sacrament in their own private oratories.[48] It is true that such chapels enjoy the privilege of semi-public oratories.[49] However, the reservation of the Blessed Sacrament is not a privilege of a semi-public oratory as such, but rather the privilege of the principal oratory, public or semi-public, of a *domus pia* or a *domus religiosa.* The private chapel of a cardinal or of a bishop cannot properly be included under either classification.[50] Furthermore, in the recently prepared new formulas of faculties which the Sacred Congregation for the Propagation of the Faith customarily grants to missionary ordinaries, faculty 50 of the *Formula Maior* reads thus: *"Asservandi in sacello domus stabilis suae residentiae SSmum Eucharistiae Sacramentum."*[51] This faculty, and the other

---

[46] Cappello, II, 288.

[47] Guiniven, *The Precept of Hearing Mass,* The Catholic University of America Canon Law Studies, n. 158 (Washington, D. C.: The Catholic University of America Press, 1942), pp. 126-132.

[48] Coronata, II, 166; Ayrinhac, p. 134; Augustine, VI, 217.

[49] Can. 1189.

[50] Vermeersch-Creusen, II, 413; Bouscaren-Ellis, p. 652.

[51] Winslow, p. 219.

faculties of the *Formula Maior,* it is to be noted, are issued only to those ecclesiastical superiors who possess the episcopal character.[52]

ARTICLE IV. THE RESERVATION OF THE BLESSED SACRAMENT IN THE CHURCH OR THE MAIN ORATORY OF A RELIGIOUS OR PIOUS HOUSE

> Can. 1267. *Revocato quolibet contrario privilegio, in ipsa religiosa vel pia domo sanctissima Eucharistia custodiri nequit, nisi vel in ecclesia vel in principali oratorio; nec apud moniales intra chorum vel septa monasterii.*

The Blessed Sacrament may not be reserved in a religious or pious house, except in the church or in the principal oratory. Moreover, nuns may not reserve the Blessed Sacrament within the choir or elsewhere in the convent enclosure. The Code expressly revokes privileges contrary to these provisions.

Section I. ". . . nisi vel in ecclesia vel in principali oratorio . . ."

Many doubts arose concerning the interpretation of the words, *"nisi vel in ecclesia vel in principali oratorio,"* of canon 1267. Accordingly on June 3, 1918, the Pontifical Interpretation Commission[53] attached the following authentic signification to this disputed phrase:

> *Si religiosa vel pia domus adnexam habeat publicam ecclesiam eaque utatur ad ordinaria et quotidiana pietatis exercitia explenda, SS. Sacramentum in ea tantum asservari potest; secus in oratorio principali eiusdem religiosae vel piae domus (sine praeiudicio iuris ecclesiae, si quod habet); in eoque tantum, nisi in eodem materiali aedificio sint distinctae ac separatae familiae, ita ut formaliter sint distinctae religiosae vel piae domus.*

It is clear from this interpretation that when the church which is connected with the religious house is the place wherein the community gathers for its ordinary and daily spiritual exercises, then

---

[52] Winslow, p. 31.
[53] *AAS,* X (1918), 346-347.

in that church alone can the Blessed Sacrament be reserved. However, if the main oratory is the place where the daily spiritual exercises are held, then the Blessed Sacrament can be reserved in two places, namely, in the church and also in the main oratory. Finally, if in one and the same material complex of buildings distinct and separate groups of religious have residence, so that the religious houses to which they pertain are formally distinct and separate, then each such group may reserve the Blessed Sacrament in its own proper oratory. The same prerogative exists for groups which in the same material residence pertain to distinct and separate pious houses in view of their prosecution of distinct and separate ends and aims in the fostering of religious worship or in the exercise of Christian charity.

There are situations in which groups of persons living in the same material house may be classified as distinct and separate groups. Different institutes of religious engaged in one and the same work, for example, in a large city hospital, constitute without question distinct and separate groups. Again, without question, several different groups of persons which follow a different kind of spiritual life and work constitute distinct and separate units. Thus in a hospital or in an orphanage the sisters and their charges constitute distinct groups; in a college or in an academy conducted by religious, the religious and their pupils; in a seminary, the clerics and the sisters engaged in the domestic work.[54]

According to Cappello,[55] even members of the same religious institute under one and the same superior can constitute distinct and separate groups as contemplated by the Interpretation Commission. This would be true, he declared, if the community were divided into groups for the purpose of executing different kinds of work. Thus a community of sisters could be divided into a group which habitually engages itself in catechetical work, into another group which habitually occupies itself in teaching, and into still another group which habitually devotes itself to missionary work.

This opinion of Cappello seems to be very liberal and, in fact,

---

[54] Cappello, I, 298; Vermeersch-Creusen, II, 414; Ayrinhac, pp. 136-137.

[55] *Tractatus Canonico-Moralis de Sacramentis,* I, 298.

not at all tenable. The Interpretation Commission measured the distinction between groups by their pertinence to distinct religious or pious houses. In the situation described above, there is no question of the religious in the sense of belonging to distinct religious houses. In spite of their multiple tasks, they still belong to one and the same community, and are ruled exclusively by one and the same local superior. The mere fact that a religious community prosecutes multiple ends does not destroy the oneness of that community.

There are, however, other situations in which members of the same religious institute under one and the same local superior can constitute distinct and separate groups as contemplated by the Commission. This would be true if members from the various houses of an institute assembled at the provincial house for a retreat that did not coincide with the time of retreat for the members of the provincial house.[56] This would also be true if one specific house of a religious institute, in addition to other uses, served as the infirmary for the whole province.[57]

There is, however, considerable doubt regarding the existence of a differentiated status between professed members, novices, and lay brothers of an institute who live in the same material house and under the same local superior. Some authors claim that they form separate and distinct groups as contemplated in the explanation given by the Commission.[58] Thus Köster[59] maintains that if the discipline of the novices suffers because of the use of one and the same oratory with the professed members, then these novices can be considered as a separate and distinct group. The cause for the hardship, he asserts, may be an external cause, such as the small size of the main oratory, or also an internal cause, such as the conflicting times of the spiritual exercises.

In the mind of the present writer such a difficulty could furnish a just cause for the seeking of an apostolic indult, but it could not

[56] Ayrinhac, pp. 136-137.

[57] Vermeersch-Creusen, II, 414.

[58] Köster, p. 201; Cappello, I, 286; Cocchi, *Commentarium in Codicem Iuris Canonici* (8 vols. in 5, Vol. V, 4. ed., recognita, Taurinorum Augustae: Marietti, 1942), V, 194 (hereafter cited as Cocchi).

[59] *De Custodia Sanctissimae Eucharistiae,* p. 201.

serve to constitute the novices as a group which is separate and distinct from the professed members. The Commission abstracted from all consideration of the *iusta causa* in its delineation of what constitutes a separate and distinct group, and adhered to only one yardstick, namely, the presence of a formally distinct religious house. The novices even in the face of such difficulty form one and the same community with the professed members, are ruled by one and the same local superior, and therefore in the full juridical sense constitute with the professed members one and the same religious house.[60]

Section II. ". . . nec apud moniales intra chorum vel septa monasterii . . ."

The second provision of canon 1267, namely, that the Blessed Eucharist should not be reserved within the choir or elsewhere within the walls of the monastery, refers to only those nuns who are under the observance of the strict papal cloister.[61] The reason for this restriction is at once apparent. The place where the Blessed Sacrament is reserved must remain approachable to a priest. If that place were within the papal enclosure, the priest's entry would be barred.

---

[60] Cf. Beste, p. 638; Vermeersch-Creusen, II, 414.

[61] Bouscaren-Ellis, p. 645.

CHAPTER IV

The Altar of Reservation

Can. 1268. § 1. *Sanctissima Eucharistia continuo seu habitualiter custodiri nequit, nisi in uno tantum eiusdem ecclesiae altari.*

§ 2. *Custodiatur in praecellentissimo ac nobilissimo ecclesiae loco ac proinde regulariter in altari maiore, nisi aliud venerationi et cultui tanti sacramenti commodius et decentius videatur, servato praescripto legum liturgicarum quod ad ultimos dies hebdomadae maioris attinet.*

§ 3. *Sed in ecclesiis cathedralibus, collegiatis aut conventualibus in quibus ad altare maius chorales functiones persolvendae sunt, ne ecclesiasticis officiis impedimentum afferatur, opportunum est ut sanctissima Eucharistia regulariter non custodiatur in altari maiore, sed in alio sacello seu altari.*

§ 4. *Curent ecclesiarum rectores ut altare in quo sanctissimum Sacramentum asservatur sit prae omnibus aliis ornatum, ita ut suo ipso apparatu magis moveat fidelium pietatem ac devotionem.*

The Code of Canon Law has made the following provisions relative to the altar of the Blessed Sacrament:

1. The Blessed Eucharist may not be kept constantly or habitually on more than one altar in the same church.

2. The Blessed Eucharist should be kept in the most honorable and prominent place in the church, and therefore generally on the main altar, unless some other altar be considered more convenient and more suitable for the veneration and the worship due to this great Sacrament.

3. In cathedral, collegiate or conventual churches, where choral functions must be celebrated at the main altar, it is advisable that the Blessed Sacrament be kept as a rule on side altars or in side chapels, in order that ecclesiastical offices may be conducted with more freedom.

4. Rectors of churches must take care that the altar of the

Blessed Sacrament is more elaborately adorned than all the other altars in the church, so that by its very appointments such an altar may more effectively excite the piety and the devotion of the faithful.

ARTICLE I. ONE ALTAR

The Blessed Eucharist may not be kept constantly or habitually on more than one altar in the same Church. This one altar should be designated by the local ordinary.[1]

This restriction to one altar is modified by the words *"continuo seu habitualiter."* In other words, for some transient reason it is not forbidden to temporarily reserve the Blessed Sacrament on more than one altar. For example, on the occasion of some special feast, of May Devotions, of a triduum, and of a novena, a pastor could legitimately reserve the Blessed Eucharist on several altars in order to provide more conveniently for the distribution of Holy Communion and for Benediction of the Blessed Sacrament.[2]

Moreover, the Sacred Congregation of Rites[3] has allowed one exception to the prohibition of canon 1268, § 1, in favor of churches of perpetual or of temporary exposition of the Blessed Sacrament. The reason for such an exception is that only in the presence of a grave cause or in a case of necessity may Holy Communion be distributed from an altar where the Blessed Sacrament is exposed.[4]

ARTICLE II. THE ALTAR IN A PROMINENT PLACE OF HONOR

The Blessed Sacrament should be kept in the most prominent and the most honorable place in the church, and therefore generally on the main altar, unless some other altar be considered more con-

---

[1] S.R.C., *Augustae Praetoriae,* 21 iul. 1696, ad 3—*D.A.,* n. 1946.

[2] S.R.C., *Cuneen.,* 2 iun. 1833, ad VI—*D.A.,* n. 3576; S.R.C., *Montis Regalis,* 10 maii 1890, ad I—*D.A.,* n. 3728.

[3] *Papien.,* 23 nov. 1880, ad IV—*D.A.,* n. 3525; *Gandaven.,* 18 maii 1878, ad III—*D.A.,* n. 3449.

[4] S.R.C., *Societatis Iesu,* 11 maii 1878, ad I—*D.A.,* n. 3448; S.R.C., *Marianopolitana,* 17 apr. 1919—*AAS,* XI (1919), 246.

venient and more suitable for the veneration and the worship due to this great Sacrament.

This restriction of canon 1268, § 2, is modified by the word *"regulariter."* In virtue of this choice of words, the Code does not demand that the pastor always and necessarily reserve the Blessed Sacrament on the main altar.[5] For example, on the occasion of great feasts, of triduums, and of May Devotions, a pastor would be justified in temporarily transferring the Blessed Sacrament to a side altar that proved more convenient and more fitting for the distribution of Holy Communion and for Benediction of the Blessed Sacrament.[6] In the face of a special difficulty continuous in character a pastor would be permitted, and even obliged, to permanently transfer the Blessed Sacrament to such a side altar.[7] A difficulty of this kind would exist if the main altar, because of its artistic beauty, became the center of attraction to many visitors, both Catholic and non-Catholic.

ARTICLE III. THE MAIN ALTAR AND CHORAL FUNCTIONS IN CATHEDRAL, COLLEGIATE AND CONVENTUAL CHURCHES

In cathedral, collegiate, or conventual churches, where choral functions must be celebrated at the main altar, it is advisable that the Blessed Sacrament be kept as a rule on side altars or in side chapels, in order that ecclesiastical offices may be conducted with more freedom.

The text of canon 1268, § 3, uses the word *"opportunum,"* which, beyond doubt, indicates that there is no question of a rigorous precept.[8]

Furthermore, the use of the word *"regulariter"* indicates that as a general rule the Blessed Sacrament more advisedly belongs on a side altar in such churches. However, circumstances in particular churches may be such that a reservation of the Blessed Sacrament on the main altar would be more fitting and at times

---

[5] Cappello, I, 293.

[6] S.R.C., *in Cuneen.*, 2 iun. 1883, ad VI—*D.A.*, n. 3576.

[7] S.R.C., *Gandaven.*, 18 maii 1878, ad I, II—*D.A.*, n. 3449; S.R.C., *Angelopolitana,* 26 april 1901, ad III—*D.A.*, n. 4071.

[8] Augustine, VI, 220; Cappello, I, 296.

even necessary.[9] The lack of a decent side chapel, or the necessity of repairing a side altar, would be examples of circumstances justifying a departure from the general rule of canon 1268, § 3.

When for a just and reasonable cause the Blessed Sacrament is reserved on the main altar in such churches, at least during the times of solemn Mass and of solemn Vespers It must be transferred to a side altar or to a side chapel, in order that full compliance with the ceremonies demanded at these solemn functions may the more readily be achieved.[10]

ARTICLE IV. THE ALTAR AND ITS ADORNMENTS

Rectors of churches must take care that the altar of the Blessed Sacrament is more elaborately adorned than all the other altars in the church, so that by its very appointments such an altar may more effectively excite the piety and the devotion of the faithful.

Another reason why the altar of the Blessed Sacrament should be so adorned is that it may the more easily be recognized by the faithful as the altar of reservation. For the sake of forestalling all possible emergence of irreverence and abuse, the Sacred Congregation of the Sacraments in its Instruction of March 28, 1929,[11] demanded that the altar of the Blessed Sacrament be distinguished from other altars by "some certain and conspicuous mark." Now, elaborate ornamentation is one way of effecting a "certain and conspicuous mark."

The altar of the Blessed Sacrament, therefore, should, as much as possible, have more steps leading to it, finer linens, more candlesticks, more flowers, and more of the other ornaments allowed by the rubrics, in order to attract the attention of the faithful to their Eucharistic Lord.[12]

Other altars must be less ornamented. The fact that a particular

---

[9] Cappello, I, 296.

[10] *Caeremoniale Episcoporum,* lib. I, c. XII, n. 8; Cappello, I, 297.

[11] S.C. de Sacramentis, *Instructio ad Revmos Ordinarios de Quibusdam Vitandis atque Observandis in Conficiendo Sacrificio Missae et in Eucharistiae Sacramento Distribuendo et Asservando* (hereafter cited *Instruction of 1929*), 23 mart. 1929, (adnotatio 12)—*AAS,* XXI (1929), 642.

[12] Augustine, VI, 221.

parish has a special devotion to St. Anthony, to Our Lady of Lourdes, or to the Little Flower, is no justification for a pastor to ignore the prescript of canon 1268, § 4. No doubt the devotion of the faithful in some places has become the occasion for establishing altars other than the altar of the Blessed Sacrament as the center of attraction to those who enter the church. However, such customs, when they exist, must be disapproved as abuses, inasmuch as they are based either on error or on a false devotion.[13]

[13] Cappello, I, 298.

CHAPTER V

The Tabernacle

ARTICLE I. THE POSITION OF THE TABERNACLE ON THE ALTAR

Can. 1269, § 1. *Sanctissima Eucharistia servari debet in tabernaculo inamovibili in media parte altaris posito.*

The Most Blessed Eucharist must be kept in an immovable tabernacle placed in the middle of the altar.

Section I. The Tabernacle Must Be Set on an Altar

In 1614, the *Roman Ritual*[1] demanded that the tabernacle be set on an altar. The Code of Canon Law has extended this obligation even to those churches which up to that time had not accepted the *Roman Ritual.*

In spite of this prescript of the Code, however, certain ancient methods of reserving the Blessed Sacrament may, in virtue of immemorial custom, be continued.[2] Thus, if an ordinary judges that the practice of reserving the Blessed Eucharist at the side of the altar, in a wall or a pillar of the church, or in a Sacrament House, cannot be prudently abolished, he may tolerate such prac-

---

[1] "Hoc autem tabernaculum . . . in altari maiori vel in alio, quod venerationi et cultui tanti Sacramenti commodius ac decentius videatur, sit collocatum. . . ."—*Rituale Rom.*, tit. IV, c. 1, *de sanctissimo Eucharistiae sacramento,* n. 6.

[2] Köster, p. 209; Vermeersch-Creusen, II, 416; Cavanaugh, p. 56; Woywod, "The Tabernacle,"—*The Homiletic and Pastoral Review* (New York: 1900—), XXVII (1926-1927), 150.

Cappello (*Tractatus Canonico-Moralis de Sacramentis,* I, 298) and Coronata (*Institutiones Iuris Canonici ad Usum Utriusque Cleri et Scholarum,* II, 170) assert the contrary, but they apparently base their opinion on a letter which the Sacred Congregation of Rites sent on August 21, 1863, to the Bishops of Belgium in the name of the Holy Father. In this letter the Sacred Congregation reprobated merely the reintroduction of such methods of reservation.

tices in accordance wth the norm of canon 5. Neither the Code of Canon Law nor liturgical law has expressly reprobated these methods of reservation.

An ordinary does not enjoy a similar liberty relative either to the movable tabernacle or to the suspended dove-shaped receptacle. The Sacred Congregation of the Sacraments in its Instruction of May 26, 1938,[3] explicitly reprobated the construction and use of movable tabernacles. In view of the intention of the Sacred Congregation, namely, the safe custody of the Blessed Eucharist, this reprobation would at least implicitly apply to the suspended dove-shaped receptacle, inasmuch as such a receptacle of its very nature is movable.

Section II. The Tabernacle Must Be Immovable

The prescript of the Code of Canon Law, that the tabernacle be immovable, is an ordinarily grave obligation.[4] Absolute immovability, of course, is not meant. It is sufficient that thieves would find it difficult to lift the tabernacle from the altar and carry it off.[5] To this end the Sacred Congregation of the Sacraments in its recent Instruction[6] has suggested that the tabernacle be securely fastened by iron bolts either to the lowest gradine of the altar or to the wall at the back of the altar.

Section III. The Tabernacle Must Be Set in the Middle of an Altar

The Code of Canon Law prescribes that the tabernacle stand directly in the middle of the altar. It should not be set over the altar stone nor over the table of the altar.[7] Furthermore enough room must be left in front of the tabernacle, so that the priest at Mass may easily spread the corporal and be able to open the tabernacle door safely and conveniently.[8]

---

[3] *Instruction,* n. 4—*AAS,* XXX (1938), 199.

[4] *Instruction,* n. 4—*AAS,* XXX (1938), 199.

[5] Vermeersch-Creusen, II, 415; Ayrinhac, p. 140; Beste, p. 639.

[6] *Instruction,* n. 4—*AAS,* XXX (1938), 199.

[7] Blat, IV, 166.

[8] Collins, *The Church Edifice and Its Appointments* (2. ed., reprinted, Westminster, Md.: The Newman Bookshop, 1946), p. 86 (hereafter cited Collins).

ARTICLE II. THE MATERIAL AND THE STRUCTURE OF THE TABERNACLE

Can. 1269, § 2. *Tabernaculum sit affabre exstructum, undequaque solide clausum. . . .*

The tabernacle must be of expert construction and solidly enclosed on all sides.

Section I. Affabre Exstructum

In order to safeguard the Blessed Sacrament more securely, the Sacred Congregation of the Sacraments in its instruction of 1938[9] suggested the use of metal safes. However, by this suggestion the Sacred Congregation did not intend to dispense from the prescript of the Code that the tabernacle be a well-finished piece of work. According to the Instruction, when such tabernacles are used, they are to be manufactured in the form of a tabernacle, covered with marble and embellished with other ornaments, or at least they are to be so constructed that they can be placed within a well-finished tabernacle.

A tabernacle *affabre exstructum* implies that the tabernacle is a work of skill, of beauty and of elegance, executed by a professional workman in accordance with the rules of Christian art.[10]

The legislation of the Church has never determined any special shape for this well-finished tabernacle.[11] So the tabernacle may be round, square, hexagonal, or of any other shape that may fit the design of the altar.[12]

For the determining of the shape, however, the following positive requirements should be kept in mind:

---

[9] *Instruction,* n. 4—*AAS,* XXX (1938), 199-200.

[10] Berutti, IV, 251; Ayrinhac, p. 140; Blat, IV, 166; Sipos, *Enchiridion Iuris Canonici* (Pecs: Ex Typographia "Haladás R. T.," 1926), p. 663 (hereafter cited Sipos); Cance, *Le Code de Droit Canonique* (5. ed., 3 Vols., Paris: J. Gabalda et Fils, 1930), III, p. 92 (hereafter cited Cance).

[11] Cappello, I, 298.

[12] Collins, p. 90; Regatillo, *Ius Sacramentarium* (2 vols., Santander: Sal Terrae, 1945-1946), I, 202 (hereafter cited Regatillo).

1. The tabernacle must be completely covered on all sides by a veil or canopy.[13]

2. The top of the tabernacle should not serve as a base for relics, flowers or statues;[14] nor should it be used as a support of a permanent canopy for the exposition of the Blessed Sacrament.[15]

Section II. Undequaque solide Clausum

The prescript of the Code of Canon Law that the tabernacle must be solidly enclosed on all sides implies an ordinarily grave obligation. Not even an immemorial custom can justify a pastor's neglect of this precept.[16] At times in the past, indeed, for the sake of beauty, tabernacle doors were constructed or fabricated with perforations.[17] Such a practice today, even though it have the status of an immemorial custom, cannot be tolerated by the ordinary.

This complete enclosure of the tabernacle is required for many reasons. Due protection must be afforded the Sacred Species against profanation by thieves, against disturbance by insects, against irreverence in consequence of the collecting dust, against destruction through fire, and against the process of quick corruption in consequence of heavy moisture.

To ensure the complete enclosure of the tabernacle, first and above all a material that is strong and solid must be used. Liturgical laws have sanctioned the use of wood, of metal, and of marble.[18] If wood is used, then the exterior of the tabernacle must be gold-plated,[19] or at least artistically painted.[20]

It is of the utmost importance that a solid material be chosen

---

[13] *Rituale Rom.*, tit. IV, c. 1, *de sanctissimo Eucharistiae sacramento*, n. 6. *Tridentina*, 12 mart. 1836, ad I—*D.A.*, n. 2740.

[14] S.R.C., *Decretum Generale*, 2 april 1821, ad 6—*D.A.*, n. 2613; S.R.C.,

[15] S.R.C., *Westmonasterien*, 27 maii 1911, ad 4—*D.A.*, n. 4269.

[16] *Instruction*, n. 4—*AAS*, XXX (1939), 199.

[17] Provincial Council of Prague (1860)—Mühlbauer, III, pars II, 366, s.v. *tabernaculum*.

[18] *Instruction*, n. 4—*AAS*, XXX (1938), 199.

[19] Cappello, I, 298; Cocchi, V, 195.

[20] Cappello, I, 298.

for the construction of the tabernacle, but it is just as important that the parts of the tabernacle be firmly joined together.

Consequently a very particular attention should be paid to the door of the tabernacle. The door should fit snugly. The lock must be as secure as possible. The hinges must be strongly made and firmly attached both to the door itself and to the tabernacle.[21]

Provided that a similar care is exercised, the presence of a rear door does not offend against the demand of the Code of Canon Law for a well-enclosed tabernacle. In fact, tabernacles with two doors were at times recommended in the earlier law.[22] Furthermore, the Sacred Congregation of Rites in its official collection has never forbidden such a practice.

In 1908, the Rauwald Ecclesiastical Art Manufacturing Company of the United States designed a fine example of a well-enclosed tabernacle. Externally this tabernacle resembled all others of its time. Its walls, however, were made up of solid metal plates separated by a lining of asbestos. Furthermore, the door of this tabernacle revolved on ball bearings, and therefore could be opened only by a key. When Father Baumgarten of Milwaukee demonstrated this new tabernacle to the Sacred Congregation of Rites, the Congregation praised the inventor. Doctor Piacenza, Officialis of the Congregation, noted three especial advantages of this new tabernacle, namely, security against fire, safety against theft, and protection against insects and dust. In consequence of such advantages, he recommended that churches acquire this type of tabernacle, provided the price was comparable to that of the older types of tabernacles.[23]

The Sacred Congregation of the Sacraments in its Instruction of 1938 stated its preference for metal as the material of the tabernacle. Furthermore, this Congregation recommended the new type of tabernacle as designed by the Rauwald Ecclesiastical Manufacturing Company, and declared that it in no way offended

---

[21] *Instruction,* n. 4—*AAS,* XXX (1938), 199.

[22] *Instructiones Fabricae Ecclesiasticae—Acta Ecclesiae Mediolan,* I, pars IV, p. 472.

[23] Pauwels, *"Annotationes ad Instructionem de Eucharistiae Custodia"*—*Periodica,* XXVII (1938), 387.

against liturgical law. In detail, the Sacred Congregation recommended that the tabernacle be a real safe or strong-box, so that it cannot be pierced with a drill, nor dismantled with a chisel, nor easily broken open by other means commonly employed by thieves. Such a safe should be strongly attached by iron bolts either to the lowest gradine of the altar or to the wall at the back of the altar. Finally, such a safe should be either constructed in the form of a tabernacle and then encased in marble and decorated artistically in accord with the norm of canon 1269, § 2, or, at least, be constructed so as to fit into the tabernacle already made.[24]

The Sacred Congregation in this Instruction of 1938 did not however do more than offer a recommendation in respect to the choice of these new tabernacles. The Sacred Congregation did not insist that they be placed in churches already built, but strongly recommended that they be placed in churches of the future.[25] So the ordinary tabernacle now in use which offers solid prospects of genuine security may certainly be retained.

The Sacred Congregation, indeed, left it to the discretion and to the prudence of the local ordinary to enact legislation on the choice of tabernacles. From the tenor of the Instruction, he is the real legislator on the matter. Thus, for example, if he prescribes the use of metal tabernacles, or if he prescribes that tabernacle doors be set on ball-bearings, or if he prescribes the removal of tabernacles insufficiently secure, then these regulations must be absolutely obeyed.[26]

Recently an American ecclesiastical church goods firm has constructed and placed on the market a tabernacle very much in compliance with the suggestions and the recommendations of the Sacred Congregation of the Sacraments. This tabernacle has for its purpose a burglar-proof, a fire-proof, and a dust-proof receptacle of the Blessed Eucharist. It has been described as follows:

> It is circular in form, and is constructed of cast bronze with two walls, the outside being bronze and the inner

[24] *Instruction,* nn. 4-5—*AAS,* XXX (1938), pp. 199-201.
[25] *Instruction,* n. 4—*AAS,* XXX (1938), 199.
[26] *Instruction,* n. 4—*AAS,* XXX (1938), 199.

being steel. Between these two steel walls is an air-chamber so designed as to protect the contents from fire. The inside steel walls are lined with asbestos, cedar-wood and silk. There is neither groove nor slot on the floor of the tabernacle in which a Host or Particle might fall. The door is one solid piece of cast bronze, which instead of opening out towards the front, revolves inside on ball-bearings, so that it could not be opened without a key. The door has a four-way locking device which cannot be forced, pried or jimmied as all the parts are concealed under the double floor and bottom of the tabernacle. To assure further the utmost safety, this tabernacle has a two-way burglar alarm which operates on both door and key.[27]

ARTICLE III. THE LITURGICAL LAWS OF ORNAMENTATION FOR THE TABERNACLE

Section I. The Exterior of the Tabernacle

The exterior of the tabernacle should be decorated in some be fitting manner. The ornamentation should be limited to representations of the mystery of the Eucharist, or of the Passion, or of the Resurrection of Our Lord.[28]

From a practical point of view this pictorial ornamentation should not be excessive, for the true exterior ornamentation of the tabernacle is the veil. This veil, canopy, or curtain was prescribed by the *Roman Ritual.*[29] On several occasions the Sacred Congregation of Rites insisted on the strict observance of this Ritual rubric.[30] At one time the Sacred Congregation of Rites denied a dispensation from this prescript even though the tabernacle was of precious metal or of rich workmanship.[31] At another time the Sacred Congregation forbade the pursuit of a custom contrary to this Ritual rubric.[32]

---

[27] Collins, p. 88.

[28] Collins, p. 90.

[29] *Rituale Rom.*, tit. IV, c. 1, *de sanctissimo Eucharistiae sacramento*, n. 6.

[30] *Sancti Iacobi De Cile*, 28 apr. 1866—*D.A.*, n. 3150; *Mexicana*, 10 sept. 1898, ad III—*D.A.*, n. 4000; *Auxitana*, 7 aug. 1880—*D.A.*, n. 3520; *Dubium*, 1 iul. 1904—*D.A.*, n. 4137.

[31] *Auxitana*, 7 aug. 1880—*D.A.*, n. 3520.

[32] *Dubium*, 1 iul. 1904—*D.A.*, n. 4137.

On occasion, a physical or a moral impossibility of retaining this tabernacle veil may exist. For example, the form or structure of the tabernacle may render the use of a veil impossible.[33] In the presence of this just cause the veil may then be disregarded.[34]

In such cases of moral or physical impossibility the baldachin placed over the tabernacle may serve as a substitute for the canopy.[35] However, it seems more in keeping with the spirit of liturgical legislation to hang curtains before the door of the tabernacle, in the absence of a veil that can cover the whole exterior.[36]

The material of the tabernacle veil has not been determined by liturgical law.[37] Silk, cotton, wool, hemp, and other decent materials may be used.[38] Rich fabrics, such as brocade and cloth of gold, or soft and beautiful materials, such as silk, damask, and silk poplin are commonly used.[39]

Moreover, the color of the tabernacle veil has not been determined. The Sacred Congregation of Rites[40] has admitted two opinions: the first which demands that the color be always white; the second which allows the color to change according to the office and the season. This latter opinion was the more favored of the two. In practice it requires the use of four different colors, namely, white, red, green, and violet. The veil of violet color also serves the tabernacle on All Souls' Day and at Requiem functions.[41]

In spite of what has been said about the tabernacle veil, its value is much more than merely ornamental. It serves two practical purposes. First of all, as a covering, the veil protects the tabernacle from dust and insects.[42] A well-enclosed tabernacle, secure against theft, may indeed prove excellent in that regard,

---

[33] Cappello, I, 300.

[34] S.R.C., *Vicariatus Apostolici Utriusque Guineae*, 27 iul. 1878—*D.A.*, n. 3456. Cf. Cappello, I, 300; Ayrinhac, p. 141; Beste, p. 639.

[35] Ayrinhac, p. 141; Vermeersch-Creusen, II, 416; Coronata, II, 169.

[36] Collins, p. 99.

[37] Augustine, VI, 222; Collins, p. 99.

[38] S.R.C., *Briocen.*, 21 iul. 1855, ad 1°—*D.A.*, n. 3035.

[39] Collins, p. 99.

[40] *Briocen.*, 21 iul. 1855, ad 10—*D.A.*, n. 3035.

[41] S.R.C., *Nesqualien*, 1 dec. 1882—*D.A.*, n. 3562. Cf. Beste, 639; Augustine, VI, pp. 222-223; Collins, p. 100.

[42] Regatillo, I, 202.

but may nevertheless prove inadequate with reference to other sources of irreverence. So any additional safeguard, such as the covering of the tabernacle veil, is most desirable.

Secondly, the veil is a certain sign that the Blessed Eucharist is contained within the tabernacle. In fact, in Europe the veil is the only sign that the Blessed Sacrament is contained within the tabernacle. In the United States, of course, there is another common sign, the red-colored sanctuary lamp. However, such lamps may also be found before other altars in the church, before relics, and before images.[43]

From this point of view it is apparent that the necessity of the tabernacle veil is important, inasmuch as reverence and care for the Blessed Sacrament demand that the altar of the Blessed Sacrament be clearly recognizable.[44]

Section II. The Interior of the Tabernacle

In accordance with the liturgical law the interior of the tabernacle should be covered either with white silk cloth, or gilded, or else lined with gold or silver plate.[45] A lining of gilt wood is permissible. Furthermore, if silk cloth is the choice, it may be attached to wooden boards.[46]

This interior lining of the tabernacle has a practical as well as an ornamental value. This lining is a safeguard against heavy moisture and thus militates against any quick corruption of the Sacred Species.[47]

ARTICLE IV. THE USE OF THE TABERNACLE FOR THE BLESSED EUCHARIST

The tabernacle has for its only purpose the custody of the Blessed Sacrament.[48] In view of this sublime purpose, it should

---

[43] Collins, p. 97.

[44] *Instruction of 1929*, adnotatio 12—*AAS*, XXI (1929), 642.

[45] S.R.C., *Calven et Theanen.*, 5 iun. 1889—*D.A.*, n. 3709; S.R.C., *Urgellen*, 7 aug. 1871, ad VII—*D.A.*, n. 3254; *S.R.C.*, Romana, 20 iun. 1899, ad IV—*D.A.*, n. 4035.

[46] Collins, p. 91.

[47] Regatillo, I, 202.

[48] ". . . ab omni alia re vacuum. . . ."—canon 1269, § 2.

be blessed[49] with the form found in the *Roman Ritual* under the title *"Benedictio tabernaculi seu vasculi pro sacrosancta Eucharistia conservanda."*[50] This blessing may be imparted even by pastors and rectors of churches.[51]

This single purpose of the tabernacle demands that it should contain nothing else but the Sacred Species and those objects necessary, fitting, or useful for the proper custody of the Sacred Species. Both the interior and the exterior of the tabernacle should be free from all encumbrances that do not serve this proper purpose of the tabernacle.

Section I. External Encumbrances of the Tabernacle

The liturgical laws strictly prescribe that the exterior of the tabernacle be covered on all sides with a canopy or a veil. Furthermore, the outside of the tabernacle should be ornamented in a suitable manner.

Relative to other encumbrances on the exterior of the tabernacle, the Sacred Congregation of Rites has been very specific.

1. The tabernacle must not serve as a base for flowers, for relics, for images, or for statues. Customs contrary to this regulation must be eliminated as abuses.[52]
2. A permanent canopy for Exposition of the Blessed Sacrament should not be placed over the tabernacle.[53]
3. The use of the tabernacle as a support for the altar cross may be tolerated.[54]
4. Relics and images of the saints cannot at any time be exposed for veneration before the door of the tabernacle. Even an immemorial custom contrary to this regulation must be eliminated as an abuse.[55]

---

[49] S.R.C., *in Romana*, 20 iun. 1899, ad IV—*D.A.*, n. 4035.

[50] Tit. VIII, c. 23.

[51] Can. 1304, § 3°.

[52] S.R.C., *Decretum Generale*, 3 apr. 1821, ad 6—*D.A.*, n. 2613; S.R.C., *Tridentina*, 12 mart. 1836, ad I—*D.A.*, n. 2740.

[53] S.R.C., *Westmonasterien.*, 27 maii 1911, ad 4—*D.A.*, n. 4268.

[54] S.R.C., *Ordinis FF. Minorum Provinciae Portugaliae*, 11 iun. 1904, ad II—*D.A.*, n. 4136.

[55] S.R.C., *Sancti Angeli in Vado*, 6 sept. 1845—*D.A.*, n. 2906.

5. It is not forbidden to place a statue of the Sacred Heart on the altar of the Blessed Sacrament, provided that it is located against the wall and not on the tabernacle itself.[56]

6. A vase of flowers may not be placed before an image of Our Lord on the door of the tabernacle.[57]

Section II. Internal Encumbrances of the Tabernacle

The *Roman Ritual*[58] and the Code of Canon Law[59] demand that the tabernacle be "... *ab omni alia re vacuum*. ..." Therefore the interior of the tabernacle should be free from all encumbrances that do not directly serve the custody of the Sacred Species.

Certainly those vessels which actually serve as a *custodia* of the Blessed Sacrament may be retained within the tabernacle. Also those vessels, as yet unpurified, such as the lunette, the pyx and the ciborium, which have served as a *custodia,* may be retained within the tabernacle.[60] Furthermore, the chalice with all its covering, that is when it is to be used in the Mass of bination, may be placed within the tabernacle during the period of intermission between the two Masses.[61]

Another requirement for the interior of the tabernacle has been indirectly suggested by the Sacred Congregation of the Sacraments in its Instruction of March 26, 1929.[62] The Congregation demanded that pastors and rectors of churches strive to protect the tabernacle of the Blessed Sacrament as much as possible from dampness and extreme cold in order to forestall the bad effects of excessive moisture or cold on the Sacred Species.

At times the effect of humidity can be eliminated only when special attention is given to the interior of the tabernacle. Liturgical laws, for this reason as well as for the reason of ornamentation, have demanded that the interior be covered with a white

---

[56] S.R.C., 13 apr. 1926—*AAS,* XVIII, 291.

[57] S.R.C., *Congregationis Montis Coronae,* 22 ian. 1701, ad X—*D.A.,* n. 2067.

[58] Tit. IV, c. 1, *de sanctissimo Eucharistiae sacramento,* n. 6.

[59] Can. 1269, § 2.

[60] Cappello, I, 300; Köster, p. 222.

[61] Köster, p. 222.

[62] N. 4—*AAS,* XXI (1929), 638.

silk cloth, or that it be gilded, or else that it be lined with gold and silver plate.

At times, however, additional requirements may be necessary in order to offset the effects of humidity. For example, if marble is used in the construction of a tabernacle, silk cloth would hardly be a lining sufficient to protect the Sacred Hosts from excessive moisture. From the tenor of the Instruction of March 26, 1929, in such a case the pastor would be bound to seek other means of protection. He could, e.g., line the interior of the tabernacle with cedarwood,[63] or else place some drying agent within the tabernacle.[64]

Such additional requirements depend entirely upon the circumstances in each case. The material of the tabernacle, the climate, the season of the year, and other circumstances will determine the obligation of the pastor in this matter.

So the phrase ". . . *ab omni alia re vacuum* . . ." permits the presence within the tabernacle of vessels which actually contain the Blessed Sacrament, or of vessels, as yet unpurified, which have contained the Blessed Sacrament, and of inner linings and drying agents which serve to offset the effect of heavy moisture on the Sacred Species. These things directly serve the custody of the Blessed Sacrament.

Furthermore, this phrase allows the use of a corporal to cover the floor of the tabernacle. However, the presence of a corporal is the result of laudable practice rather than the result of legislation.[65]

Finally, this phrase allows the use of an interior veil placed at the door of the tabernacle.[66] The use of this veil is indeed allowable but it can in no way be considered as a substitute for the use of the canopy.

All objects and furnishings other than those mentioned are excluded from the tabernacle by the force of the phrase ". . . *ab omni alia re vacuum*. . . ."[67] Thus, for example, the Sacred Oils,

---

[63] Collins, p. 92.

[64] Regatillo, I, 202.

[65] Bouscaren-Ellis, p. 648; Cappello, I, 308.

[66] S.R.C., *Sancti Iacobi De Cile*, 28 apr. 1866—*D.A.*, n. 3150.

[67] Cappello, I, 300; Köster, p. 222; Blat, IV, 161; Beste, p. 639.

relics of the Holy Cross, purificators, keys, electric lights, and other unnecessary encumbrances may not be placed within the tabernacle.[68]

Moreover, the Sacred Congregation of the Sacraments[69] demanded that as far as it was possible rectors of churches were not to retain any sacred vessels of great intrinsic worth within the tabernacle. The retention of vessels of this quality within the tabernacle would not violate the ". . . *ab omni alia re vacuum* . . ." prescription of the Code of Canon Law, but would certainly offend against the proper safeguarding of the Blessed Eucharist, for the known presence of such vessels could stimulate the daring and the desire of unscrupulous men to break into the tabernacle in order to steal them.

ARTICLE V. THE TABERNACLE LAMP

Can. 1271. *Coram tabernaculo, in quo sanctissimum Sacramentum asservatur, una saltem lampas diu noctuque continenter luceat, nutrienda oleo olivarum vel cera apum; ubi vero oleum olivarum haberi nequeat. Ordinarii loci prudentiae permittitur ut aliis oleis commutetur, quantum fieri potest, vegetabilibus.*

At least one lamp must be kept burning constantly day and night before the tabernacle in which the Blessed Sacrament is reserved. The burning flame must feed upon olive oil or beeswax. However, when olive oil cannot be had, other oils, of vegetable origin if possible, may be used according to the prudent judgment of the local ordinary.

The text of the Code and the new edition of the *Roman Ritual*[70] require as a minimum the presence of one tabernacle lamp. There can be no doubt, therefore, that the prescript of the *Caeremoniale Episcoporum* which requires the presence of at least three tabernacle lamps is merely of a directive nature and is applicable only on feast days in cathedral and collegiate churches when pontifical functions are celebrated in such churches.[71]

---

[68] S.C. Ep. et Reg., 3 maii 1693—Cappello, I, 300; Gasparri, II, 265.

[69] *Instruction*, n. 5—*AAS*, XXX (1938), 202.

[70] Tit. IV, c. 1, *de sanctissimo Eucharistiae sacramento*, n. 5.

[71] Köster, p. 242.

Nothing has been prescribed relative to the material or to the color of this tabernacle lamp. Glass lamps, red or green in color, are in common use.[72] These two colors have been approved by the Sacred Congregation of Rites.[73]

Section I. The Necessity of the Tabernacle Lamp

The prescript of the Code of Canon Law which requires a tabernacle lamp is commonly interpreted by canonists as a grave prescript.[74] Some authors think that the rector of a church would commit a mortal sin if he failed for one whole day of twenty-four hours to keep this tabernacle lamp burning.[75] Cappello,[76] on the contrary, classifies such a neglect as simply tantamount to a venial sin. It seems difficult to reconcile this opinion with the fact that such a failure to keep the tabernacle lamp burning could readily lead to grave irreverence towards the Blessed Sacrament. The tabernacle lamp is a sign to the faithful that the Blessed Sacrament is reserved within the tabernacle.[77] The absence of this sign would move many people to make a contrary judgment.

ARTICLE VI. THE POSITION OF THE TABERNACLE LAMP

The tabernacle lamp should be placed near the tabernacle in which the Blessed Sacrament is reserved, in order that the faithful may easily recognize this sign as pointing to the nearby proper receptacle of the Sacred Species.[78] It has been explicitly forbidden, however, to place it either on the altar, above the altar, or behind the altar.[79]

---

[72] Köster, p. 243.

[73] *Cuneen.*, 2 iun. 1883, ad V—*D.A.*, n. 3576.

[74] Coronato, II, 172; Köster, p. 239; Blat, IV, 167; Augustine, VI, 225; Cance, III, 93; Cocchi, V, 201; Gasparri, II, 272; Van Hove, *Tractatus de Sanctissima Eucharistia* (Editio Altera Aucta et Recognita, Mechlinae: H. Dessain, 1941), p. 159 (hereafter cited Van Hove).

[75] Köster, p. 239; Van Hove, p. 159; Cance, III, 93.

[76] *Tractatus Canonico-Moralis De Sacramentis*, I, 309.

[77] Köster, p. 239; Collins, p. 165.

[78] S.R.C., *Cuneen*, 2 iun. 1883, ad IV—*D.A.*, n. 3576. Cf. Bouscaren-Ellis, p. 648; Cappello, I. 310.

[79] S.R.C., *Romana*, 20 iun. 1899, ad VI—*D.A.*, n. 4035; S.R.C., *Ordinis Capuccinorum*, 20 aug. 1699—*D.A.*, n. 2033; S.R.C., *Cuneen.*, 2 iun. 1883, ad IV—*D.A.*, n. 3576.

The tabernacle lamp may have one of three positions in the sanctuary.

1. It may be suspended from the ceiling by the aid of a chain.[80]
2. It may be attached to a side wall by means of a metal bracket.[81]
3. It may be placed on a stand or pedestal at one side of the sanctuary.[82]

Section III. The Contents of the Tabernacle Lamp

Under ordinary circumstances either olive oil or a beeswax candle must be used in the tabernacle lamp. A mixture of these two has also been approved for use by the Sacred Congregation of Rites.[83]

Other oils are permitted only when neither olive oil nor a beeswax candle is available. When the cost of these two commodities is prohibitive, or when they can be had only with grave difficulty, they may be regarded as unavailable.[84] These "other oils" must be, as far as possible, vegetable oils, such as linseed oil. If necessary, however, even mineral oil, such as petroleum, may be used.[85]

Some authors[86] exclude the use of petroleum. The Code of Canon Law, however, makes no distinction among mineral oils.

In such a substitution of "other oils," the local ordinary, and not the pastor or the rector of a church, is competent to judge regarding the availability or the unavailability of olive oil and beeswax candles. The archbishops and Bishops of Quebec made such a judgment when they authorized the use of mineral oils or their extracts, such as paraffin, in the sanctuary lamp.[87]

During World War I, on February 23, 1916, the Sacred Congre-

---

[80] S.R.C., *Cuneen.*, 2 iun. 1883, ad IV—*D.A.*, n. 3576.

[81] S.R.C., *Cuneen.*, 2 iun. 1883, ad IV—*D.A.*, n. 3576.

[82] Collins, p. 168.

[83] *Carcassonen.*, 8 nov. 1907—*D.A.*, n. 4205.

[84] Ayrinhac, p. 142; Coronata, II, 172.

[85] S.R.C., *Plurium Diocesium,* 9 iul. 1864—*D.A.*, n. 3121. Cf. Ayrinhac, p. 142; Beste, p. 642; Köster, p. 241.

[86] Cappello, I, 309; Gasparri, II, 274.

[87] *"Decrees and Decisions"—The Jurist* (Washington, D. C., 1941—), III (1943), 158.

gation of Rites[88] in a response ratified by Pope Benedict XV allowed a temporary derogation of canon 1271:

> *Inspectis circumstantiis enunciatis, iisque perdurantibus, remittendum prudentiae Ordinariorum, ut lampas, quae diu noctuque collucere debet coram Sanctissimo Sacramento, nutriatur, in defectu olei olivarum, aliis oleis, quantum fieri potest, vegetalibus, aut cera apum pura vel mixta, et ultimo loco etiam luce electrica adhibita; si Sanctissimo placuerit.*

According to many authors,[89] this concession, whereby as a last resort even an electric light could be used for the tabernacle lamp, did not automatically cease at the end of World War I. Inasmuch as the war was not explicitly mentioned in the rescript, and inasmuch as the indult was granted "... *ob peculiares circumstantias sive ordinarias sive extraordinarias . . . inspectis circumstantiis enunciatis, iisque perdurantibus...*," they maintain that this indult is still in force wherever the "peculiar circumstances, ordinary or extraordinary," named in the rescript, still prevail.

The opinion of these canonists has been corroborated to a certain extent in that the decree of February 23, 1916, was inserted in Appendix II of the *Decreta Authentica.*[90] These decrees of Appendix II were approved and declared authentic by Pope Pius XI on January 23, 1927.[91]

However, the present writer contends that the concession as made on February 16, 1916, terminated at the end of World War I. The "peculiar circumstances, ordinary or extraordinary," mentioned in this rescript, were limited to a single interpretation, namely, the circumstances of war. This is very evident from a rescript of the Sacred Congregation of Rites on March 13, 1942,[92] in which a similar indult was granted for the duration of World War II. In this second rescript the Sacred Congregation mentioned the "cir-

---

[88] *AAS,* VIII (1916), 72.

[89] Köster, p. 241; Cappello, I, 310; Vermeersch-Creusen, II, 417; Ayrinhac, p. 142; Beste, p. 642; Coronata, II, 172.

[90] N. 4334.

[91] *AAS,* XIX (1927), 109.

[92] *AAS,* XXXIV (1942), 112.

cumstances of war" as the reason for the temporary indult of 1916; it mentioned that the "same circumstances" recurred; and it granted a second indult as long as the "peculiar circumstances, ordinary or extraordinary, of this war" continued.

Therefore the present writer thinks that it is never within the normal competence of the local ordinary to allow the use of an electric light. Only by apostolic indult can such a derogation of the prescript of canon 1271 be allowed.

CHAPTER VI

The Pyx

Can. 1270. *Particulae consecratae, eo numero quo infirmorum et aliorum fidelium communioni satis esse possit, perpetuo conserventur in pyxide ex solida decentique materia, eaque munda et suo operculo bene clausa, cooperta albo velo serico et, quantum res feret, ornato.*

A number of consecrated Particles, sufficient for the Communion of the sick and of the other faithful, shall always be kept in a pyx made of some solid and suitable material, kept clean and well-enclosed with a cover, and draped with a white silken and, if possible, ornamented veil.

ARTICLE I. THE NECESSITY OF THE PYX

The prescript of the *Roman Ritual*[1] and of the Code of Canon Law to keep the Blessed Sacrament in a pyx implies an ordinarily grave obligation.[2] This prescript, however, does not mention the receptacle for the Sacred Host of Exposition. The Sacred Congregation of Rites,[3] nevertheless, has approved the practice of keeping the Sacred Host of Exposition within a lunette. So the Blessed Sacrament may be kept either within a pyx or within a lunette. The pyx may be a large ciborium or else the small pyx commonly used on sick-calls. The lunette may be placed within a monstrance, and the monstrance itself may then be placed within the tabernacle.[4]

The Blessed Sacrament must be kept at all times within one of these receptacles.[5] Not even the intention of averting a sacrilegious theft can permit the rector of a church to place the Sacred Species

[1] Tit. IV, c. 1, *de sanctissimo Eucharistiae sacramento,* n. 5.

[2] Cappello, I, 306.

[3] *Dubium seu Galliarum,* 14 ian. 1898—*D.A.,* n. 3974. Cf. De Herdt, III, 251.

[4] De Herdt, III, 251.

[5] Coronata, II, 171; Augustine, VI, 225; Blat, IV, 167.

within the folds of a corporal.[6] Not even persecution can allow a priest to carry the Blessed Sacrament privately without the use of at least a small pyx.[7] Even during the Forty Hours' Devotion and during processions of the Blessed Sacrament one of these receptacles is mandatory for containing the Sacred Species.[8]

ARTICLE II. THE CONSTRUCTION OF A PYX

The Code of Canon Law has not determined the material of which the pyx is to be constructed. Provided that the material is sufficiently solid and suitable, the choice is left to the discretion of the pastor or of the rector of the church. Such materials as iron, lead, brass, stone, and ivory are commonly considered as unsuitable.[9] And such materials as cardboard, glass, wood and aluminum are not sufficiently solid.[10] But such materials as gold and silver, and also bronze, copper, and pewter, interiorly gilded, are considered both solid and suitable.[11]

There is a dispute relative to the need of the interior gold-plating of materials lesser in suitability than gold and silver. Many authors declare this gold-plating as obligatory.[12] They base their conclusion on a decree which the Sacred Congregation of Rites issued in 1867. This decree, however, in no way whatsoever demanded the inner gilding of the pyx. The bishop of St. Pölten had merely asked whether a pyx, a monstrance, or a lunette, made of copper and gold-plated, was permissible for use in reserving the Blessed Sacrament, and to this query the Sacred Congregation answered in the affirmative.[13]

---

[6] S.R.C., *Altonen.*, 17 febr. 1881—*Fontes*, n. 6127; *D.A.*, n. 3527.

[7] S.C. de Prop. Fide, *litt. encycl.*, 25 febr. 1859, ad 3—*Fontes*, n. 4846.

[8] Coronata, II, 171; Augustine, VI, 225; Blat, IV, 167.

[9] Bouscaren-Ellis, p. 647; Cappello, I, 306; Collins, p. 198.

[10] Bouscaren-Ellis, p. 647; Cappello, I, 306; Collins, p. 198.

[11] Gasparri, II, 270; Collins, p. 198; Bouscaren-Ellis, p. 647; Cappello, I, 306.

[12] Augustine, VI, 224; Ayrinhac, p. 141; Vermeersch-Creusen, II, 417; Van Hove, p. 159; Cocchi, V, 200; Cance, III, 93.

[13] *Sancti Hippolyti*, 21 aug. 1867, ad VI: "An permitti possit Ciborium, seu sacra Pyxis ex cupro deaurato? 'Affirmative.'"—*D.A.*, n. 3162.

Many other authors[14] declare that the interior gold-plating of pyxes made from such materials as bronze, copper and pewter, is certainly a desirable suggestion, but not at all a prescript of law.

Inasmuch as the authors of the first group base their conclusion on a questionably pertinent basis, the present writer supports the authors of the second group. Moreover, if such an inner gilding of the pyx were obligatory, it seems strange that the Sacred Congregation of Rites did not have occasion during the several centuries since the publishing of the *Roman Ritual* to stress that requirement explicitly.

As a matter of fact, however, pyxes are usually made of gold or of silver.[15] This practice is to be encouraged, inasmuch as it best fulfills the prescript of the *Roman Ritual* and of the Code of Canon Law. Poverty, nevertheless, may, in some churches, prompt the use of pyxes made of less expensive materials, such as copper, bronze, and pewter. They too would fulfill the prescript of law. They may be gilded on the inside, or may not be gilded on the inside. Because of the *dubium iuris,* the practice of not gilding the interior of such pyxes can rightly be sustained, or at least be tolerated.

A certain freedom, therefore, prevails in the choice of material for the pyx. Even more freedom prevails in the choice of a form for the pyx. Nothing has been prescribed concerning the general shape of the ciborium.[16] The large ciborium commonly used for the reservation of the Blessed Sacrament is generally of the same design as the chalice. It consists of a cup, a knob, a lid, and a cross surmounting the lid.[17]

Now the Roman Ritual[18] and the Code of Canon Law[19] definitely prescribe the presence of this lid, a cover that closely and snugly fitted the ciborium, and constitutes the ciborium as a well-enclosed receptacle for the Blessed Sacrament. Only a transitory necessity

---

[14] Regatillo, I, 204; Cappello, I, 306; Many, p. 288; Gasparri, 270; Coronata, 171; Bouscaren-Ellis, p. 648.

[15] Collins, p. 198.

[16] Köster, p. 232; Collins, p. 198.

[17] Collins, p. 198.

[18] Tit. IV, c. 1, *de sanctissimo Eucharistiae sacramento,* n. 5.

[19] Canon 1270: ". . . suo operculo bene clausa. . . ."

can allow the pastor or the rector of a church to ignore this prescript and to substitute a corporal or a pall for the closely fitting lid.[20]

In the construction of the lunette, the same material may be used as in the construction of the pyx.[21] However, the lunette may also be faced with glass, provided that the glass in no way contacts the Sacred Species.[22] Moreover, the size of the lunette should correspond to the common size of the large host, so that the Sacred Species may be held firmly in place within the receptacle.[23] If the lunette is too large, there is considerable danger of the detaching of some Sacred Particles from the body of the Host.

ARTICLE III. THE CLEANLINESS OF THE PYX

Natural reverence for the Eucharistic Body of Christ demands that the pyx, which has contact with the Sacred Species, be kept scrupulously clean at all times. Care must be taken lest extraneous matter, such as dust, verdigris, insects, and rust, violate the cleanliness of the pyx.[24] To this end the rector or the pastor of a church should not only purify the pyx at each renewal of the Sacred Hosts, but he should also from time to time thoroughly wash the receptable.[25]

ARTICLE IV. THE VEIL OF THE PYX

The pyx which contains the Blessed Sacrament must be covered with a white silken veil which, if possible, is also ornamented. This prescript of the Code of Canon Law involves an ordinarily light obligation.[26] The veil should be a real veil, and not merely a partial joining together of four pieces of silk cloth with an opening left at the base of the juncture.[27] The ornamentation of this

---

[20] Köster, p. 232; Cappello, I, 306.

[21] Cavanaugh, p. 70.

[22] S.R.C., *Dubium seu Galliarum,* 14 ian. 1898—*D.A.*, n. 3974; S.R.C., *Vicariatus Apostolatus De Dania,* 4 febr. 1871, ad IV—*D.A.*, n. 3234.

[23] Cavanaugh, p. 70.

[24] Augustine, VI, 225; Köster, p. 232.

[25] Köster, p. 232.

[26] Cappello, I, 307.

[27] Collins, p. 201.

veil should be fitting and suitable, but not excessive.[28] The veil indeed, may be painted or embroidered with figures referring to the Eucharistic Presence.[29] The hem of the veil and also the opening at the top of the veil may be finished with a fringe which[30] thus can serve a practical as well as an ornamental purpose inasmuch as it will facilitate the handling of the veil.

ARTICLE V. THE BLESSING OF THE PYX

It has been contended that, since there is a *dubium iuris* regarding the need of any blessing for the pyx inasmuch as the Code of Canon Law has not settled the point, the pastor or the rector of a church who would use an unblessed pyx for the Sacred Species would be excused from sin, provided that he was not influenced by any motive of contempt.[31]

It is difficult, however, to understand why it is held that there exists a *dubium iuris* on this matter. In 1649 the Sacred Congregation of Rites was questioned concerning the blessing of the pyx, the ostensorium, and the lunette. The Congregation answered: *"Servandae sunt rubricae."*[32] And indeed a rubric of the *Roman Missal*[33] definitely states: *"Si sacerdos esset consecraturus plures hostias . . . , locat eas super corporale ante calicem, aut in aliquo calice consecrato, vel vase mundo benedicto. . . ."*

Whether such a *dubium iuris* does or does not exist, the pastor or rector as motivated by a sense of reverence for the Blessed Eucharist should always bless a new pyx with the form found in the *Roman Ritual* under the title: *"Benedictio tabernaculi seu vasculi pro sacrosancta Eucharistia conservanda."*[34]

---

[28] Augustine, VI, 225.

[29] Cavanaugh, p. 68; Augustine, VI, p. 225.

[30] Collins, p. 200.

[31] Cappello, I, 308.

[32] S.R.C., *Ianuen.*, 16 nov. 1649, ad V—*D.A.*, n. 926.

[33] *Missale Romanum Ex Decreto Sacrosancti Concilii Tridentinum Restitutum S. Pii V Pontificis Maximi Jussu Editum Aliorum Pontificum Cura Recognitum A Pio X Reformatum et Benedicti XV Auctoritate Vulgatum* (Editio IV, Juxta Typicam Vaticanam, New-Eboraci: Benziger Brothers, Inc., 1944), Tit. II, *De Ingressu Sacerdotis ad Altero*, n. 3.

[34] Tit. VIII, c. 23.

CHAPTER VII

The Careful Custody of the Holy Eucharist

Can. 1269, § 2. *Tabernaculum . . . tam sedulo custodiatur ut periculum cuiusvis sacrilegae profanationis arceatur.*

Can. 1269, § 4. *Clavis tabernaculi, in quo sanctissimum Sacramentum asservatur, diligentissime custodiri debet, onerata graviter conscientia sacerdotis qui ecclesiae vel oratorii curam habet.*

The tabernacle must be so carefully guarded that all danger of sacrilegious profanation is precluded.

The key of the tabernacle in which the Blessed Sacrament is kept must be most carefully guarded. This precept is a grave obligation in conscience for the priest who has charge of the church or of the oratory.

ARTICLE I. THE GUARDIAN

The presence of a guardian is the starting point in effecting a careful custody of the Blessed Sacrament. The Holy See has insistently urged, and has never dispensed from the rule, that there must always be a person charged with the security of the Blessed Eucharist.[1]

Section I. The Primary Guardian

The primary guardian of the Blessed Sacrament should be a priest.[2] He should be the priest who is responsible for the tabernacle key. This is a safe presumption, for the guardianship of the tabernacle key is certainly the principal duty incumbent upon the person of the guardian

Prudence demands that the primary guardian expressly delegate the acting guardian and inform him of the specific duties of

[1] *Instruction*, n. 3—*AAS*, XXX (1938), 199.

[2] Blat, IV, 160; Köster, p. 223; Cavanaugh, p. 13; Wernz-Vidal, IV, pars 1, 537, footnote 17.

guardianship that are entrusted to his care. No special acting guardian, however, need be so designated in the churches or in the oratories of religious communities, since the community itself performs the duties of the acting guardian.[3]

The primary guardian, when he so acts through the agency of others, should always remain as an overseer of their work. He should supervise the safe guardianship of the Blessed Sacrament at all times. He should take care that the acting guardian, especially if he is a layman, does not become independent in the exercise of such a privileged charge.[4]

When the primary guardian acts through the agency of a layman, it is evident that he should reserve to himself or to another priest those duties of guardianship which only a priest can properly perform. One example is the examination of the tabernacle door to ascertain whether it is properly locked. At times a visiting priest may have trouble with the mechanism of a strange lock and inadvertently leave the tabernacle door open. The examining of the tabernacle door after the Mass of a visiting priest unquestionably devolves as a duty upon the primary guardian or upon another priest. Another example is the custody of the tabernacle key, the subject of which shall be treated in a later section of this chapter.

Moreover, when the primary guardian acts through the agency of a lay person, it is expedient that he carefully instruct the lay guardian on what is to be done if some grave harm threatens the security of the Blessed Eucharist. For example, in the absence of the priest a fire may threaten destruction to the church or to the oratory. In such a situation the well-informed lay guardian would, in so far as it would be possible, remove the Sacred Species to a safe place. Again, in the absence of a priest the tabernacle may be broken open, the ciborium stolen, and the Sacred Species scattered in many profane places. In such a situation the well-informed lay guardian would organize a search for the scattered Hosts, and provide a safe place for the ones that are found.[5]

---

[3] Augustine, VI, 216.

[4] Blat, IV, 160; Köster, p. 223; Cavanaugh, p. 13; Wernz-Vidal, IV, pars 1, 537, footnote 17.

[5] Cf. S.C. de Sacramentis, *Epistula ad Ordinarios de Custodia et Protectione Sanctissimae Eucharistiae adversus Bellicos Incursos,* 15 sept. 1943, n. 7—*AAS,* XXXV (1943), 284.

Once having made the distinction between the primary guardian and the acting guardian of the Blessed Sacrament, the present writer deems it unnecessary to continuously remind the reader of the distinction. In the pages that immediately follow the word "guardian" will often appear. The context, if not the express words of the text, will clearly show whether the subject of the primary guardian or the subject of the acting guardian is under discussion.

Section II. The Lay Guardian

The Code of Canon Law[6] did not specify that a priest must be the guardian of the Blessed Sacrament. The Code, therefore, mitigated the severe norm that was established by the *Caeremoniale Episcoporum*[7] the *Roman Ritual*,[8] and the decisions of the Sacred Congregation of Rites,[9] and confirmed the milder practice that had prevailed since the latter part of the nineteenth century, whereby even a lay person often exercised custody of the Holy Eucharist.[10]

This mitigation in discipline was imperative in order that a practical contradiction in the Code of Canon Law might be avoided. In post-Code law many more churches were given the opportunity of reserving the Blessed Sacrament. Yet, if the stricter norm of the earlier law relative to the person of the Eucharistic guardian still prevailed, such an opportunity in countless cases would prove worthless, for the number of available priests would be inadequate to provide lawful guardians sufficient in number to care for so many more places in which the Blessed Sacrament could be reserved.

Most canonists admit that a mitigation in the discipline relative to the person of the Eucharistic guardian was effected by the Code of Canon Law.[11] Cappello,[12] however, maintains that the strict ap-

---

[6] Can. 1265, § 1.

[7] Lib. I, c. VI, nn. 1-2.

[8] Tit. IV, c. 1, *de sanctissimo Eucharistiae sacramento*, n. 2.

[9] *Firmana*, 16 mart. 1883—*D.A.*, n. 2700; *Papien.*, 23 nov. 1880, ad III—*D.A.*, n. 3525.

[10] S.R.C., *Alton.*, 17 febr. 1881—*Fontes*, n. 6127; S.C.C., *Fulden.*, 17 febr. 1883—*ASS*, XV (1883), 528; Köster, p. 154.

[11] Sipos, p. 663; Blat, IV, 160; Augustine, VI, 216; Vermeersch-Creusen, II, 411; Coronata, II, 163; Cance, III, 88; Cavanaugh, p. 12; Köster, p. 223.

[12] *Tractatus Canonico-Moralis de Sacramentis*, I, 283. Cf. also Prümmer, *Manuale Iuris Canonici in Usum Scholarum* (3. ed., Friburgi Brisgoviae: Herder and Co., 1922), p. 470 (hereafter cited Prümmer).

plication of the earlier norm still prevails. At the present time this contrary opinion of Cappello is no longer tenable, for the Sacred Congregation of the Sacraments in its Instruction of 1938 has definitely settled the question as follows:

> *Quod vero attinet ad custodem, hic, licet sit optandum ut sit clericus, immo sacerdos, non prohibetur quod sit laicus, modo clericus respondeat de clavi, qua est reserandus locus ubi Eucharistia asservatur.*[13]

In accord, therefore, with the less strict norm of the Code of Canon Law as interpreted by the Sacred Congregation of the Sacraments, a lay person may certainly be appointed as guardian of the Blessed Sacrament. Natural prudence demands that the lay guardian so appointed be above suspicion of any kind, and especially not addicted to over-indulgence in drink. Furthermore, fidelity and zeal in caring for the Blessed Sacrament is more surely expected of a guardian who is not only a Catholic but also a fervent Catholic who has a lively devotion to the real presence of Christ in the Eucharist.[14]

Section III. The Duties of the Guardian

The designated guardian, whether he be a priest, a religious, or a lay person, need not exercise all the duties of guardianship personally. He may delegate others to habitually perform some of the functions necessarily connected with a proper safeguarding of the Blessed Eucharist, and for those periods of time in which he himself is absent from the vicinity of the church or of the oratory he may delegate others to perform all the functions demanded of the guardian.[15]

In the delegation of his duties, however, the designated guardian should be careful to discern in the substitute the qualifications necessary for the proper execution of the entrusted functions. Moreover, the primary guardian should certainly supervise such substitutions.

---

[13] *Instruction*, n. 5—*AAS*, XXX (1938), 201.

[14] Blat, IV, 160.

[15] Köster, p. 224.

In parishes of the United States, the church sexton performs many duties of the guardian. This practice is certainly legitimate, provided that the sexton has qualifications proportionate to the functions that are entrusted to him. He may, for example, lock the church at night. The sexton, then, should not only be a Catholic, but, what is more, a fervent Catholic. He should also be punctual, trustworthy, and above all not addicted to over-indulgence in drink.[16]

The first duty of the guardian is to safeguard the Blessed Sacrament from all danger of irreverence. He must take the precautions that are advisedly necessary against the danger of fire and against the danger of theft. He must, therefore, watchfully heed the vigil lights, closely guard against other possible sources of fire within the church, and also carefully attend to the secure locking of the church at night. Moreover, he should effectively counteract what constitutes a very common source of irreverence to the Blessed Eucharist, namely, untidiness and uncleanliness.

The duties, proper even to a lay guardian, also include a careful attention to the proper decorum of the altar, to the continued burning of the sanctuary lamp, and to the opening of the church, so that at least a few hours each day the faithful may have access to the Blessed Sacrament.[17]

In practice, the various duties of the guardian demand that he retain a key to the place where the Blessed Sacrament is reserved. Always, however, a cleric is to be responsible for this key.[18] The primary guardian remains truly responsible also when he has prudently judged that the lay guardian is so reliable that he can at all times be trusted with a key to the church or to the oratory where the Blessed Sacrament is reserved.

ARTICLE II. CONSTANT VIGILANCE

Sedulous custody of the Holy Eucharist demands more than the possession of a strong, solidly enclosed tabernacle, and more also

---

[16] *Instruction*, n. 5—*AAS*, XXX (1938), 201.

[17] Woywod, "Custody and Cult of the Blessed Sacrament"—*The Homiletic and Pastoral Review*, XXVII (1926-1927), 36.

[18] *Instruction*, n. 5—*AAS*, XXX (1938), 201.

than the presence of a guardian. Constant vigilance must be exercised against the possibility of theft. In other words, the guardian, or his qualified substitute, must remain day and night near the place where the Blessed Sacrament is reserved, so that he may be promptly at hand in any case of emergency. Furthermore, every other possible precaution must be employed for the purpose of insuring security at all times for the Sacramental Species.[10]

Section I. Precautions during the Day

The guardian shall never depart from the church during those periods of time in which the church is open to the faithful, but is not at the same time visited by worshippers.

This provision of the Sacred Congregation of the Sacraments in its Instruction of 1938 is to be especially urged in city churches, where men with evil intentions are not so readily identified as thieves. These men can pose as devout Catholics, or as beggars, and frequent the place where the Blessed Sacrament is reserved, in the hope that they may find the church empty. Given the least opportunity, they will break open the tabernacle, or else make preparations so that they may easily gain entrance to the church at night for the perpetration of their evil designs.

So, in city churches the pastor or the rector must be especially solicitous about the presence of the Eucharistic guardian. Unless there is a constant stream of visitors, the guardian should be constantly on duty during those hours when the church is open to the faithful. He should remain in the church, or near enough to the church, so that he may be able to notice everyone who enters or leaves the church. Since a thief can, as it were in the twinkling of an eye, perpetrate a sacrilegious theft, the guardian, if he remains outside the church, should follow in and watch the movements of every suspicious stranger.

The daytime perpetration of a sacrilegious theft or the daytime preparation for a sacrilegious theft rarely occurs in country places, where the presence of a stranger in his walking around and entering the church is more readily noticed and more easily arouses the suspicion of the priests and of the lay people. This fact, however,

[10] *Instruction,* n. 5—*AAS,* XXX (1938), 201.

does not relieve the pastor or the rector from the duty of effecting constant vigilance. The pastor or the rector, according as the local circumstances may suggest, should prudently determine the most effective manner and method of exercising constant vigilance. For example, he may either personally, or through some other qualified individual, the housekeeper in many instances, visit the church from time to time during the day. Again, he may commission certain reliable housewives who live near the church to keep close watch on the church when he is absent. Again, he may arrange for the parishioners to make private visits at set hours during the day.

Although strangers should be watchfully observed by the eucharistic guardian, whoever he may be, other persons who by their employment or for other reasons frequent the church, the sacristy, or the adjacent house of the priest or of the guardian should also be subject to vigilance. Thus, for example, such persons as plumbers, electricians, converts, school children, no matter how familiar they are with the pastor or his assistants, should be subject to vigilance. Such persons, because of their familiarity with the routine of the church or of the oratory, could very easily and with a considerable degree of safety execute a sacrilegious theft.[20]

Section II. Precautions during the Night

The careful custody of the Blessed Eucharist as prescribed by canon 1269, § 2, should be unremitting, and therefore precautions must be employed for the protection of the Blessed Sacrament even during the night, when the church is locked.

The Sacred Congregation of the Sacraments in its Instruction of 1938 has enumerated three precautions that must be employed as ordinary means of effecting security for the Blessed Sacrament at night.

1. All the entrances to the church should be so designed that they offer sufficient protection against the attempts of thieves. Therefore the doors should be made of a strong and solid material, equipped with firm locks and bars and so constituted that from the inside they can be opened only with a key. Moreover, as a remedy

[20] *Instruction*, n. 5—*AAS*, XXX (1938), 201.

against the condition of their breakable glass the windows should be equipped with bars or with gratings.

In a country church, as sometimes happens, the upper half of the front door may be made of glass, unprotected by an inner grating or by bars. Furthermore, the lock on the door may open on the inside without the use of a key. This is an example of a serious infraction of the prescription established by the Sacred Congregation of the Sacraments. The great number of easily perpetrated auto thefts in the United States clearly prove the inadequacy of such a door, and clearly prove that the pastor or the rector of such a church is gravely negligent in his office as the primary guardian of the Blessed Sacrament.

2. When the church is closed in the evening, the acting guardian must be careful to ascertain that the church is truly empty of all visitors.

In order that he may faithfully comply with this prescription of the Sacred Congregation, the guardian should not be content with merely closing the door. He should enter the church and walk through the church. Furthermore, he should carefully examine all possible entrances to the church, and also carefully scrutinize all possible places of concealment, such as the confessionals and the choir loft.

3. The duty of closing the church and of guarding the keys should be entrusted to persons who are above suspicion, and who are, above all, not addicted to over-indulgence in drink.

Furthermore, the Sacred Congregation of the Sacraments strongly recommended another precaution for the security of the Blessed Sacrament at night, namely, the installation of special safety devices, controlled by electricity, which suddenly illuminate the church or cause the ringing of a bell when the doors are opened, or when certain parts of the altar are touched.

These burglar alarms, the Sacred Congregation cautioned, should be carefully and skillfully concealed, so that they may not arouse suspicion, and should be daily inspected, so that they may be certain to function properly in time of necessity.

A final precaution, an extraordinary one, that has been recommended by the Sacred Congregation is the use of the concession granted in canon 1269, § 3. This precaution, since it entails the reservation of the Blessed Sacrament outside the church, shall be more fully dealt with in a later chapter.[21]

ARTICLE III. SACRED VESSELS AND VOTIVE GIFTS OF GREAT VALUE

The rector of a church should exhaust every possibility in order that he may insure a proper and safe guardianship of the Blessed Eucharist. Not only should he employ the positive measures that have already been discussed, but he should also employ a very important negative measure that has been brought to his attention by the Sacred Congregation of the Sacraments in its Instruction of 1938. In so far as it is possible, he is not to retain pyxes and other sacred vessels of great intrinsic worth within the tabernacle.

The reason for this recommendation is immediately evident. The known presence of such vessels can stimulate the daring, the desire and the ingenuity of unscrupulous men to break into the tabernacle in order to steal them.

When such vessels are used on the occasion of a great feast, they should be purified at the last Mass and deposited in some place of security other than the tabernacle.

Furthermore, the presence of valuable votive gifts in the vicinity of the altar, such as gold and silver rings, chains, necklaces, ear rings and pearls, may stimulate men to rob not only these objects but also the contents of the tabernacle. The presence of such valuable objects outside the protection of the enclosed tabernacle can lead men to the conclusion that objects of yet greater value are protected within the tabernacle.

So the rector of a church must refrain from decorating the altar, the statues and the paintings with expensive votive gifts. If the celebration of some great feast prompts this type of decoration, then the rector should take care that the objects of great value be immediately removed at the conclusion of the ceremonies. The faithful, of course, should be informed of the reason for the removal out of due consideration for the generosity which prompted them to make these offerings.[22]

---

[21] *Instruction,* n. 5—*AAS,* XXX (1938), 201-202.
[22] *Instruction,* n. 5—*AAS,* XXX (1938), 202-203.

ARTICLE IV. THE CUSTODY OF THE TABERNACLE KEY

Many precautions and recommendations for the proper safeguarding of the Blessed Eucharist have already been discussed. These precautions, no matter how exactingly they are executed, are nevertheless useless if a very special attention is not directed to the careful custody of the tabernacle key.[23]

Section I. General Principles Relative to the Custodian of the Tabernacle Key

It is imperative for a clear understanding of this article to keep in mind some general principles relative to the custodian of the tabernacle key.

1. A priest must have charge of the tabernacle key. This principle had its origin in the earlier law[24] and received confirmation in the Code of Canon Law.[25]

2. The priest to whom the custody of the tabernacle key pertains need not exercise his charge personally.[26]

3. A lay person may never retain the tabernacle key if he does not possess an apostolic indult which authorizes him to do so.[27] This principle also had its origin in the earlier law.[28]

Some canonists[29] have apparently taken exception to this general principle, and have at least in a general way admitted the lawful retention of the tabernacle key by a lay person. The reason for their contrary opinion is that canon 1269, § 4, definitely designated

---

[23] *Instruction*, n. 6—*AAS*, XXX (1938), 203.

[24] S.R.C., 22 sept. 1593—André-Wagner, III, 580; S.R.C., *Pacen.*, 30 ian. 1610—André-Wagner, III, 582; S.R.C., *Civitaten.*, 6 dec. 1631—*Fontes*, n. 5341; S.R.C., *Tiburtina*, 7 dec. 1737—*Fontes*, n. 5774.

[25] Can. 1269, § 4.

[26] Can. 1269, § 4. Cf. Beste, p. 639; Augustine, VI, 223; Cavanaugh, p. 64; Cance, III, 93; Sipos, p. 664; Coronata, II, 170; Ayrinhac, p. 141.

[27] *Instruction*, n. 6—*AAS*, XXX (1938), 203.

[28] S.R.C., *Civitaten.*, 6 dec. 1631—*Fontes*, n. 5341; S.R.C., *Hispalen.*, 22 nov. 1636—*Fontes*, n. 5363; S.R.C., *Calaguritana*, 13 sept. 1642—*Fontes*, n. 5422; S.R.C., *Atrebaten.*, 13 sept. 1866—Reiffenstuel, lib. III, tit. 44, n. 1, adnotatio XLIV.

[29] Sipos, p. 664; Many, p. 287; Cavanaugh, p. 64; Cance, III, 93; Ayrinhac, 141; Coronata, II, 170.

the person who was to be responsible for the tabernacle key, but did not in so many words designate the person who was to retain the key.

The Sacred Congregation of the Sacraments in its Instruction of 1938 settled any further question on the matter by the following express declaration: "*. . . sine apostolico indulto laici per se clavem ciborii retinere nequeunt.*"[30]

Section II. The Grave Obligation of the Custodian of the Tabernacle Key

The care of the tabernacle key is a grave obligation in conscience for the priest who has care of the church or of the oratory.[31] The gravity of the obligation is immediately evident from the purpose of the law, and also from the very words of the law.[32]

In order that the priest who has care of the church may the more effectively fulfill this grave obligation, the Sacred Congregation of the Sacraments in its Instruction of 1938 has prescribed three possible methods of safeguarding the tabernacle key.[33]

1. The rector may keep the key in the rectory.
2. He may carry the key on his person, provided that he takes precautions against losing it.
3. He may leave the tabernacle key in the sacristy in some secure and secret place that is locked with another key. The second key must then be guarded in the same way as the tabernacle key itself, namely, it must either be kept in the rectory or retained by the rector himself.

The tabernacle key, therefore, must not be left carelessly in the sacristy. It must be locked in a safe and secret place with another key. Even during the hours of morning Mass the tabernacle key, contrary to what so often happens, should not be left on the vestment case, especially if no one continuously remains in the sacristy, and especially if the doors to the sacristy are usually left open for

[30] *Instruction,* n. 6—*AAS,* XXX (1938), 203. On this point cf. also Beste, p. 639; Köster, p. 224; Vermeersch-Creusen, II, 416; Gasparri, II, 267.

[31] Can. 1269, § 4.

[32] *Instruction,* n. 6—*AAS,* XXX (1938), 203; Can. 1269, § 4; Cappello, I, 303.

[33] *Instruction,* n. 6—*AAS,* XXX (1938), 203.

the convenience of the many priests who say Mass in the church. Such a practice is altogether to be reprobated.[34]

It is also to be noted that the Sacred Congregation made no mention of sacristy safes equipped with combination locks. However, it does not seem contrary to the purpose of the law, nor does it appear contrary to the mind of the Sacred Congregation, to so retain the tabernacle key, provided that the combination of the safe is known only to the rector, to the priests who usually say Mass in the church, and to the trustworthy sacristan or sexton.[35]

The Sacred Congregation not only prescribed positive measures that must be employed by the priest who has care of the church, in order that he might fulfill the grave obligation in conscience to safeguard the key of the tabernacle, but also prescribed that he should never leave the key on the table of the altar or in the lock of the tabernacle door. According to the Instruction the unguarded leaving of the key on the table of the altar or in the lock of the tabernacle is not to be countenanced even during the morning hours when Mass is celebrated and Holy Communion is distributed at the altar of reservation, especially if the altar is not in a conspicuous place.[36]

It is to be well noted that the Sacred Congregation said: ". . . *praesertim si hoc altare haud in conspicuo sit.*"[37] This stress leads the present writer to conclude that the custodian, if during the morning hours of Mass and Holy Communion he carelessly leaves the tabernacle key on the altar, can hardly be excused from mortal sin if the altar is not continuously and easily visible either to himself, to another priest, or to trustworthy lay people.

Section III. The Custodian of the Tabernacle Key According to the Instruction of the Sacred Congregation of the Sacraments

The Sacred Congregation of the Sacraments in its Instruction of 1938 was quite explicit relative to the custodian of the taber-

---

[34] Cappello, I, 303.

[35] "Studies and Conferences"—*The Ecclesiastical Review* (Philadelphia, 1905-1943), XCVIII (1938), 372 (hereafter cited *ER*).

[36] *Instruction*, n. 6—*AAS*, XXX (1938), 203.

[37] *Instruction*, n. 6—*AAS*, XXX (1938), 203.

nacle key. In determining the custodian, however, the Sacred Congregation apparently abstracted from the distinction between the responsible custodian, who must always be a priest, and the actual custodian, who may be even a lay person. So the present writer, in the course of dealing with the custodian of the tabernacle key according to the Instruction, shall endeavor to maintain the distinction. The distinction has some importance in that the responsible custodian of the tabernacle key is the primary guardian of the Blessed Sacrament.

Before further venture into the subject, however, the writer desires to remark that the term "responsible" custodian is perhaps misleading, since it connotes the presence of responsibility in the responsible custodian to the exclusion of anyone else. There is no doubt that responsibility in varying degrees devolves upon all who in any way deal with the guardianship of the Blessed Sacrament, since penalties are enacted without distinction for all who are guilty of negligence in the matter.[38] So in view of this fact it may be better to speak of the "primary" custodian of the tabernacle key, rather than of the "responsible" custodian of the tabernacle key.

According to the Instruction, the general rule relative to the primary custodian of the tabernacle key is that the rector of the church or of the oratory is responsible for its safety. However, the Sacred Congregation determined the person of the primary custodian more specifically.

a. In a parish church the pastor has the right and the duty of safeguarding the tabernacle key. Indeed, even when a Confraternity of the Blessed Sacrament has been erected in the church, the pastor is still possessed of this right and of this duty. However, if the parish church is also a cathedral or a collegiate church, the custody of the tabernacle key pertains to the chapter. In this case, nevertheless, a second key must be entrusted to the pastor.[39]

It is to be noted that the Sacred Congregation did not take cognizance of a religious church which at the same time is a parochial church.[40] In this case it is apparent that the custody of the

[38] *Instruction,* n. 10—*AAS* (1938), 206.

[39] *Instruction,* n. 6—*AAS,* XXX (1938), 203.

[40] Cf. can. 609, § 1.

tabernacle key pertains to the religious community.[41] However, if the superior of the religious community is not a priest, the custody of the tabernacle key would devolve upon the chaplain of the community.[42] Under all circumstances, nevertheless, a second key must be entrusted to the pastor.[43]

b. In a non-parochial church where the Blessed Eucharist is reserved by virtue of an apostolic indult the chaplain or the rector must safeguard the tabernacle key. Lay persons, even though they are patrons, cannot enjoy such a right. Indeed, without an apostolic indult laics can never have immediate charge of the tabernacle key.[44]

c. In oratories of seminaries, in ecclesiastical colleges, in schools for the religious instruction and training of the young of either sex, in hospitals and in other such institutions which may have the privilege of reserving the Blessed Sacrament, the tabernacle key must be kept by the rector or by the moderator of each institution, provided that he is a priest. If the rector or the moderator is not a priest, then the key must be kept by the spiritual director or by the chaplain who has charge of the regular celebration of Mass and of the sacred functions.

It is to be noted that the Sacred Congregation did not speak of a resident spiritual director or of a resident chaplain. To the mind of the writer, therefore, in such a case any priest who has charge of the regular celebration of Holy Mass and of the sacred functions becomes the primary custodian of the tabernacle key.

In addition to this more specific determination of the primary custodian of the tabernacle key the Sacred Congregation enumerated two situations in which the actual custodian of the tabernacle key almost independently looks to the custody of the tabernacle key.

a. According to the Instruction, some special observations must be made relative to the custody of the tabernacle key in the churches of nuns or of women religious, and in the religious or the pious houses of women. The tabernacle key must never be kept within the walls of the monastery, nor elsewhere in the house. The tabernacle key must be kept in the sacristy, where it will be easily

[41] Can. 609, § 1; Can. 415, § 3, 1°.

[42] Köster, p. 226.

[43] Can. 415, § 3, 1°.

[44] *Instruction*, n. 6—*AAS*, XXX (1938), 203.

available whenever it is needed. After the conclusion of the sacred functions which demand the use of the tabernacle key, and especially at night, it must be deposited and locked with two keys in a safe, strong and secret place within the confines of the sacristy. One of these keys must be kept by the superioress of the community, or by the substitute whom she appoints. The other must be kept by one of the nuns, for example, by the sacristan. Such an arrangement is desirable in that it demands the concurrence of at least two persons in order that access may be had to the tabernacle key.[45]

It must be noted that these rules for the custody of the tabernacle key in the churches of women do not apply if a proper rector is assigned to the church and lives in the near vicinity, or if a resident chaplain is assigned to the community of women.[46] In such cases the rector or the chaplain is to exercise the custody of the tabernacle key in accordance with the ordinary methods suggested by the Sacred Congregation.

However, in the event that there is no rector or chaplain so assigned, may it be assumed that the women in question are completely in charge of the tabernacle key? Are they independent in the exercise of their charge? Are they the primary guardians of the Blessed Sacrament? Affirmative answers to these questions would hardly be consonant with the general principle that a priest must always have charge of the tabernacle key, or, in other words, with the general principle that a priest must always be the primary guardian of the Blessed Sacrament.

Some priest, therefore, must be the primary guardian of the tabernacle key. In the event that there is no rector assigned to the church and living in the near vicinity, or in the event that there is no resident chaplain assigned to the community, this priest must be the one who regularly celebrates Mass and conducts sacred functions in the place of reservation. Apparently the Sacred Congregation made such a disposition relative to the custody of the tabernacle key in the oratories of seminaries, colleges, hospitals, and other institutions in which the rectors or moderators were not priests. To the mind of the present writer an analogous application

[45] *Instruction*, n. 7—*AAS*, XXX (1938), 204.

[46] Can. 1269, § 4. Cf. also Köster, p. 226; "Studies and Conferences"—*ER*, XCVIII (1938), 372.

of this disposition to the churches and to the oratories of women seems plainly warranted.[47]

So, for the sake of an example, in the sisters' convent where he or one of his assistants regularly celebrates Mass and conducts the sacred functions, the pastor must be the primary custodian of the tabernacle key. He should, therefore, supervise the carrying out of the special regulations that were made by the Sacred Congregation relative to the safekeeping of the key in such situations.

As the primary custodian of the tabernacle key, however, may the pastor in such a situation presume to change the method of safeguarding the key? May he for the sake of greater safety insist that the tabernacle key be carried to the priest's house after every celebration of Mass? Even though the reason for the change may be just and grave, such as the negligence of the sisters or the lack of a safe, strong and secret place in the sacristy of the convent, the pastor may not insist that the tabernacle key be carried to the priest's house after every celebration of Mass. The special observations of the Sacred Congregation relative to the custody of the key in such situations are ordinarily a matter of prescript.[48]

What, therefore, may be done when a change of method becomes imperative in the presence of a just and grave cause? The pastor as the primary custodian of the tabernacle key and as the primary guardian of the Blessed Sacrament should report the circumstances that demand a change to the local ordinary. The present writer is persuaded that the local ordinary may act in such a case and may legitimately authorize another method of safeguarding the tabernacle key. The writer bases his conclusion on the following data: 1) Whenever grave and continued negligence is the cause for the desired change, the local ordinary is empowered to inflict a suspension *a munere* on the guilty parties.[49] 2) The local ordinary is empowered to authorize such a change in the case of private oratories whenever it seems more desirable to him that the holder of the apostolic indult for the reservation of the Blessed Sacra-

---

[47] *Instruction,* n. 8—*AAS,* XXX (1938), 204.

[48] *Instruction,* n. 7: "Huiusmodi praescriptum probe inspiciant Excm̃i Episcopi. . . ."—*AAS,* XXX (1938), 204.

[49] *Instruction,* n. 10—*AAS,* XXX (1938), 205.

ment should not retain the actual custody of the tabernacle key.[50] 3) The Sacred Congregation pointed out that the local ordinary is in no way limited to the application of the specific norms and precautions that are contained in the Instruction to the exclusion of other added regulations. He may employ and urge other measures of safety, which according to the circumstances of time and of place may seem better suited for the fuller attainment of the proper guardianship of the Blessed Sacrament.[51]

A final note should be made relative to the special regulations that were established by the Sacred Congregation for the custody of the tabernacle key in churches and oratories of women. In the mind of the present writer, these rules are not to be analogically applied to the churches and to the oratories of men. If the Sacred Congregation desired that the tabernacle key be so safeguarded in the churches and oratories of lay communities of men, the presumption is that the Sacred Congregation would have expressed this desire.[52] Therefore, in such churches and oratories the ordinary norms that have been established by the Sacred Congregation for the safe custody of the tabernacle key should be followed.

b. In private oratories, if by apostolic indult they have the privilege of reserving the Blessed Sacrament, the key of the tabernacle is usually kept in the sacristy in the care of the family rather than in the care of the chaplain. However, if the bishop thinks that it is more advisable that the key should not be entrusted to the holder of the indult, then he may entrust it to the priest who celebrates Mass in the oratory, especially if he does so regularly, or else to the pastor in whose territory the private oratory is located. When the pastor is entrusted with the tabernacle key, he should deliver it each time, if it is conveniently possible, to the priest who is to celebrate Mass in the private oratory.

Lay persons who while enjoying the privilege of a private oratory also exercise the custody of the tabernacle key have the grave obligation to see to it that the key does not fall into the hands of

---

[50] *Instruction*, n. 9—*AAS*, XXX (1938), 204.

[51] *Instruction*, n. 10—*AAS*, XXX (1938), 206.

[52] Cf. Köster, p. 227.

anyone else, not even of the members of their own family or of their own household.[53]

These lay persons, it is to be noted, even though they exercise the actual custody of the tabernacle key, nevertheless remain under the supervision of the primary custodian. This is imperative in view of the general principle that a priest must always have charge of the tabernacle key. This priest, as the Sacred Congregation has suggested, must be the chaplain assigned to the private oratory, or the priest who regularly says Mass there, or else the pastor in whose territory the private oratory is located.

Section IV. The Actual Custody of the Tabernacle Key

From the things that have been said in the course of this article, it is evident that the priest who is responsible for the tabernacle key need not exercise the custody personally. It is also evident that he may entrust the actual custody of the key to persons other than priests. Thus, in churches and oratories of women which have no chaplain, the sisters themselves must be the actual guardians of the tabernacle key. Furthermore, in private oratories the holders of the apostolic indult are usually charged with the actual custody of the tabernacle key.

Moreover, the Sacred Congregation of the Sacraments in its Instruction of 1938 has established two norms of procedure that are to be followed in the absence of the rector of a church or of an oratory. The second of these norms involves the actual custody of the tabernacle key by a lay person. The norms have been stated as follows:

> *Sacerdos, cui ius et officium ordinarie et per se competit custodiendi clavem, est rector ecclesiae vel oratorii: quodsi discedat, potest et debet pro tempore absentiae alio sacerdoti committere custodiam; et si clavem in sacrario retineat sub alia clavi, potest hanc tradere aedituo, pro tempore quo ipse abest, et clavis tabernaculi necessaria esse queat.*[54]

---

[53] *Instruction*, n. 9—*AAS*, XXX (1938), 204.

[54] *Instruction*, n. 6—*AAS*, XXX (1938), 203.

These two norms of procedure are of general application in all churches and in all oratories where the Blessed Sacrament is reserved. It is true that the Sacred Congregation spoke of the absence of the "rector"; but, in the mind of the present writer, the term "rector" was employed to refer to any custodian of the tabernacle key. So these norms can be followed not only in the absence of rectors, but also in the absence of pastors, chaplains, moderators and spiritual directors, if these be the custodians of the tabernacle key.[55]

Apparently the first norm of procedure applies only when the absence of the rector is of such duration that the designation of another priest to take his place in the exercise of the sacred functions in the church becomes imperative. In this case the rector can and must entrust the custody of the tabernacle key to the substitute. The substitute then becomes the responsible custodian of the key, and accordingly acquires all the rights and all the obligations of the rector.[56]

The second norm evidently applies when the rector himself continues to be the responsible custodian of the tabernacle key. Thus the rector of a church may be unable to be present in the sacristy during all the hours of the morning Masses. Again, the chaplain of a religious community of women may go away on a few days' vacation. Again, the pastor who has the care of an oratory that belongs to a lay community of men may almost always be absent from the oratory. During these periods of absence the key may be necessary in order that the priest from a neighboring institution, or from a neighboring parish, may celebrate Mass, give Benediction, take Holy Communion to the sick, or carry Holy Viaticum to the dying. In these cases the rector, the pastor, or the chaplain may somewhere in the sacristy lock up the tabernacle key, and then entrust the second key to the sacristan. The second key, however, must be returned to the rector, to the pastor, or to the chaplain at the conclusion of the period of his absence.

In small parishes it is ordinarily the pastor himself who performs the duties of the sacristan. So, strictly taken, there is no available

---

[55] Cf. Köster, p. 225.

[56] Köster, p. 225.

sacristan to whom the second key may be entrusted when the pastor desires to be away from the parish for a few days. Yet the pastor, with due regard for the needs of the parishioners, may desire to have Mass celebrated during his absence by a neighboring priest. In such a case the pastor can appoint his housekeeper, provided that she has the proper qualifications, or else a trustworthy parishioner, as temporary sacristan. This does not seem to be in any way whatsoever an extension of the regulation of the Sacred Congregation of the Sacraments.

CHAPTER VIII

The Duties of the Local Ordinaries Relative to the Careful Custody of the Holy Eucharist

The Sacred Congregation of the Sacraments in its Instruction of 1938 determined many canonical norms and precautions that are to be employed for the proper custody of the Blessed Sacrament. The Sacred Congregation enjoined these norms and precautions principally upon the local ordinaries in order that they in turn may more insistently urge their execution upon pastors and upon others who have the custody of the Blessed Sacrament. The local ordinaries, however, as the Sacred Congregation pointed out, are in no way limited to the application of these specific canonical norms and precautions to the exclusion of other added regulations. They may employ and urge other measures of safety, which according to the circumstances of time and of place may seem more suitable for the fuller attainment of the proper safeguardianship of the Blessed Sacrament.[1]

In addition to these general duties and these general prerogatives, the Sacred Congregation imposed four special precepts upon the local ordinaries. These precepts, the first three of which contain also penal sanctions, shall be stated in full and then commented upon in the following articles.

ARTICLE I. THE DILIGENT INQUIRY AND THE OBSERVATION OF THE LOCAL ORDINARIES RELATIVE TO THE CAREFUL CUSTODY OF THE HOLY EUCHARIST

Section I. The First Precept

Especially during the course of their diocesan visitations, but also on other occasions as circumstances demand, the local ordinaries, either in person or through the agency of qualified and

[1] *Instruction*, n. 10—*AAS*, XXX (1938), 206.

prudent ecclesiastics, shall diligently inquire and actually observe what provisions are being made for the proper safeguarding of the Blessed Sacrament in all churches and oratories. Whenever they discover that the provisions of law are not being observed, the local ordinaries shall command that those persons upon whom rests the duty of providing every means of security for the Blessed Sacrament, put them into execution within a certain period of time and under threat of penalty. The penalty shall be a fine and, if the gravity of the negligence demands it, a suspension *a divinis* in the case of priests, or a suspension *a munere* in the case of others. Moreover, the local ordinaries shall not relieve any persons from the obligation of observing the regulations of the law for the safeguarding of the Blessed Sacrament on the plea that no profanation or untoward accident has previously occurred; for things that have not yet happened may well occur in the course of time and in consequence of the malice of men, if the necessary precautions are neglected.[2]

Section II. Notes of Commentary on the First Precept

1. The first precept is not restricted in its application solely to priests, who are the primary guardians of the Holy Eucharist; for in the text of the first precept a distinction is made between priests and others upon whom rests the duty of providing every means of security for the Blessed Sacrament.[3] Thus the precept, the fine and the suspension *a munere* can evidently be imposed upon lay guardians of the Blessed Sacrament.

The suspension *a munere* which may be imposed even upon a lay guardian apparently implies the discontinuance of the specific duties of guardianship that had been entrusted to his care.

2. The penal sanctions that are contained in the first and third precepts of the Instruction can be applied by the local ordinaries

[2] *Instruction*, n. 10—*AAS*, XXX (1938), 205.

[3] *Instruction*, n. 10: ". . . eadem praecipiant [episcopi locorumque ordinarii] quam exsequenda, brevi tempore ad id praestituto, sub poena mulctae pecuniariae et etiam suspensionis a divinis pro sacerdotibus aut a munere, pro gravitate culpae, ab iis incurrendae, quibus officium competit omnia securitatis praesidia subministrandi."—*AAS*, XXX (1938), 205.

to the delinquent religious of either sex, even though they may be exempt regulars. At the conclusion of the third precept the Sacred Congregation granted the local ordinaries, cumulatively with the major superiors of these religious, special faculties for penal prosecution in such cases. The major superiors, it is to be well noted, were not dispossessed of the duty and right of penal prosecution in such cases. Their obligation in the matter continues and is to be faithfully executed.[4]

3. The Code of Canon Law limits the scope of the canonical visitation of exempt religious by the local ordinaries.[5] Therefore it is apparent that the diligent inquiry and the observation of the local ordinaries relative to the careful custody of the Holy Eucharist by exempt religious is considerably circumscribed.

However, in the following cases the local ordinaries may conduct a canonical visitation of exempt religious:

a. They may visit the monasteries of nuns who are subject to regular superiors whenever these regular superiors have failed to visit the monasteries within a five year period.[6]

b. They may visit all houses of pontifical clerical congregations which are exempt, but only concerning those matters which pertain to the church, to the sacristy, to the public oratory, and to the confessional.[7]

c. The local ordinaries may make a canonical visitation of the churches and of the public oratories of all exempt religious in order that they may enforce any special statutes which they have enacted concerning divine worship.[8]

However, this canonical visitation cannot be made in the same manner as the usual quinquennial visitation of non-exempt

---

[4] *Instruction,* n. 10: "Ut autem locorum Ordinarii poenis prosequi queant et delinquentes religiosos utriusque sexus etiam exemptos iuxta has apostolicas praescriptiones in negotio, de quo agimus, vi huius Instructionis facultates committimus necessarias cumulative cum eorum Superioribus religiosis Maioribus, quibus pariter haec S. Congregatio idem onus imponit, reservata tamen uni Episcopi facultate processum conficiendi, de quo sub litt. b) in casu ibi descripto."—*AAS,* XXX (1938), 206.

[5] Cans. 512 and 615.

[6] Can. 512, § 2, 1°.

[7] Can. 512, § 2, 2°.

[8] Can. 1261, § 2.

churches. As a general rule the local ordinaries may use the right of visitation in such cases only insofar as they have positive information that the particular laws which have been enacted by them are not being observed in the churches of the exempt regulars.[9]

d. The local ordinaries may visit the parochial churches of regulars in all things that pertain to the care of souls. The ambit of the visitation therefore includes an inspection of the altar of the Blessed Sacrament, of the tabernacle, and of the sacred vessels that are used for the purpose of preserving the consecrated particles.[10]

In the cases just enumerated the local ordinaries may, either in person or through the agency of qualified and prudent ecclesiastics, diligently inquire and actually observe what provisions are being made concerning the careful custody of the Holy Eucharist. Moreover, in these particlular cases the local ordinaries may coerce the exempt religious by means of other penalties as well as by means of the penalties sanctioned in the Instruction.[11]

In other than the cases here enumerated, for example, in the case of semi-public oratories of regulars, the local ordinaries may neither personally nor through the agency of others visit the exempt religious. Such visitations are the proper right and duty of the major religious superiors. In these other cases, therefore, only when abuses come to their attention may the local ordinaries presume to inflict the penalties sanctioned in the first and third precepts of the Instruction.

This faculty, of course, is a derogation of canon 617, which provided that the local ordinaries should in such cases first warn the superiors of the exempt religious to provide remedies against abuses, and then, if the warnings have failed in their purpose, refer the matter immediately to the Holy See. However, in a house of

---

[9] A private reply of the Code Commission, 8 apr. 1924—Bouscaren, *The Canon Law Digest* (2 vols., Milwaukee, Wis.: The Bruce Publishing Co., 1934-1943), II, 374 (hereafter cited *Digest*).

[10] Can. 1425, § 2; Reilly, *The Visitation of Religious*, The Catholic University of America Canon Law Studies, n. 112 (Washington, D. C.: The Catholic University of America, 1938), pp. 138-139.

[11] Can. 619.

exempt religious which still lacks its full juridical development (*domus non-formata*), the local ordinaries are allowed by canon 617 to deal provisionally with abuses that have become a source of scandal to the faithful.

ARTICLE II. THE LOCAL ORDINARIES AND THE VIOLATION OF THE BLESSED SACRAMENT

Section I. The Second Precept

If for any cause whatsoever a sacrilegious theft in which the Holy Eucharist is violated should occur in his diocese, the bishop of the place shall, either in person or through the *officialis* of the curia, who must be specially delegated for the task, conduct an administrative process against the pastor or against any other priest, even an exempt religious, who had charge of the Blessed Sacrament. The bishop of the place shall then send a record of the trial to the Sacred Congregation of the Sacraments, together with his own opinion on the matter. In this furnished report he first of all shall carefully describe the circumstances of the time and the place of the theft. Then, in accordance with the record of the trial, he shall name the persons to whose fault or to whose culpable negligence the commission of the crime is to be attributed. Finally, he shall propose which canonical penalties he deems it imperative to inflict on the guilty parties. No further action should be taken by the bishop of the place. Instead, he shall await the mandates of the Sacred Congregation relative to the case.[12]

Section II. Notes of Commentary on the Second Precept

1. Only the bishop of the place may conduct the administrative process that has been described in the second precept. Other local ordinaries and even major religious superiors are incompetent in the matter.[13]

2. The administrative process which receives mention in connection with the second precept is directed against the primary guardian, and not against the acting guardian, of the Holy Eucha-

[12] *Instruction*, n. 10—*AAS*, XXX (1938), 205.

[13] *Instruction*, n. 10—*AAS*, XXX (1938), 206.

rist. The primary guardian who is so arraigned may even be an exempt regular.[14]

ARTICLE III. THE LOCAL ORDINARIES AND THE USE OF CANON 2382

Section I. The Third Precept

The local ordinaries shall give mature consideration to the severity of the penalties which are enacted by canon 2382 against a pastor who is gravely negligent in the custody of the Most Blessed Sacrament, even though his negligence does not result in a sacrilegious violation of the Sacred Species.

In consideration of the aim of the law, the local ordinaries should see to it that analogous penalties (*congrua congruis referendo*) be likewise imposed upon other rectors of churches who are gravely negligent in the discharge of the exalted duty that has been entrusted to them. For so adopting the provisions of canon 2382 with reference also to other rectors of churches, the local ordinaries can readily obtain the necessary and proper faculties from the Sacred Congregation of the Sacraments, should ever the need arise.

The pastors or the others who are charged with the care of the Blessed Sacrament cannot escape these penalties through the plea that it was owing to the negligence of some other priest that the tabernacle was left open and that the keys were not kept in a secure place. For they themselves are charged with the duty of a diligent and solicitous care of the sacred vessels and of the Holy Eucharist, and, moreover, they have the personal duty of seeing that, when the divine services are concluded, the ciboria shall not be exposed to the danger of any desecration or sacrilegious pillage. The priest here contemplated as also any other person who is guilty of a like negligence lay themselves open to, and invite the

---

[14] *Instruction,* n. 10: ". . . oeconomicum semper conficiat processum (Episcopus loci) adversus parochum aliumve sacerdotem tam saecularem quam religiosum exemptum SSmi Sacramenti custodiae praepositum. . . ."—*AAS,* XXX (1938), 205. Cf. also Woywod, *A Practical Commentary on the Code of Canon Law* (revised by Callistus Smith, revised and enlarged edition, 2 vols., New York: Jos. F. Wagner, Inc., 1948), II, 75.

infliction of similar punishments, since through their fault they furnished the occasion for so grave a crime.[15]

Section II. Notes of Commentary on the Third Precept

1. The penal sanctions as mentioned in the third precept are applicable to the primary guardian of the Blessed Sacrament, even though the acting guardians or other persons are guilty of negligence in the care of the Blessed Sacrament.[16] This is not an unreasonable regulation, for the first step in the penal procedure sanctioned in the third precept consists simply in a warning.[17]

2. The penal sanctions mentioned in connection with the third precept may be applied also to the acting guardians of the Blessed Sacrament, and to anyone else who is guilty of negligence in the careful custody of the Holy Eucharist. Thus, for example, even visiting priests who are careless in the disposal of the tabernacle key may be visited with the penalties contemplated for the violation of the third precept.[18]

3. Canon 2382 has reference to the grave neglect of parochial duties. If a pastor is gravely negligent in the administration of the sacraments, in the care of the sick, in the instruction of the children and of the people, in preaching on Sundays and on Holydays, in the care of the parish church, in the care of the Most Blessed Sacrament, and in the care of the holy oils, he shall be punished by the ordinary according to the norms of canons 2182-2185.[19]

Canons 2182-2185 concern the manner of procedure that may

---

[15] *Instruction*, n. 10—*AAS*, XXX (1938), 205-206.

[16] *Instruction*, n. 10: ". . . Quibus aufugiendis poenis haud suffragatur causa forte a parocho aliisve (rectoribus cappellanis, etc.), quibus SS. Species custodiendae incumbunt, allata qua tabernacula patentia relinquantur clavesque in loco tuto non custodiantur alius sacerdotis incuria."—*AAS*, XXX (1938), 205-206.

[17] Can. 2182.

[18] *Instruction*, n. 10: "Equidem est animadvertendum et in memoratum sacerdotem et in quemlibet alium huius neglegentiae reum similibus poenis, quippe qui occasionem tanto sceleri sua culpa dederint."—*AAS*, XXX (1938), 206.

[19] Can. 2382.

be employed against a pastor who is negligent in the fulfillment of his pastoral duties. If a pastor gravely neglects his pastoral duties, the bishop shall issue a warning in which he shall remind the pastor of his strict obligation in conscience and of the penalties which the law decrees against his negligence.[20]

If such a warning has failed in its purpose, and if upon consulting with two of the synodal examiners, and after having given the pastor a chance to defend himself, the bishop finds that the pastor has repeatedly neglected his duties or has committed serious violations of his duties for a notable length of time without any just cause, he shall then rebuke the pastor and impose on him an appropriate penalty in proportion to his guilt.[21]

If both the rebuke and the penalty prove a failure, then the ordinary, when in accordance with the norm of canon 2183 he has verified the culpable continuance of the pastor in the neglect or in the serious violation of his duties, may immediately deprive a removable pastor of his parish; he may, furthermore, deprive an irremovable pastor of the income of his benefice, either in whole or in part, in proportion to the seriousness of his guilt. The income so appropriated by the ordinary shall then be distributed among the poor.[22]

If the contumacy of the irremovable pastor still continues and likewise is proved in the manner that has just been described, the ordinary shall deprive him of his parish.[23]

ARTICLE IV. THE LOCAL ORDINARIES AND THE PLACES OF RESERVATION

Section I. The Fourth Precept

The local ordinaries shall diligently inquire whether the churches and the oratories which are not entitled to reserve the Blessed Sacrament under the common law possess this faculty by an apostolic indult, by a papal brief that has been conceded in per-

[20] Can. 2182.
[21] Can. 2183.
[22] Can. 2184.
[23] Can. 2185.

petuity, or by a rescript that has been conceded for a time. Whenever the local ordinaries discover that the privilege does not rest on a legitimate claim, they shall take action to stamp out the supposititious privilege as an abuse. Moreover, they shall not show themselves over complaisant in receiving and in recommending petitions for the faculty of reserving the Most Blessed Sacrament in those places which have not that faculty in the common law.

Unless very grave reasons are present, they should rather refrain entirely from encouraging such petitions, especially in the case of private oratories and churches that are far removed from the homes of the faithful, whether in rugged mountain territory or on expansive plains, when there are not at hand all the factors which contribute to a responsible and utterly secure custody of the Sacred Species. For it can indeed be more readily condoned that even a notable number of the faithful should at times be deprived of the advantage of adoring the Blessed Eucharist than that the Most Blessed Sacrament should admittedly be exposed to a probable danger of profanation.

In the concluding part of this fourth precept the Sacred Congregation granted to local ordinaries the power to revoke the faculty of reserving the Blessed Sacrament both from churches and from oratories, even private ones, if they held this apostolic privilege by indult, whenever these ordinaries discovered that grave abuses had occurred, or that not all the conditions for the safe custody, the reverence, and the worship which are due to the Most Blessed Sacrament had been verified.[24]

Section II. Notes of Commentary on the Fourth Precept

In the granting of the faculty at the end of the fourth precept, the Sacred Congregation employed the following expression: *"Potestas hisce litteris committitur Excmis Episcopis locorumque Ordinariis. . . ."* It is immediately evident that the word *"locorum"* modifies both *"Episcopis"* and *"Ordinariis,"* for the general provisions of canon 1265, which constitute the basis for the fourth precept, take only local ordinaries into consideration.

[24] *Instruction*, n. 10—*AAS*, XXX (1938), 206.

Scholion: The Vicars Forane and the Careful Custody of the Holy Eucharist

Canon 447, § 1, 4° simply implies that over the non-exempt churches of his district the dean (vicar forane) shall exercise a general supervision relative to the careful custody of the Holy Eucharist. The canon, however, specifically states that he is to exercise vigilance regarding proper adornment and neatness in these churches, especially with regard to the reservation of the Blessed Sacrament and the celebration of the Holy Mass.

CHAPTER IX

The Renewal of the Sacred Species

Can. 1272: *Hostiae consecratae, sive propter fidelium communionem, sive propter expositionem sanctissimi Sacramenti, et recentes sint et frequenter renoventur, veteribus rite consumptis, ita ut nullum sit periculum corruptionis, sedulo servatis instructionibus quas Ordinarius loci hac de re dederit.*

The consecrated Hosts, both for the Communion of the faithful and for the Exposition of the Most Blessed Sacrament, must be fresh and must be frequently renewed, the old ones being properly consumed, so that there may be no danger of corruption. Upon this matter the instructions that are given by the local ordinary must be scrupulously observed.

ARTICLE I. ". . . [HOSTIAE] RECENTES SINT ET FREQUENTER RENOVENTUR. . ."

Section I. ". . . [hostiae] frequenter renoventur. . ."

In the post-Tridentine legislation it was evident that a renewal of the Sacred Species once a week was the norm for the universal discipline of the Latin Church.[1] In practice, however, the Holy See did not urge this norm inflexibly, but oftentimes allowed a renewal of the Sacred Species every two weeks,[2] and at times even once a month.[3]

---

[1] Van der Stappen, IV, 137; S.R.C., *Conchen.*, 3 sept. 1672, ad 3—Gardellini, n. 2602; S.R.C., *Sanctorien.*, 12 sept. 1884, ad II—*Fontes*, n. 6162.

[2] Van der Stappen, IV, 137; S.C. Ep. et Reg., *Ravennaten.*, 5 aug. 1573—*Fontes*, n. 1308; Benedictus XIV, const., *Etsi pastoralis*, 26 maii 1742, § VI, n. II—*Fontes*, n. 308; Provincial Council of Embrun (1727), c. X, n. IV—*Coll. Lac.*, I, 629; Provincial Council of Avignon (1725), tit. XXVII, c. II—*Coll. Lac.*, I, 528; Provincial Council of Prague (1860), tit. V, c. VII—*Coll. Lac.*, V, 542.

[3] Köster, pp. 167-170; Provincial Council of Vienna (1858)—*Coll. Lac.*, V, n. 163; Provincial Council of Utrecht (1865)—*Coll. Lac.*, V, n. 920.

The Code of Canon Law[4] also departed from the norm of the post-Tridentine legislation in that it omitted the statement of any determined period of time for the renewal of the Sacred Species and adopted the prescription of the *Roman Ritual,*[5] which merely demanded that the Sacred Hosts be renewed frequently. According to the common opinion of canonists this frequent renewal period of the Code of Canon Law may certainly be extended beyond one week.[6]

It is true that canon 1272 did not expressly deny the continued existence of the weekly norm of the earlier law. However, it specified only one norm of determining the frequency of renewal, namely, "*. . . et* [*hostiae*] *recentes et frequenter renoventur, ita ut nullum sit periculum corruptionis.*" Moreover, it expressly demanded that the instructions of the local ordinary should be scrupulously observed in the matter of renewing the Sacred Hosts. This concession, if it may be so called, evidently granted to the local ordinaries the liberty of following or of not following the weekly norm of the earlier law.

Confirmation of the fact that the Code of Canon Law did not demand the observance of the weekly norm of the post-Tridentine legislation relative to the renewal of the Sacred Species is found in a recent response of the Sacred Congregation of the Sacraments,[7] and also in a recent Instruction of the same Congregation.[8] These sources treated the subject of the renewal of the Sacred Species, and yet made no mention of a determined period of time. In fact, they merely repeated the prescription of the Code of Canon Law to the effect that the Sacred Hosts should be renewed frequently.

---

[4] Can. 1272.

[5] Tit. IV, c. I, *de sanctissimo Eucharistiae sacramento,* n. 7.

[6] Cavanaugh, p. 72; Beste, p. 643; Berutti, IV, 257; Vermeersch-Creusen, II, 418; Claeys Bouuaert-Simenon, *Manuale Juris Canonici* (3 vols., Vol. III, 4. ed., Gandae et Leodii: Dessain, 1934), III, 76 (hereafter cited Claeys Bouuaert-Simenon); Noldin-Schmitt, *Summa Theologiae Moralis* (3 vols., Vol. I, 29. ed., 1944, Vol. II, 28. ed., 1944, Vol. III, 28. ed., 1945, Heidelberga: Sumptibus F. H. Kerle Monachii), III, 129 (hereafter cited Noldin-Schmitt); Köster, p. 235; Sipos, p. 645; Cocchi, V, 201.

Cappello (I, 312) and Cance (III, 94, footnote 3) are in opposition to the common opinion.

[7] S.C. de Sacramentis, responsum, 7 dec. 1918—*AAS,* XI (1919), 8.

[8] *Instruction of 1929—AAS,* XXI (1929), 638.

Although canonists commonly admit that the weekly norm of the earlier law no longer prevails, nevertheless a great number of them rigorously restrict the renewal of the Sacred Hosts within a time period of no more than fifteen days.[9] Even such a restriction should not be made a general rule, since canon 1272, to repeat, adverts to but one factor for determining the frequency of renewal, namely, the danger of corruption, and furthermore, grants to the local ordinary much liberty relative to the determination of the danger of corruption.

Although it is apparent, therefore, that in the absence of the danger of corruption there is no strict obligation to follow any determined time for the renewal of the Sacred Hosts, it must be well remembered that it is the special desire of the Holy See that the Sacred Species be renewd at least once a week.[10] Certainly the norm of the weekly renewal is more in conformity with the prescript of the *Caeremoniale Episcoporum,*[11] and also with the mind of the Sacred Congregation of Rites.[12] Moreover, the norm of the weekly renewal is certainly suggested by the fact that canon 1265 established the weekly celebration of Holy Mass as a condition for the reservation of the Blessed Sacrament in churches and in oratories.

Section II. ". . . et [hostiae] recentes sint. . ."

The Code of Canon Law [13] prescribed that the consecrated Hosts which are used for the Communion of the faithful and for the Exposition of the Most Blessed Sacrament should be fresh or recently baked. In this the Code merely adopted the norm of the *Roman Ritual,*[14] and thereby avoided the determination of a set period of time beyond which altar breads are not to be consecrated.

---

[9] Beste, p. 643; Claeys Bouuaert-Simenon, III, 76; Cavanaugh, p. 72; Vermeersch-Creusen, II, 418; Berutti, IV, 257; Sipos, p. 665, footnote 11; Cocchi, V, 201.

[10] Köster, p. 237.

[11] Lib. I, c. VI, n. 2.

[12] S.R.C., *Conchen.,* 3 sept. 1672, ad 3—Gardellini, n. 2602; *Sanctorien.,* 12 sept. 1884, ad II—*Fontes,* n. 6161; Cappello, I, 312.

[13] Can. 1272. Cf. also, can. 815, § 1.

[14] Tit. IV, c. I, *de sanctissimo Eucharistiae sacramento,* n. 7.

However, on December 17, 1918, the Sacred Congregation of the Sacraments reprobated the custom in certain dioceses of consecrating hosts that were two or three months old.[15] In other words, altar breads of such an age were, as a rule, not to be used for consecration, even though they showed no signs of disintegration.[16]

The Sacred Congregation in this response, however, did not have in mind the determination of a period of time beyond which the altar breads in a particular case could no longer be classified as *"recentes."* So, in a particular case, especially in a case of necessity when fresher ones were not available, altar breads of such an age could be used, provided, of course, that the danger of corruption was not imminent.[17]

Although this response had for its object the reprobation of one concrete custom, nevertheless, according to Cappello,[18] it should be applied at all times to all churches and to all dioceses. In this matter the present writer in large part agrees with Cappello. However, there comes to mind the wartime practice whereby altar breads were used for as many as six months after their baking. These altar breads were carefully and tightly sealed in cellophane wrappers, a method of preservation that made the danger of corruption far more remote than the methods that are ordinarily employed by the pastors and the rectors of churches. For this reason the present writer would not apply the restriction of the Sacred Congregation to such a wartime practice. Furthermore, in any other case where exceptional and extraordinary methods of forestalling corruption are employed, the present writer thinks that to abstract from the restriction of the Sacred Congregation is not disallowed.

---

[15] S.C. de Sacramentis, responsum, 7 dec. 1918—*AAS,* XI (1919), 8. Cf. also, S.R.C., *Gandaven.,* 16 dec. 1826—*D.A.,* n. 2650.

[16] Woywod, "The Tabernacle"—*The Homiletic and Pastoral Review,* XXVII (1926-1927), 155; Beste, p. 643.

[17] Köster, p. 236.

[18] *Tractatus Canonico-Moralis de Sacramentis,* I, 314. Cf. also, Durieux-Dolphin, *The Eucharist, Law and Practice* (Chicago: Lakeside Press, 1926), p. 226 (hereafter cited Durieux).

ARTICLE II. "... ITA UT NULLUM SIT PERICULUM CORRUPTIONIS..."

Section I. The Canonical Standard for the Renewal of the Sacred Species

Although canon 1272 did not specify a determined time for the renewal of the Sacred Species, nevertheless it did establish a standard by which to judge the proper time for the renewal of the Sacred Species. The factor to which one must advert in every case is the danger of corruption. Whatever the circumstances may be, the Sacred Species must be renewed within a period of time that not only anticipates the actual corruption of the Sacred Hosts, but also obviates the very danger of corruption in the Sacred Hosts.[19]

Since this danger of corruption is the guiding factor to which one must advert, it is at once apparent that the local ordinary who by diocesan statute specifies a determined time for the renewal of the Sacred Species must always take into consideration the age of the altar breads that are used for consecration.[20] The phrasing of canon 1272, "... *et recentes sint et frequenter renoventur, ita ut nullum sit periculum corruptionis* ..." clearly indicates that the time of renewal necessarily depends upon the time of baking.

The danger of corruption, however, will depend on much more than the actual age of the altar breads. Many local factors and many particular circumstances must be considered in any determination of the danger of corruption. Thus, the danger of corruption will vary according to such circumstances as the quality of the wheat that is used for the altar breads, the manner and the degree of baking that is employed in the making of the altar breads, the material of the receptacle that contains the altar breads, the atmospheric conditions of a particular locality, and so forth.[21] Therefore, the standard by which to judge the proper time for the renewal of the Sacred Species will vary from place to place and from case to case.

---

[19] Cavanaugh, p. 72.

[20] Noldin-Schmitt, III, 129; Cocchi, V, 201; Sipos, p. 665, footnote 11; Berutti, IV, 257; Claeys Bouuaert-Simenon, III, 76; Regatillo, I, 92; Cappello, I, 311.

[21] Woywod, "The Tabernacle"—*The Homiletic and Pastoral Review*, XXVII (1926-1927), 155; Blat, IV, 169; Claeys Bouuaert-Simenon, III, 76; Cappello, I, 313.

In treating of the matter of the renewal of the Sacred Species, Cappello[22] made the following statement: *"Quamvis forte nullum sit periculum corruptionis, tamen semel in hebdomada vel saltem bis in mense species consecratae de regula generali renovandae sint."* This statement is indeed valid as a recommendation, but it does not seem equally valid if proposed as an obligatory general rule. Canon 1272 speaks of only one factor in the light of which to judge the frequency of the renewal, namely, the danger of corruption. Therefore, in the absence of this danger, if one considers only the expressed prescript of canon 1272, there is no obligation of renewing the Sacred Hosts so frequently. The practice of the earlier centuries, and the approbation by the Holy See of the provincial councils which allowed a monthly renewal of the Sacred Species, support this conclusion.[23]

Section II. The Monthly Standard for the Renewal of the Sacred Species

The greater number of canonists[24] teaches that as an ordinary rule the consecrated Hosts should be renewed within a period of one month after Their baking. Apparently these canonists maintain that as a general rule the danger of corruption exists after the period of one month.

Regatillo, for example,[25] based his conclusion, namely that the Sacred Hosts should be renewed within a period of one month after Their baking, on the following data: 1) Leibig (+1873), a chemist, maintained that it was not certain that Hosts even in favorable atmospheric conditions could remain perfectly incorrupt after a period of six weeks, and 2) in a synod of Piacenza (1899), the bishop declared that most expert chemists could, under ordinary circumstances by the aid of a microscope, detect the beginnings of corruption in altar breads that were only one month old.

---

[22] *Tractatus Canonico-Moralis de Sacramentis,* I, 313.

[23] Köster, p. 237.

[24] Cappello, I, 312; Cocchi, V, 202; Claeys Bouuaert-Simenon, III, 76; Regatillo, I, 92; Berutti, IV, 257.

[25] *Ius Sacramentarium,* I, 92.

In the mind of the present writer, too much importance must not be attached to the proofs that were offered by Regatillo in support of the standard of the monthly renewal of the Sacred Species.[26] No information was given by Regatillo relative to the extent and the nature of the experiments that led these chemists to their conclusions concerning the danger of corruption in the altar breads. The questions that immediately come to mind are these: How thorough were these chemists in their experiments? Did they make tests beyond their own locality? Did they vary the circumstances of the experiments? Unless these chemists were very detailed in their experiments, and unless they investigated the matter in many different localities, their conclusions can hardly have validity as universal rules. In fact, the establishing of a universal rule relative to a determined time for the renewal of the Sacred Species would entail countless experiments over a period of years by expert chemists in all parts of the world.

Furthermore, the Code of Canon Law is apparently opposed to any general rule on the matter, for canon 1272 states very clearly: "*. . . sedulo servatis instructionibus quas Ordinarius loci hac de re dederit.*" Apparently the Code of Canon Law desires the establishment of local regulations relative to any determination regarding the danger of corruption in altar breads.

The present writer, however, contends that the monthly standard must not be immediately disregarded. Although it does not have the validity of a universal rule, nevertheless it is a working standard. In other words, in the absence of a better interpretation of what constitutes the danger of corruption in each locality, it should serve as a guiding norm. Only under expert advice should the local ordinary presume to exceed this monthly standard that has been favorably accepted by the greater number of canonists.

ARTICLE III. ". . . SEDULO SERVATIS INSTRUCTIONIBUS QUAS ORDINARIUS LOCI HAC DE RE DEDERIT"

Owing to the great number of factors that may in a given locality and under given circumstances hasten or delay the process of cor-

[26] Vermeersch-Creusen (II, 418) made the following statement: "Scriptores ultra quam veri simile est, periculum corruptionis urgere solent." Cf. also Noldin-Schmitt, III, 129; Cance, III, 94, footnote 2; Köster, p. 237.

ruption in the altar breads, the Code of Canon Law[27] prescribed that the regulations of the local ordinary relative to the renewal of the Sacred Species should be scrupulously observed. The Code, in fact, insinuated that the local ordinary should consider it his duty to enact special regulations on the matter.[28]

The regulations that are so enacted by the local ordinary will also bind exempt religious.[29] Moreover, in order that the local ordinary may ascertain whether such regulations are being effectively executed by the exempt religious of his diocese, he may visit their churches and their public oratories.[30] In the churches of regulars, however, he may use the right of visitation in this matter only insofar as he has positive information that the regulations which have been enacted by him are not being observed.[31]

In these regulations it is conceivable that the local ordinary can allowably set a longer period than that of one month between the baking of the altar breads and their subsequent renewal as the Sacred Species.[32] Thus, for example, he may enact a diocesan statute to the effect that the Sacred Species may be renewed once a month, provided that the altar breads were consecrated within two weeks from the time they were baked.

In enacting diocesan statutes on the matter, however, the local ordinary must keep the following principles in mind: 1) Altar breads which are two or three months old, even though they show no signs of disintegration, should not, as a general rule, be consecrated,[33] and 2) the danger of corruption in the altar breads must at all times be scrupulously forestalled.[34]

In determining what constitutes the danger of corruption in his

---

[27] Can. 1272.

[28] Woywod, "The Tabernacle"—*The Homiletic and Pastoral Review,* XXVII (1926-1927), 155.

[29] Can. 1261, § 2; Cocchi, V, 202.

[30] Can. 1261, § 2.

[31] A private reply of the Interpretation Commission, 8 apr. 1924—*Digest,* II, 374.

[32] Merkelbach, *Summa Theologiae Moralis* (Editio Quinta Aucta et Emendata, 3 vols., Parisiis: Typis Declée de Brouwer et Soc., 1947), III, 333 (hereafter cited Merkelbach); Noldin-Schmitt, III, 129; Köster, p. 237.

[33] S.C. de Sacramentis, responsum, 7 dec. 1918—*AAS,* XI (1919), 8.

[34] Can. 1272.

locality, the local ordinary must not be arbitrary in his decision. It must be remembered that according to the common opinion of the canonists the danger of corruption under ordinary circumstances is present within one month after the baking of the altar breads. This norm should be kept in mind and should be made even stricter when the atmospheric conditions and the other peculiar circumstances of his diocese indicate that the danger of quick corruption is more imminent than under ordinary circumstances in other places. In some extremely warm and humid localities, for example, altar breads may begin to putrify within three days after they were baked.[35]

In order to determine, therefore, the special effects that the local conditions may have upon the altar breads, and in order to determine whether he may extend or whether he should restrict the monthly standard that has been established by the greater number of canonists as the standard period in which to expect the danger of corruption, it would be highly advisable and at times even necessary for the local ordinary to consult experts on the matter. Thus, for example, in an extremely warm and humid region, the local ordinary should consider it his grave duty to consult experts. Relying on their authoritative investigations, he should then determine at what time the altar breads may no longer be classified as *"recentes"* in his diocese. In view of this determination he should then set a definite date beyond which the altar breads may not be consecrated, and should also set a definite date for their renewal as the Sacred Species.

In the United States, however, the liberty that a particular local ordinary may exercise relative to any determination regarding the renewal of the Sacred Species has been restricted by the II Plenary Council of Baltimore.[36] Decree n. 268 of this Council reads as follows:

> *Rituale Romanum jubet particulas Sanctissimae Eucharistiae frequenter renovari; et Caeremoniale. Episcoporum id semel saltem in hebdomada faciendum praecipit. Hanc regularm quam S. Rituum Congregatio nedum*

---

[35] Köster, p. 237.

[36] Ayrinhac, p. 143.

> *saepius confirmavit, verum "stricte et rigorose obligare" declaravit, sacerdotibus omnibus fideliter servandam serio inculcamus. "Ubi sacerdos novas consecraverit hostias, veteres primo distribuat, vel sumat," minime vero in tabernaculo servet. Curet, insuper, ut particulae consecrandae recentes sint.*[37]

So, in the United States a particular local ordinary may not enact a diocesan statute to the effect that the Sacred Species need to be renewed only every other week. He may, however, enact a statute which would specify the age of the altar breads that may be used for consecration, since the Council merely demanded that the altar breads be fresh or recently baked.

Cavanaugh[38] and Beste[39] evidently contend that this decree of the II Plenary Council of Baltimore is no longer in force, since they admit that the Sacred Hosts may be renewed every other week in the United States. It is difficult, however, to understand their apparent contention, since the Code of Canon Law neither implicitly nor explicitly forbade a stricter rule on the renewal of the Sacred Species.[40] In fact, the Code clearly paved the way for a stricter rule, since it demanded that the regulations of the local ordinary on the matter should be scrupulously observed. Furthermore, the Code did not limit the liberty of making a stricter rule as a matter in which each individual local ordinary alone was competent in his own diocese. Room was left for legislation which emanated from them as a group. So, in the mind of the present writer, there is no reason to support the contention that the law of the II Plenary Council of Baltimore relative to the renewal of the Sacred Species no longer remains in force.

Therefore, in the matter of the weekly renewal of the Sacred Species, a particular local ordinary of the United States has no freedom of action. Certainly he may make no diocesan statute to the effect, for example, that the Sacred Hosts need to be renewed only every two weeks.

---

[37] II Plenary Council of Baltimore (1866), tit. V, cap. IV, n. 268—*Coll. Lac.*, III, 469.

[38] *The Reservation of the Blessed Sacrament*, p. 72.

[39] *Introductio in Codicem*, p. 643.

[40] Can. 1272.

It may be questioned whether any exception to this rule of the weekly renewal of the Sacred Hosts may be allowed. In accord, of course, with the norm of canon 291, § 2, the local ordinary may for a just cause dispense from the decree of the Plenary Council in a particular case. This power the local ordinary may further commit to pastors and rectors of churches. Moreover, in the event that a contrary custom has become fully established in a certain diocese, such a custom could warrant a modification of the strict law of the Plenary Council. In such a case the local ordinary could legitimately enact a diocesan statute to the effect, for example, that the Sacred Hosts need be renewed only every two weeks. Finally, in particular cases of urgency pastors and rectors should keep in mind the use of *epikeia*. For example, a new pastor who is unaware of the small number of the communicants in his parish may consecrate a superabundant number of altar breads. Must he at the end of one week consume the Sacred Hosts that remain? *Epikeia* would dictate that he continue to dispense Them in the normal way until They are consumed, provided, of course, that the danger of corruption is not present.

ARTICLE IV. "... VETERIBUS [HOSTIIS] RITE CONSUMPTIS ..."

At the proper time for the renewal of the Sacred Species, the priest should either distribute to the faithful the older Hosts that remain or else consume Them.[41]

Section I. The Mixing of the Newly Consecrated Hosts with the Older Hosts

In and of itself it is never lawful to mix the newly consecrated Hosts with the older Hosts. The altar breads that are to be consecrated should be placed in a separate ciborium or on the corporal. To mix the newly consecrated Species indiscriminately with the older Species would render the very purpose of the renewal fruitless.[42] If, however, the older Hosts are few in number, They

---

[41] Can. 1272; *Rituale Rom.*, tit. IV, c. 1, *de sanctissimo Eucharistiae Sacramento*, n. 7; Cappello, I, 315.

[42] Köster, p. 238.

may be placed on top of the newly consecrated Hosts, provided that there is the moral certitude that They will be the first to be distributed.[43]

Under certain conditions even a commingling of the Sacred Hosts That have been consecrated at different times may be allowed. Today the practice of frequent Holy Communion is very widespread. So, very often the purpose of renewing the Sacred Species is not that the danger of corruption may be precluded but rather that a sufficient number of Hosts may be furnished for the great numbers who desire to receive Holy Communion. As a result, many times the new Hosts and Those that remain from the previous renewal are of the very same age relative to the time of Their baking. In such a case a mixture is not unlawful.[44]

In the United States, of course, a definite renewal period of one week has been enacted by the II Plenary Council of Baltimore. Can, therefore, the priests of the United States ever avail themselves of such a commingling of the Sacred Hosts that have been consecrated at different times, but are of the same age relative to the time when They were baked as altar breads? In the mind of the present writer they may do so in cases of special urgency, provided, of course, that the danger of corruption is always absent. Thus the great number of communicants on a Sunday or a Holyday of obligation in a busy city parish may demand the services of several priests in the distribution of Holy Communion. The tabernacle may be too small to contain all of the ciboriums that are put to use. So the Sacred Contents of several ciboriums may be emptied into one or two ciboriums. Or, again, some of the ciboriums may be emptied at one Mass in order that they may be refilled and thereby furnish an adequate supply of the Sacred Hosts for the following Masses. In the mind of the present writer such a situation that has been occasioned by the practice of frequent Holy Communion lay beyond the prevision of the lawgiver, the II Plenary Council of Baltimore. If the Fathers of this Council had envisioned such circumstances, undoubtedly they would have approved a commingling of the Sacred Hosts in these special cases.

---

[43] Köster, p. 238; Cappello, I, 315; Cavanaugh, p. 74; Gasparri, II, 276-277.
[44] Köster, p. 238.

Section II. The Consumption of the Sacred Hosts Which have Become Corrupt

If the Sacramental Species for any reason have become corrupt, it must be determined whether the corruption is total or partial. If total, then the Sacred Species must be burnt, and the ashes must be disposed of in the sacrarium. Furthermore, the water that was employed for washing the vessel which contained the corrupt Species must also be disposed of in the sacrarium. If, however, the corruption is partial, the Sacred Species can be consumed by the priest, provided that he does not suffer nausea as a result. If the priest feels that he is unequal to this manner of consumption, he must preserve the Sacred Species in a ciborium, or in some other clean vessel, which must be kept in the tabernacle until the Species are totally corrupt. When the priest realizes for a certainty that the Species no longer contain the Real Presence of Christ, he should then burn the remains and dispose of the ashes in the sacrarium.[45]

[45] Cappello, I, 316; Regatillo, I, 205.

CHAPTER X

The Custody of the Blessed Eucharist Outside the Church

Can. 1265, § 3: *Nemini licet sanctissimam Eucharistiam apud se retinere aut secum in itinere deferre.*

Nobody is allowed to reserve the Blessed Sacrament in his home or to carry It with him on a journey.

ARTICLE I. "NEMINI LICET SANCTISSIMAM EUCHARISTIAM APUD SE RETINERE. . . ."

Section I. The Severity of the Present Law Relative to the Private Reservation of the Blessed Sacrament

The Code of Common Law[1] confirmed the earlier law which strictly forbade the private reservation of the Blessed Sacrament.[2] First of all, canon 1265, § 1 and § 2, envisions only churches and oratories as the proper places for the reservation of the Blessed Sacrament. Secondly, canon 1265, § 3, explicitly forbids the retention of the Blessed Sacrament *"apud se."* Thirdly, canon 1267 explicitly restricts the reservation of the Holy Eucharist in a pious or in a religious house to the church or the main oratory. Therefore it is certain that the law of today proscribes any type of private reservation of the Blessed Sacrament.

The rule of canon 1265, § 3, is so strict that only in virtue of an apostolic indult or only in virtue of special faculties may it be ignored. The use of the word *"nemini"* bespeaks the universal need of a dispensation before the law relative to the private reservation of the Blessed Sacrament can give way to any opposite practice.[3] Thus, even cardinals, missionaries and military chaplains may not presume to exempt themselves in this matter.[4]

[1] Can. 1265, § 3.

[2] Benedictus XIV, const. *Etsi pastoralis,* 26 maii 1742, § VI, n. VII—*Fontes,* n. 328; Ayrinhac, p. 139; Köster, p. 187.

[3] Blat, IV, 162.

[4] Blat, IV, 162; Berutti, IV, 249.

The intervention of the Holy See in special cases, however, is not altogether uncommon. Thus faculty 15 of the *Formula Maior* of a recently prepared formula of faculties which are customarily granted to mission ordinaries reads in this way: *"Permittendi, si sit periculum sacrilegii, ut Sanctissimum Sacramentum pro infirmis sine lumine in loco tamen decenti retineri possit."*[5] Again, in the first World War the military chaplains were given special faculties whereby they could reserve the Blessed Sacrament *"extra sacram aedem"* on board warships and in hospital camps.[6] In the second World War the military chaplains of the United States were granted faculties to reserve the Blessed Sacrament not only in chapels but also in respectacle and suitable places on military posts, provided that the buildings were suitably and sufficiently furnished with ecclesiastical equipment.[7] Furthermore, during the recent war the Sacred Congregation of the Sacraments established special provisions for the custody of the Blessed Sacrament in air-raid shelters or in the basements of churches, whenever there was danger of bombardment.[8]

In the lack of a special intervention by the Holy See, the failure to observe the prohibition of canon 1265, § 3, beyond doubt constitutes a gravely sinful matter. Thus ordinarily a priest who even for the shortest time reserves the Blessed Sacrament in his own home would be guilty of a mortal sin. Cappello,[9] however, completely excuses from any sin the priest who for a short time and for a just cause reverently reserves the Blessed Sacrament in a chapel within his own home.

The present writer does not entirely agree with the contention of Cappello. Very often a just cause may exist for removing the Blessed Sacrament from the church. Thus non-Catholic workmen may be repairing the church and may without any malice be disturbing the adorers of the Real Presence. Can the pastor in such

---

[5] Winslow, p. 59.

[6] S.C. Consist., decr., 22 febr. 1919—*AAS*, XI (1919), 74.

[7] *Digest*, II, 593.

[8] *Epistula ad Ordinarios de Custodia et Protectione Sanctissimae Eucharistiae adversus Bellicos Incursus*, 15 sept. 1943—*AAS*, XXV (1943), 282-285.

[9] *Tractatus Canonico-Moralis de Sacramentis*, I, 277. Cf. also Durieux, p. 216.

a situation presume to dispense himself from the common law and remove the Blessed Sacrament to the private chapel in his own home? Certainly not. The local ordinary himself can not grant such a permission. In virtue of canon 1265, § 2, the local ordinary has a *per modum actus* power for the granting of a dispensation relative to the place of reservation, but this *per modum actus* power is restricted in extent to the reservation of the Blessed Sacrament in churches and in public oratories. Furthermore, the local ordinary in such a situation cannot invoke the exceptional power that he has in virtue of canon 81, since the provisions of that canon demand the presence of the following circumstances, namely, "*in mora sit periculum gravis damni.*"

Suppose however, that more than a just cause exists, or, in other words, suppose that there exists a danger of grave harm if the Blessed Sacrament is not removed from the church. If the danger is immediate, the pastor on his own authority may dispense himself from the prescript of canon 1265, § 3. He may at once remove the Blessed Sacrament to the sacristy, to his own home, or to any other safe and decent place.[10] Common sense dictates this solution. However, if the danger is grave but not immediate, or if the danger is likely to continue for some time as a grave danger, then the pastor must invoke the ordinary means that have been constituted by the common law for such cases. In other words, let him consult the local ordinary who may grant the necessary dispensation from the common law whenever recourse to the Holy See is difficult and there exists a danger of grave harm in delay.[11]

According to the present law, if such a pastor, or for that matter anyone else, unlawfully contravenes the prescript of canon 1265, § 3, he does not become subject to any determined ecclesiastical penalty, provided that he is without evil intention in his action. However, if he does have some evil purpose in mind, he then becomes suspect of heresy; he incurs an excommunication *latae sententiae* most specially reserved to the Holy See; he becomes

---

[10] Köster, p. 190.

[11] Can. 81.

ipso facto infamous; and furthermore, if he is a cleric, he is to be deposed.[12]

Section II. The Concession of Canon 1269, § 3

Under the earlier law, even apart from any apostolic indult, the Blessed Sacrament in many places was at night transferred from the church to some safer place.[13] The Holy See indirectly approved this relaxation of the law, since several Provincial Councils contained statutes to the effect that such a practice could be lawfully continued.[14] By the present law of canon 1269, § 3, however, the Holy See has clearly and directly sanctioned this precautionary practice for the universal Church. This canon reads as follows:

> *Gravi aliqua suadente causa ab Ordinario loci probata, non est vetitum sanctissimum Eucharistiam nocturno tempore extra altare, super corporali tamen, in loco tutiore et decenti, asservari, servato praescripto can. 1271.*

From the reading of this third part of canon 1269 it is to be noted that six conditions must be fulfilled before a pastor or a rector of a church can avail himself of this exceptional method of reserving the Blessed Sacrament outside the tabernacle and outside the altar.[15]

1. The cause must be just and also grave. Although commonly the cause will be the danger of a sacrilegious theft, nevertheless other grave causes may also suffice for the application of canon 1269, § 3.[16]

2. The cause must be previously recognized and approved by the local ordinary in order that the pastor or the rector of a church may not act *contra Codicem.* The local ordinary may approve the

---

[12] Can. 2320.

[13] Gasparri, II, 263; Many, p. 285.

[14] I Provincial Council of Australia (1884), decr. XI—*Coll. Lac.,* III, 1048-1049; III Provincial Council of Tuam, cap. XV, n. 1—*Coll. Lac.,* III, 886. Cf. also, Many, p. 285.

[15] Cappello, I, 302.

[16] Köster, p. 188.

grave cause in each particular case, or else he may approve the grave cause through the medium of a general decree.[17] Thus the local ordinary by a general decree may state, for example, that the Blessed Sacrament may at night be removed from those churches in which the doors are partly made of glass but are unprotected by any inner grating or by bars.

3. The reservation of the Blessed Sacrament *extra altare et extra tabernaculum* may be allowed only during the night, for it is presumed that men will be well able to guard the Blessed Sacrament against any grave danger during the day. If, however, a grave danger continues even during the day, the intervention of the Holy See must be sought.[18]

Thus in 1943 the Sacred Congregation of the Sacraments made special provisions for wartime and extended the concession as regulated by canon 1269, § 3, so that the Blessed Sacrament on the occasion of air-raids could also be reserved *extra altare et extra tabernaculum* during the day. In the absence of such an intervention of the Holy See, however, the pastor of a church may not presume to so extend the concession which canon 1269, § 3 makes available, unless the danger is urgent and unless there is no time to have recourse to the local ordinary so that he, in virtue of canon 81, may dispense from the common law.

4. The Blessed Sacrament under these circumstances must be placed on a corporal. It is true that the placing of a corporal within the tabernacle derives, not from any strict law, but rather from a laudable practice.[19] But in this case, when the Blessed Sacrament is reserved *extra tabernaculum,* the use of a corporal derives not simply from a laudable practice, but rather from an explicit requirement of law.

5. The Blessed Sacrament under these circumstances must be kept in some place that is becoming and, above all, more secure than the place from which It is removed. The place in question is usually the sacristy,[20] provided, of course, that it really is a suit-

[17] Blat, IV, 166.

[18] Köster, p. 188; Cappello, I, 302; Sipos, p. 664; Blat, IV, 166.

[19] Bouscaren-Ellis, p. 648; Cappello, I, 308.

[20] *Instruction,* n. 5—*AAS,* XXX (1938), 202; Regatillo, I, 203; Sipos, p. 664.

able and a safer place. Preference, however, may also be given to a very strong and well enclosed safe that is built into some wall of the church.[21]

The Sacred Congregation of the Sacraments in its Instruction of 1938 stipulated that, if neither the church nor the sacristy afforded the proper security, then the Blessed Sacrament could be removed to a private place, such as a room in the priest's rectory.[22]

It is to be well noted that the Sacred Congregation stated its preference for either the church or the sacristy. The reason for the preference is at once apparent. If it is at all possible, the sacristy or the church must be chosen, since the removal of the Blessed Sacrament to these places entails shorter distances and thereby lessens the possibility of irreverence to the Blessed Sacrament.[23]

6. A tabernacle lamp must be kept burning continuously before the Blessed Sacrament so reserved.

In addition to these six conditions that have been established by the Code of Canon Law for the lawful reservation of the Blessed Sacrament *extra altare et extra tabernaculum,* the following monitions of the Sacred Congregation of the Sacraments must be kept in mind in the application of canon 1269, § 3:[24]

1. Whenever the safer place in question is some place other than the church or the sacristy, the pastor must take care that the Blessed Sacrament is guarded with the greatest reverence and honor. He must also take care that the faith of the people in the Real Presence is not diminished because of this unwonted method of reserving the Blessed Sacrament.

2. The Sacred Species shall not touch the corporal, but shall always be enclosed in a vessel or in a pyx.[25]

3. Whenever the Sacred Species are taken from the tabernacle,

---

[21] *Instruction,* n. 5—*AAS,* XXX (1938), 202.

[22] *Instruction,* n. 5—*AAS,* XXX (1938), 202. Cf. also, Sipos, p. 664; Regatillo, I, 203.

[23] Köster, p. 188.

[24] *Instruction,* n. 5—*AAS,* XXX (1938), 202.

[25] Cf. S.R.C., *Altonen.,* 17 febr. 1881—*D.A.,* n. 3527; *Fontes,* n. 6127.

or whenever They are replaced in the tabernacle of the church, the priest must be vested in surplice and in stole, and, as a general rule, must be accompanied by a cleric carrying a lighted candle.

Finally, in connection with the concession which canon 1269, § 3, makes available, there arises the question of whether the local ordinary may order such an unusual method of reserving the Blessed Sacrament during the night. One pre-Code canonist[26] without any restriction maintained that the local ordinary possessed such a power. Coronata[27] maintains that the local ordinary possesses such a power at least in special and extraordinary cases.

There is no doubt that in some special and extraordinary cases the local ordinary may *per modum praecepti* demand the observance of this unwonted method of reserving the Blessed Sacrament.[28] However, if the local ordinary would make such an observance the matter of a diocesan law, he would hardly be acting within his lawful competence.[29] The concession as made available through canon 1269, § 3, is restricted to cases of true danger, and true danger can hardly be said to exist at all times in all churches of the diocese. Perhaps, however, the local ordinary may be very circumspect in the statute that he enacts. He may, for example, list a series of circumstances which he considers as furnishing a grave cause for the use of the concession that canon 1269, § 3, warrants. He may then demand that in all those churches where these circumstances exist, the pastor or the rector must reserve the Blessed Sacrament during the night *extra altare et extra tabernaculum*. Such a diocese statute, in the mind of the present writer, would be equivalent to a recognition of the true danger in each particular case and, furthermore, would be equivalent to a precept in each particular case. Such a statute would be in complete harmony with the mind of the legislator, namely, the desire to preclude all irreverence to the Blessed Sacrament by every possible means.

---

[26] Many, p. 285.
[27] *Institutiones Iuris Canonici*, II, 168.
[28] Cappello, I, 302; Köster, p. 189; Coronata, II, 168.
[29] Cappello, I, 302; Köster, p. 189.

Section III. The Reservation of the Blessed Sacrament during Holy Week

Since the liturgical laws relative to the reservation of the Blessed Sacrament on the last three days of Holy Week include provisions for a private reservation, it seems proper at this point briefly to summarize the import of these laws as illustrated in an Instruction of the Sacred Congregation of the Sacraments.[30]

During the last three days of Holy Week, the Blessed Sacrament is reserved in a special way for the Mass of the Presanctified and for Communion of the sick.

The Sacred Host for the Mass of the Presanctified is to be reserved in a chapel within the church. This chapel should be beautifully decorated with candles, draperies and flowers. Relics, however, pictures of the Blessed Mother and of the Saints, and representations of the Passion must not form part of the decorations. The tabernacle should be locked and, furthermore, so constructed that the adorers may not see the chalice which contains the Sacred Host. The key of the tabernacle should be entrusted to the priest who is to celebrate the Mass of the Presanctified on the following day.

For Communion of the sick some consecrated particles are to be reserved in a ciborium. According to the mind of the Rubrics this ciborium should be kept outside the church, that is, near the sacristy in a fitting and a convenient place. Such a place may be a chapel near the church, or the sacristy itself, or some small compartment of the sacristy. Again, such a place may even be in a part of the parish house which is separated from domestic and profane uses, and which is remote from all danger of irreverence.

A tabernacle that can be locked with a key should be previously set in the place that is chosen for the reservation of the Sacred Species for the Communion of the sick. During the time that the Blessed Sacrament remains in this tabernacle a lamp in front of it should be kept burning continuously. During this time, however, the faithful are not allowed to make visits to the Blessed Sacrament.

Whenever a fitting place outside the church is not available, the sacred ciborium with the Communion for the sick is to be kept

[30] *Instruction of 1929—AAS,* XXI (1929), 636-637.

in the same repository as the Host of the Presanctified. This ciborium may remain behind the chalice which contains the Host of the Presanctified until the Mass of the Presanctified. At that time the ciborium is to be removed to a more remote and secret chapel of the church where a lamp should be kept burning during the period of reservation in that place. If, however, such a remote and secret chapel is non-existent, then the sacred ciborium with the Communion for the sick is to be kept in the repository of the Host of the Presanctified until Saturday morning. A lamp should be kept burning there during this period, but the other lights and candles that normally decorate the repository for the Host of the Presanctified should be extinguished once the Host of the Presanctified has been removed.

In those churches where the solemnities of Holy Thursday are not observed, the sacred ciborium for the Communion of the sick may be kept in its customary place until sunset on Holy Thursday. From that time on it should be reserved in one of the places that has been indicated above.

ARTICLE II. "NEMINI LICET SANCTISSIMAM EUCHARISTIAM . . . SECUM IN ITINERE DEFERRE"

Section I. The Severity of the Present Law Relative to the Carrying of the Blessed Sacrament on a Journey

Such comments as were made in the preceding article in relation to the prescript of canon 1265, § 3, were intended simply to refer to the first part of canon 1265, § 3, namely, the prohibition against the private reservation of the Blessed Sacrament. However, more often than not, these comments were of equal application to the second part of canon 1265, § 3, namely, the prohibition against the carrying of the Blessed Sacrament on a journey.

Thus the prohibition of the present law relative to the carrying of the Blessed Sacrament on a journey is also a confirmation of the earlier law.[31]

---

[31] Benedictus XIV, const. *Etsi pastoralis,* § VI, n. VII—*Fontes,* n. 328; S.C. de Prop. Fide, litt. encycl., 25 febr. 1859—*Fontes,* n. 4846; Ayrinhac, p. 139.

Again, this prohibition is so strict that only in virtue of an apostolic indult may anyone, even a cardinal, presume to abstract from its observance.[32] The Pope, it is true, had retained until modern times the practice of taking the Blessed Sacrament with him on a journey, but it must be remembered that no other dignitary had, or now has, the right to use the same privilege.[33] Thus the practice of many military chaplains in the recent wars whereby for long periods of time they carried the Blessed Sacrament on their persons is to be entirely reprobated.[34]

Again, the failure to observe this prohibition would, in and of itself, certainly constitute a gravely sinful matter.[35]

Finally, if one were with an evil purpose in mind to carry the Blessed Sacrament on a journey, he would fall prey to the penal sanctions enacted in canon 2320.

Section II. The Lawful Transferral of the Blessed Sacrament from Its Customary Place of Reservation

There are many occasions when the Blessed Sacrament may be lawfully transferred from Its customary place of reservation. Thus the Blessed Sacrament may for a just cause be transferred from one altar to another altar within the same church.[36] Furthermore, at times the Blessed Sacrament may even be lawfully transferred outside the church.

It is immediately evident that in a case of emergency, such as a fire in the church, and also in the cases of private reservation that were discussed in the preceding article, a transferral *extra ecclesiam* is certainly lawful. Ordinarily, however, the Blessed Sacrament may be transferred outside the church only on the occasion of the solemn procession of the Feast of Corpus Christi and during its octave, on the occasion of the procession of the

---

[32] Blat, IV, 162; Gasparri, II, 248; Prümmer, p. 470; Ayrinhac, p. 139.

[33] Ayrinhac, p. 139.

[34] Vermeersch-Creusen, II, 413.

[35] Cappello, I, 277.

[36] S.R.C., *Cuneen.*, 2 iun. 1883, ad IV, XII—*D.A.*, n. 3576; Blat, IV, 162.

Forty Hours Devotion when the church is small, and on the occasion of distributing Holy Communion to the sick.[37]

Other causes than those that have been just enumerated do not justify the transferral of the Blessed Sacrament outside the church or outside the oratory in which It is reserved. However, it must be noted that in the distribution of Holy Communion to the sick a priest at times may also distribute Holy Communion to those who are physically well. This fact is certain from the replies that the Sacred Congregation of the Sacraments issued to the Bishop of Mondovì in Piedmont. The English translation of these replies is as follows:

> I. May the faithful who live in mountain hamlets be given Holy Communion in a sacred place whenever Holy Communion is brought to the sick, or, since there is question of so sacred a matter, may this even be done in a decent and suitable place along the way, when they are unable on that day to go to the church?
>
> Reply: In the affirmative according to c. 869 in connection with c. 822, § 4, that is, provided the Ordinary of the place grants the faculty according to the provision cited, namely, for each case and by way of act.
>
> II. May Holy Communion and the sacrament of confession be administered to those who are in the house of the sick person?
>
> Reply: As regards Communion, the answer is provided for in the reply to I.[38]

From the text of these replies and also from the annotations of the secretary of the Sacred Congregation on these replies[39] it is apparent that the following conditions must be present in order that a priest may lawfully distribute Holy Communion to those who are physically well.

---

[37] S.R.C., *Sulmonen.*, 12 iun. 1638—*D.A.*, n. 648; "Notes and Queries"—*The Irish Ecclesiastical Record* (Dublin, 1864—), 5 series, XXXIII (1929), 535 (hereafter cited *IER*); "Cases and Studies"—*ER*, LXXIX (1928), 412; Beste, p. 636.

[38] *Digest*, I, 391. Cf. also, S.C. de Sacramentis, *Montis Regalis in Pedemonte*, 5 ian. 1928—*AAS*, XX (1928), 79.

[39] *AAS*, XX (1929), 79-81.

1. The occasion must be the distribution of Holy Viaticum or the distribution of Communion to the sick. In the mind of the present writer this condition is essential and can in no way be disregarded in view of the strict law of the sacred liturgy relative to the carrying of the Blessed Sacrament outside the church.[40]

2. The healthy persons must live a long distance from the church and must be unable on that day to approach the church. Since, however, the secretary of the Sacred Congregation spoke of "similar circumstances,"[41] the present writer thinks that this second condition can be fulfilled if, for example, a healthy person, such as a nurse tending the sick, lived close to the church but found it gravely inconvenient to approach the church.

3. The healthy persons must receive the Sacred Species in a place that has been designated by the common law for the distribution of Holy Communion. In other words, under these circumstances Holy Communion must be distributed in accordance with the norms of canons 869 and 822.

Section III. Some Practical Applications of the Law Relative to the Transferral of the Blessed Sacrament

From the preceding section it is apparent that the law relative to the transferral of the Blessed Sacrament is a strict law. In fact, the legitimate transferral of the Blessed Sacrament outside the church is restricted to a very few instances. Many problems, however, do arise. This section, therefore, will deal with some of these problems and their practical solutions.

1. Under what circumstances is it allowable for a priest on a weekday to take several consecrated particles from the church in order that he may distribute Holy Communion to the sisters who live ten blocks away, and who otherwise would not be able to receive Our Blessed Lord on that day? Or, on the other hand, sup-

---

[40] S.R.C., *Sulmonen.*, 12 iun. 1638—*D.A.*, n. 648. Cf. also, Beste, p. 502; Vermeersch-Creusen, II, 94; Davis, *Moral and Pastoral Theology* (3. ed., 4 vols., London: Sheed and Ward, 1938), III, 232; Aertnys-Damen, *Theologia Moralis* (14. ed., 2 vols., Torini: Marietti, 1944), II, 101; Merkelbach, III, 331; Cappello, I, 339.

[41] *AAS,* XX (1928), 80.

pose that these sisters could otherwise receive, but only with considerable inconvenience to themselves or to some third party?

Relative to the distribution of Holy Communion, the laws of the sacred liturgy do not allow the carrying of the Blessed Sacrament outside the church or outside the chapel where It is reserved except in the case of people who through illnesses are unable to approach the church or the chapel for the purpose of receiving.[42] Therefore, as a general rule, the priest may not bring Holy Communion to the sisters in the convent that is ten blocks away from the church.

However, one or two of the sisters in the convent may be sick. Or, again, some of the sisters may suffer from rheumatism, arthritis, or general weakness from old age. Such sisters may be physically able to approach the parish church if they live within a very short distance from it, but may be physically unable to approach the church if they live at a considerable distance away. Under the latter circumstance these sisters may be considered as persons who are sick, and are therefore entitled to the Communion of the sick.[43]

When such a situation arises, may the priest justifiably bring Holy Communion not only to the sick sisters, but also to the rest of the community? Two of the conditions that are necessary for the lawful distribution of Holy Communion outside the church or the chapel where It is reserved are certainly present. Thus, the priest in this case lawfully transfers the Blessed Sacrament for the Communion of the sick, and, secondly, he distributes Holy Communion to the community presumably in the convent chapel, a place where it is permitted to say Holy Mass. However, there is a question of whether the third condition is fulfilled? It is certain that the sisters who are well do not live at such a long distance from the church that they are unable to approach it. Nevertheless, in the mind of the present writer, if these sisters would gravely inconvenience either themselves or some third party by their approach on that day to receive Holy Communion at the parish church, they would find themselves in a situation similar to that of people who do live far from the church. So, in the mind of the writer, the priest may

---

[42] S.R.C., *Sulmonen.*, 12 iun. 1638—*D.A.*, n. 648.

[43] Woywod, "Answers to Questions"—*The Homiletic and Pastoral Review*, XXIX (1928), 649.

bring Holy Communion to all the sisters of the community under the circumstances that have just been described.

2. In the outskirts of a wide-spread country parish, a pastor on the occasion of bringing Holy Communion to a sick parishioner may see an opportunity to distribute Holy Communion to the healthy parishioners in the neighborhood who on that day may not be able to approach the church to receive. May the pastor presume to take several consecrated particles with him and on the way to the sick person distribute Holy Communion to such parishioners? If there is an oratory or a church in the neighborhood where it is permitted to celebrate Holy Mass, the pastor on his own authority may distribute Holy Communion to these people in the church or in the oratory.[44]

If, however, no sacred place of this character exists, may the pastor presume to distribute Holy Communion to these parishioners in some decent place? He may certainly do so if he enjoys by apostolic indult the privilege of the portable altar.[45] Furthermore, under certain other circumstances he may do so. Canon 822, § 4, provides:

> The ordinary of the place, or, if there is question of a house of an exempt religious institute, then the major Superior can, for a just and a reasonable cause in some extraordinary case and by way of a single act, grant permission for the celebration of Mass outside a church or an oratory upon a consecrated stone and in a decent place, but never in a bedroom.

So in the above-named circumstances, and in circumstances of a similar nature, if the local ordinary, under the terms of canon 822, § 4, can grant permission for the celebration of Holy Mass, for example in the hallway of a house, and has used his faculty for the actual grant of that permission, then the pastor may lawfully distribute Holy Communion in that place to those who desire to receive, even though for the want of a priest Holy Mass is not actually celebrated. Moreover, in accord with the norm of canon

---

[44] Cappello, I, 340.

[45] Cans. 822, § 3, and 869.

199, § 1, the local ordinary may delegate to the pastor the *per modum actus* power that he himself possesses in virtue of canon 822, § 4. In such a hypothesis, the pastor, independently of any further permission granted by the local ordinary, may distribute Holy Communion to healthy persons on the occasion of bringing Holy Communion to a sick person, provided that he does so for a just and a reasonable cause in some extraordinary case and by way of a single performance.[46]

3. May the Blessed Sacrament be carried from one church to another in order that the Sacred Species may be renewed? There should be no need for such a transferral inasmuch as canon 1265 requires the weekly celebration of Holy Mass in the place of reservation. In 1932, however, a bishop of the United States presented the following problem to the Sacred Congregation of the Sacraments for its consideration and its approval. In his diocese there were many houses of women religious whose oratories enjoyed the faculty of reserving the Blessed Sacrament. Because of the fewness of priests, however, it became impossible in many cases to celebrate Holy Mass in these places of reservation. So the bishop asked for the following faculty ". . . *permittendi ut SS. Species renoventur novas deducendo ab ecclesia(paroeciali) in memoratis oratoriis, et veteres reducendo in ecclesiam(paroecialem), quin celebratur Missa in oratoriis ipsarum Sororum a Charitate.*"

The Sacred Congregation replied to this petition of the bishop as follows:

> *SSmus D.N. Pius Papa XI audita relatione infrascripti Card. Praefecti S.C. de Sacramentis, attentis peculiaribus adiunctis in casu concurrentibus, Ordinario. . . . Oratori, benigne tribuit facultates ad triennium, permittendi ut quoties non adsit liber sacerdos pro missae celebratione in enunciatis oratoriis Sororum praedictorum, parochus aut alter sacerdos Sacrum iterare possit etiam diebus ferialibus, ad effectum renovandi SS. Species in praedictis piis domibus, vetita eleemosynae perceptione pro una e*

[46] Cf. the notes of the secretary of the Sacred Congregation relative to the response, S.C. de Sacramentis, *Montis Regalis in Pedemonte*. 5 ian. 1928—*AAS,* XX (1928), 80.

> *duabus Missis, aliisque servatis de jure servandis quoad custodiam SS.mae Eucharistiae.*
>
> *M. Card. Lega Epus Tusculanus*
> *Praef.*
> *D. Jorio, Secr.*[47]

From this reply it is apparent that the Holy See is much opposed to the omission of Holy Mass in the place of reservation and is also much opposed to the transferral of the Blessed Sacrament outside the church in order that the Sacred Species may be renewed. This is evident in that the Holy See has in this reply preferred to grant the faculty of bination rather than to approve the solution that had been presented by the bishop of the United States.

In conclusion, one may point to an exceptional situation that necessarily followed from an indult of the Sacred Congregation for the Propagation of the Faith to the Bishop of Trichinopoly. The indult stated the following:

> By this letter (from the Cardinal Prefect of the Sacred Congregation) the Sacred Congregation grants you the faculty of celebrating once a month in churches where the Most Blessed Sacrament is kept, provided that the Sacred Species be renewed every two weeks.[48]

Under such circumstances it indeed appeared imperative that the Blessed Eucharist be removed to another church in order to allow for Its renewal at duly frequent intervals. Could the Bishop of Trichinopoly justify such a practice? In accordance with the norm of canon 66, § 3, which provides that the grant of a faculty also carries with it such other powers as are postulated for the effective use of the granted faculty, the bishop indeed was authorized to do so.

[47] (Private) : S.C. de Sacramentis, 18 apr. 1932. After the word "*Ordinario*" the name of the diocese has been withheld.

A similar concession was granted to the Bishop of Cincinnati on Nov. 16, 1948. Cf. "Decrees and Decisions"—*The Jurist,* IX (1949), 262.

[48] S.C. Prop. Fide, epistula, 14 mart. 1922 (private)—*Digest,* II, 445-446.

CONCLUSIONS

The Reservation of the Blessed Sacrament:

1. The only ecclesiastical control which is necessary in order that the local ordinary may allow the reservation of the Blessed Sacrament in the principal oratory, public or semi-public, of a pious house is that a chaplain attends to the spiritual needs of the residents.

2. The local ordinary may grant permission for the reservation of the Blessed Sacrament in the main oratory, public or semi-public, of any school which functions as a Catholic school under the sole provision that the school is conducted either by the secular clergy or by religious.

3. The fact that sisters who belong to the same religious house are divided into groups for the purpose of executing different kinds of work does not entitle these sisters to enjoy the reservation of the Blessed Sacrament in separate oratories for each group. Furthermore, the novices, the lay brothers, and the professed members of a religious institute are not entitled to separate oratories in each of which the Blessed Sacrament is reserved.

The Tabernacle Lamp:

1. It is not within the competence of the local ordinary to allow the use of an electric light in place of the sanctuary lamp.

The Guardian of the Blessed Sacrament:

1. The primary guardian, or the one principally responsible for the proper custody of the Holy Eucharist, must always be a priest. Religious communities and lay persons are permitted to perform the duties of guardianship, but in the execution of these duties they must always remain under the supervision of the priest who is the primary guardian. Religious communities and lay persons who so perform the main duties of guardianship may be called the actual guardians of the Blessed Sacrament.

2. The primary guardian is the priest who is responsible for the tabernacle key.

3. The primary guardian is principally responsible for the proper safeguarding of the Blessed Sacrament. Responsibility, however, does not cease with the principal guardian. The actual guardian and anyone else who is careless in respect to the safeguarding of the Blessed Sacrament are with certain reservations punishable in accord with the penal sanctions that were established by the Sacred Congregation of the Sacraments in its Instruction of 1938.

The Pyx:

1. The pyx must be blessed.

2. The inner gold-plating of the pyx which is made of such materials as bronze, copper, and pewter is not at all a prescript of law.

The Custody of the Tabernacle Key:

1. A priest must always be the responsible guardian of the tabernacle key. As a general rule this priest is the rector of the church or of the oratory where the Blessed Sacrament is reserved. In oratories or in chapels to which no special rector, chaplain, or spiritual moderator is assigned, the priest who has charge of the regular celebration of Holy Mass and of the sacred functions is responsible for the custody of the tabernacle key.

2. The responsible guardian of the tabernacle key need not always exercise the custody of the key personally.

a. He may entrust the key to other priests.

b. During periods of absence he may entrust the custody of the key even to laymen. In this case, however, the lay person may retain, not the tabernacle key itself, but rather the key to the place where the tabernacle key is kept. At the conclusion of a period of absence the responsible custodian should demand from the layman the possession of this second key.

c. In churches and in oratories of women in which the responsible custodian of the tabernacle key serves merely as the priest who regularly says Mass and performs the sacred functions, normally the actual custody of the tabernacle key must be entrusted to the women themselves. The primary custodian may not ignore the special regulations that were established by the Sacred Congregation in its Instruction of 1938. When a just and grave cause makes a change in these regulations imperative, the primary custodian should report the situation to the local ordinary. The local ordinary may authorize a departure from the special regulations of the Sacred Congregation, provided that he recognizes the presence of a just and grave cause.

d. In private oratories the holders of the apostolic indult are usually charged with the actual custody of the tabernacle key, but in virtue of this fact they are not constituted as the primary custodians of the tabernacle key.

3. The special regulations that were established by the Sacred Congregation of the Sacraments in its Instruction of 1938 for the actual custody of the tabernacle key in the churches and oratories of women do not apply in the event that a regular chaplain is assigned to these churches and oratories. Furthermore, these special regulations are not to be analogically applied to churches and oratories of men. In both these cases the ordinary norms that have been established by the Sacred Congregation should be followed.

The Renewal of the Sacred Species:

1. The duty of declaring the time beyond which hosts may not be consecrated, and the duty of declaring the time at which the Sacred Species are to be renewed are primarily the duties of the local ordinary. The local ordinary should enact diocesan statutes relative to these questions. In such enactments he is bound by the following restrictions:

a. The danger of corruption in the altar breads must at all times be scrupulously counteracted. The local ordinary, therefore, with the help of experts, should recognize the particular effects that local conditions have upon the altar breads. Once having determined the time at which the danger of corruption exists, he must then regulate accordingly the duration of time beyond which the altar breads may not be used and also the time at which the Sacred Species must be renewed.

b. Altar breads which are two or three months old, even though they show no signs of disintegration, should not as a general rule be consecrated. However, when exceptional and extraordinary methods of forestalling corruption have been employed, such as the tight sealing of the altar breads in cellophane wrappers, the local ordinary may abstract from this restriction.

c. The liberty that a local ordinary may exercise relative to any determination regarding the age of the altar breads or the time for the renewal of the Sacred Species may be restricted by the legislation of a plenary or a provincial council. Thus in the United States a local ordinary may not enact a diocesan statute to the effect that the Sacred Species need to be renewed only every other week, since the II Plenary Council of Baltimore demanded a weekly renewal of the Sacred Species. In the event, however, that a contrary custom has become fully established in a certain diocese, such a custom could warrant a modification of the strict law of the Plenary Council.

d. The greater number of canonists maintain that as an ordinary rule the consecrated Hosts should be renewed within a period of one month after Their baking. Although this monthly standard does not have the validity of a universal rule, nevertheless it is a working standard. In the absence of a better interpretation of what constitutes the danger of corruption in each locality, it should serve as a guiding norm. Only under expert advice should the local ordinary presume to exceed this monthly standard that has been favorably accepted by the greater number of canonists.

2. Ordinarily, in the absence of any diocesan, provincial, or plenary regulation on the matter, the individual pastor should follow the monthly standard. In the United States a pastor may be bound by only one specific regulation, namely, the law of weekly renewal of the Sacred Species. He should not, therefore, presume to use altar breads that are two or three months old. Ordinarily, in accordance with the monthly standard, he should renew the Sacred Species every week and in the consecration of the new Species use altar breads that are not more than three weeks old.

Private Reservation of the Blessed Sacrament:

1. Cardinals and bishops need an apostolic indult to reserve the Blessed Sacrament in their own private oratories.

2. There is need of an apostolic indult for a pastor to reserve the Blessed Sacrament privately when his church is in need of repair, or when his church is one that is used in common with non-Catholics.

3. The priest who for a short time and for a just cause reserves the Blessed Sacrament in a chapel within his own home is not completely excused from sin. Only a cause that is grave and so urgent that there is not even time to consult the local ordinary will justify the priest in the performance of such an action.

4. The local ordinary may not demand that in all the churches of his diocese the Blessed Sacrament must be reserved outside the altar and outside the tabernacle during the night. He may, however, list a series of circumstances which he considers as furnishing a sufficient warrant for the use of this unwonted method of reserving the Blessed Sacrament, and then demand that in all those churches where these circumstances exist the Blessed Sacrament must be reserved *extra altare et extra tabernaculum* during the night.

The Transferral of the Blessed Sacrament:

1. Ordinarily the Blessed Sacrament may be transferred outside the church only on the occasion of public Eucharistic processions and on the occasion of distributing Holy Communion to the sick. In the distribution of Holy Communion to the sick, however, a priest may also distribute Holy Communion to those who are physically well but only under the following conditions:

a. The healthy persons must find it gravely inconvenient to approach the church on that day;

b. The healthy persons must receive the Sacred Species in a place that has been designated by the common law for the lawful celebration of Holy Mass. Holy Mass, however, need not be actually celebrated.

BIBLIOGRAPHY

Sources

Acta Apostolicae Sedis, Commentarium Officiale, Romae, 1909-1929; Civitate Vaticana, 1929—

Acta Ecclesiae Mediolanensis, a Sancto Carolo Cardinali S. Praxedis Achiep. Mediolan. Condita, Frederici Cardinalis Borromaei Archiepiscopis Mediolana jussu undique diligentius collecta, et edita, 2 vols., Lugduni, 1682-1683. Tom. I, 1682; Tom. II, 1683.

Acta et Decreta Concilii Plenarii Americae in Urbe Celebrati, anno MDCCXCIX, 2 vols., Romae, 1900.

Acta et Decreta Sacrorum Conciliorum Recentiorum, Collectio Lacensis, 7 vols., Friburgi Brisgoviae, 1870-1892.

Acta Sanctae Sedis, 41 vols., Romae, 1865-1908.

Bruns, Hermann, *Canones Apostolorum et Conciliorum Veterum Selecti,* 2 vols., Berolini, 1839.

Caeremoniale Episcoporum, Benedict; Papae XIV Jussu Editum et Auctum, Mechliniae, 1867.

Caeremoniale Episcoporum Clementis VIII primum, nunc denuo Innocentii Papae X Auctoritate Recognitum, Romae: Ex Typographia Rev. Camerae Apostolicae, 1651.

Codex Iuris Canonici Pii X Pontificis Maximi iussu digestus, Benedicti Papae XV auctoritate promulgatus, Praefatione, Fontium Annotatione et Indice Analytico-Alphabetico ab Emo Petro Card. Gasparri Auctus, Romae, Typis Polyglottis Vaticanis, 1917; reimpressio, 1934.

Codicis Iuris Canonici Fontes, cura Emi Petri Card. Gasparri editi, 9 vols. Romae (postea Civitate Vaticana): Typis Polyglottis Vaticanis, 1923-1939. (Vols. VII-IX, ed. cura et studio Emi Iustiniani Card. Serédi.)

Collectanea S. Congregationis de Propaganda Fide, 2 vols., Romae: Typographia Polyglotta S.C. de Propaganda Fide, 1907.

Collectio Decretorum ad Sacram Liturgiam Spectantium Ab Anno 1927 ad Annum 1946, 2. ed., Romae, Edizioni Liturgiche, 1947.

Corpus Iuris Canonici, ed. Lipsiensis secunda, post Aemilii Richteri curas . . . instruxit Aemilius Friedberg, 2 vols., Lipsiae, 1879-1881.

Corpus Iuris Civilis, 3 vols., Berolini, 1928-1929. *Institutiones, quas recognovit* P. Krueger, ed. stereotypa 15., 1928; *Digesta,* quae recognovit T. Mommsen et retractavit P. Krueger, ed. stereotypa 15., 1928; *Codex Iustinianus,* quem recognovit et retractavit P. Krueger, ed. stereotypa 10., 1929; *Novellae,* quas recognovit R. Schoell, et absolvit G. Kroll, ed. stereotypa 5., 1928.

Decreta Authentica Congregationis Sacrorum Rituum ex actis eiusdem collecta eiusque auctoritate promulgata sub auspiciis SS. Domini nostri Leonis Papae XIII, 5 vols. et 2 appendices, Romae: Ex Typographia Polyglotta, 1898-1927.

Decretales D. Gregorii Papae IX, suae integritati una cum glossis restitutae, cum privilegio Gregorii XIII, Pont. Max., et aliorum Principum, Romae, 1582.

Decretum Gratiani emendatum et notationibus illustratum cum glossis, Gregorii XIII, Pont. Max., iussu editum, 2 vols., Romae, 1582.

Gardellini, Aloisius, Decreta Authentica Congregationis Sacrorum Rituum, cura H. Capalti, 4 vols., Romae, 1856-1858.

Ius Pontificium de Propaganda Fide, ed. R. de Martinis, pars I, 7 vols., Romae, 1888-1897; pars II, Romac, 1909.

Mansi, Joannes, *Sacrorum Conciliorum Nova et Amplissima Collectio,* 53 vols. in 60, Parisiis, 1901-1927.

Missale Romanum Ex Decreto Sacrosancti Concilii Tridentinum Restitutum S. PII V Pontificis Maximi Jussu Editum Aliorum Pontificum Cura Recognitum A Pio X Reformatum et Benedicti XV Auctoritate Vulgatum, Editio IV Iuxta Typicam Vaticanam, Neo-Eboraci: Benziger Brothers, Inc., 1944.

Mühlbauer, Wolfgang, *Decreta Authentica Congregationis Sacrorum Rituum,* 4 vols., Monachii-Parisiis-Neo-Eboraci, 1863-1867.

Monumenta Germaniae Historica, 188 vols., incomplete, Hannoverae, 1826— *Leges,* 5 vols., 1835-1889. T. I, *Capitularia Regum Francorum* ed. Georgius Henricus Pertz, Hannoverae, 1863; Neudruck, 1925.

Potthast, Augustus, *Regesta Pontificum Romanorum inde ab anno post Christum natum MCXCVIII ad annum MCCCIV,* 2 vols., Berolini, 1874-1875.

Schroeder, H. J., *Canons and Decrees of the Council of Trent,* St. Louis: B. Herder Book Co., 1941.

Reference Works

Aertnys, J.-Damen, C. A., *Theologia Moralis,* 14. ed., 2 vols., Taurinorum Augustae: Marietti, 1944.

André, Msgr. M-Condis, L'Abbe P.-Wagner, Chanoine J., *Dictionnaire de Droit Canonique,* 5. ed., 4 vols., Paris, 1901.

Augustine, Charles, *A Commentary on the New Code of Canon Law,* 8 vols., Vol. VI, 2. ed., St. Louis: Herder, 1923.

Ayrinhac, H. A., *The Administrative Legislation in the New Code of Canon Law,* New York: Longmans, Green & Co., 1930.

Barbosa, Augustinus, *Animadversiones de Officiis et Potestate Parochi,* Romae, 1774.

Berutti, Christophorus, *Institutiones Iuris Canonici,* 6 vols. in 7, Vol. IV, *De Rebus,* Taurini-Romae: Marietti, 1940.

Beste, Udalricus, *Introductio in Codicem*, 3. ed., Collegeville Minn.: St. John's Abbey Press, 1946.

Blat, Albertus, *Commentarium Textus Codicis Iuris Canonici*, 6 vols., Vol. IV, Romae, 1923.

Bouscaren, T. Lincoln, *The Canon Law Digest*, 2 vols., Milwaukee, Wis.: The Bruce Publishing Co., 1934-1943.

Bouscaren, T.-Ellis, A., *Canon Law*, Milwaukee: The Bruce Publishing Co., 1946.

Bouuaert, F. Claeys-Simenon, G., *Manuale Juris Canonici*, 3 vols., Vol. III, 4. ed., Gandae et Leodii: Dessain, 1934.

Cance, Adrien, *Le Code de Droit Canonique*, 5. ed., 3 vols., Paris: J. Gabalda et Fils, 1930.

Cappello, Felix, *Tractatus Canonico-Moralis de Sacramentis*, 3 vols. in 6, Vol. I, 4. ed., Romae: Marietti, 1945.

Catholic Encyclopedia, The, 15 vols. with Index and 2 Supplements, New York, 1907-1922.

Cavanaugh, William, *The Reservation of the Blessed Sacrament*, The Catholic University of America Canon Law Studies, n. 40. Washington, D. C.: The Catholic University of America, 1927.

Cocchi, Guido, *Commentarium in Codicem Iuris Canonici*, 8 vols. in 5, Vol. V, 4. ed. recognita, Taurinorum Augustae: Marietti, 1942.

Collins, Harold, *The Church Edifice and Its Appointments*, 2. ed., reprinted, Westminster, Md.: The Newman Bookshop, 1946.

Corblet, Jules, *Histoire Dogmatique, Liturgique et Archéologique du Sacrament de l'Eucharistie*, 2 vols., Paris, 1885-1886.

Coronata, Matthaeus Conte a, *Institutiones Iuris Canonici ad Usum Utriusque Cleri et Scholarum*, 5 vols., Vol. II, 2. ed., Taurini: Marietti, 1939.

Davis, Henry, *Moral and Pastoral Theology*, 3. ed., 4 vols., London, 1938: Sheed and Ward.

De Herdt, J. B., *Sacrae Liturgiae Praxis*, 4. ed., 3 vols., Lovanii, 1863.

De Meester, A., *Juris Canonici et Juris Canonico-Civilis Compendium*, nova ed., 3 toms. in 4 vols., Brugis: Desclée de Brouwer et Soc., 1921-1928; Vol. III, Pars I, 1926.

Durieux, P.-Dolphin, O., *The Eucharist, Law and Practice*, Chicago: Lakeside Press, 1926.

Ferraris, Lucius, *Prompta Bibliotheca Canonica Iuridica, Moralis, Theologica, necnon Ascetica, Polemica, Rubristica, Historica*, 9 vols., Romae, 1885-1889.

Gasparri, Petrus, *Tractatus Canonicus de Sanctissima Eucharistia*, 2 vols., Parisiis, 1897.

Giraldi, Ubaldus, *Animadversiones et additamenta ex posterioribus Summorum Pontificum constitutionibus et Sacrarum Congregationum decretis desumptis ad Aug. Barbosa, De officio et potestate parochi descriptio*, Romae, 1774.

Guiniven, John, *The Precept of Hearing Mass,* The Catholic University of America Canon Law Studies, n. 158, Washington, D. C.: The Catholic University of America Press, 1942.

Hostiensis, Cardinalis (Henricus de Segusio), *Commentaria in Quinque Decretalium Libros,* 5 vols., Venetiis, 1581.

———, *Summa Aurea,* Lugduni, 1568.

Ioannes, Andreae, *In Quinque Decretalium Libros Novella Commentaria,* 5 vols., Venetiis, 1581.

Köster, Laurentius, *De Custodia Sanctissimae Eucharistiae,* Romae: Catholic Book Agency, 1940.

Kurtscheid, Bertrandus-Wilches, Felix, *Historia Iuris Canonici,* Tom. I, *Historia Fontium et Scientiae Iuris Canonici,* Romae: Officium Libri Catholici, 1943.

Mabillon, Ioannes, *Museum Italicum,* 2 vols., Parisiis, 1687-1689.

Many, Stephanus, *Praelectiones de Missa,* Parisiis, 1903.

Merkelbach, B. H., *Summa Theologiae Moralis,* Editio Quinta Aucta et Emendata, 3 vols., Parisiis: Typis Desclée de Brouwer et Soc., 1947.

Migne, J. P., *Patrologiae Cursus Completus, Series Graeca,* 161 vols. in 164, Parisiis, 1856-1866.

———, *Patrologiae Cursus Completus, Series Latina,* 221 vols., Parisiis, 1844-1864.

Muratori, Ludovicus, *Liturgia Romana Vetus,* 2 vols., Venetiis, 1748.

Noldin, H.-Schmitt, A., *Summa Theologiae Moralis,* 3 vols., Vol. III, 28. ed., 1945, Heidelbergae: Sumptibus F. H. Kerle Monachii.

Panormitanus, Abbas (Nicholaus de Tudeschis), *Commentaria in Quinque Libros Decretalium,* 5 vols. in 7, Venetiis, 1588.

Prümmer, Dominicus, *Manuale Iuris Canonici in Usum Scholarum,* 3. ed., Friburgi Brisgoviae: Herder and Co., 1922.

Regatillo, Eduardus, *Ius Sacramentarium,* 2 vols., Santander; Sal Terrae, 1945-1946.

Reiffenstuel, Anacletus, *Ius Canonicum Universum,* 5 vols. in 7, Venetiis, 1735.

Reilly, Thomas, *The Visitation of Religious,* The Catholic University of America Canon Law Studies, n. 112, Washington, D. C.: The Catholic University of America, 1938.

Rufinus, *Summa Decretorum,* ed. H. Singer, Paderborn, 1902.

Santi, Franciscus, *Praelectiones Juris Canonici,* 5 vols. in 1, Ratisbonae-Neo-Eboraci-Cincinatii, 1886.

Schmalzgrueber, Franciscus, *Jus Ecclesiasticum Universum,* 5 vols. in 12, Romae, 1843-1845.

Sipos, Stephanus, *Enchiridion Iuris Canonici,* Pécs: Ex Typographia "Haladás R. T.," 1926.

Smith, William-Cheetham, Samuel, *Dictionary of Christian Antiquities,* 2 vols., London, 1880.

Van der Stappen, J. F., *Sacra Liturgia,* 5 vols., Vol. IV, 3. ed., Mechliniae, 1912.

Van Hove, A., *Tractatus de Sanctissima Eucharistia,* Editio Altera Aucta et Recognita. Mechlinae: H. Dessain, 1941.

Vermeersch, A.-Creusen, J., *Epitome Iuris Canonici,* 6. ed., 3 vols., Mechliniae-Romae: H. Dessain, 1937-1946; Vol. II, 1940.

Wernz, F. X., *Ius Decretalium,* 6 vols., Romae, 1898-1904; Vol. V, 3. ed., Prati, 1914.

Wernz, Franciscus-Vidal, Petrus, *Ius Canonicum ad Codicis Normam Exactum,* 7 vols. in 8, Romae: Apud Aedes Universitatis Gregorianae; Vol. IV, *De Rebus,* Pars I, 1934.

Winslow, Francis, *A Commentary on the Apostolic Faculties,* New York: Field Afar Press, 1946.

Woywod, Stanislaus, *A Practical Commentary on the Code of Canon Law,* revised by Callistus Smith, revised and enlarged edition, 2 vols., New York: Jos. J. Wagner, Inc., 1948.

Zitelli, Zepyrinus, *Apparatus Iuris Ecclesiastici,* 2. ed., Romae, 1895.

Articles

Anonymous, "Cases and Studies"—*The Ecclesiastical Review,* LXXXIX (1928), 403-417.

———, "Decrees and Decisions"—*The Jurist,* III (1943), 154-160.

———, "Decrees and Decisions"—*The Jurist,* IX (1948), 261-276.

———, "De la Frequente Communion"—*Analecta Juris Pontificii,* VII (1864), 781-847.

———, "Notes and Queries"—*The Irish Ecclesiastical Record,* 5 ser., XXXIII (1929), 521-536.

———, "Notes and Queries"—*The Irish Ecclesiastical Record,* 5 ser., XXXV (1930), 72-93.

———, "Studies and Conferences"—*The Ecclesiastical Review,* XCIX (1938), 350-373.

Braun, Joseph, "Tabernacle"—*The Catholic Encyclopedia,* XIV, 424-425.

Pauwels, Joseph, "Annotationes ad Instructionem de Eucharistiae Custodia"—*Periodica,* XXVII (1938), 386-392.

Woywod, S., "Answers to Questions"—*The Homiletic and Pastoral Review,* XXIX (1928), 644-649.

———, "Custody and Cult of the Blessed Sacrament"—*The Homiletic and Pastoral Review,* XXVII (1926-1927), 36-44.

———, "The Tabernacle"—*The Homiletic and Pastoral Review,* XXVII (1926-1927), 150-160.

Periodicals

Analecta Juris Pontificii, Romae, 1855-1869; Parisiis, 1872-1891.

Ecclesiastical Review, The, Philadelphia, 1905-1943.

Homiletic and Pastoral Review, The, New York, 1900—

Irish Ecclesiastical Record, The, Dublin, 1864—

Jurist, The, Washington, D. C., 1941—

Periodica de Religiosis et Missionariis, Brugis, 1905-1919; from 1920: *Periodica de Re Canonica et Morali utilia praesertim Religiosis et Missionariis,* Brugis, 1920-1927; from 1927: *Periodica de Re Morali, Canonica, Liturgica,* Brugis (1927-1936) et Romae (1937—).

ABBREVIATIONS

AAS—Acta Apostolicae Sedis.

Acta Ecclesiae Mediolan.—Acta Ecclesiae Mediolanensis, a Sancto Carolo Cardinali S. Praxedis Archiep. Mediolan. Condita, Frederici Cardinalis Borromaei Archiepiscopi Mediolan. iussu undique diligentius collecta, et edita.

ASS—Acta Sanctae Sedis.

Bruns—*Canones Apostolorum et Conciliorum Veterum Selecti.*

Caeremoniale Episcoporum—Caeremoniale Episcoporum, Benedicti Papae XIV Jussu Editum et Auctum.

Collectanea—Collectanea S. Congregationis de Propaganda Fide.

Coll. Lac.—Collectio Lacensis.

D.A.—Decreta Authentica Congregationis Sacrorum Rituum ex actis eiusdem collecta eiusque auctoritate promulgata sub auspiciis SS. Domini nostri Leonis Papae XXII.

Digest—The Canon Law Digest.

ER—The Ecclesiastical Review.

Fontes—Codici Iuris Canonici Fontes.

Gardellini—*Decreta Authentica Congregationis Sacrorum Rituum*, ed. Gardellini.

IER—The Irish Ecclesiastical Record.

Instruction—The Instruction of the Sacred Congregation of the Sacraments, May 26, 1938, on the Careful Custody of the Blessed Eucharist.

Instruction of 1929—The Instruction of the same Congregation, March 26, 1929, to the Most Reverend Ordinaries regarding certain faults to be avoided and certain requirements to be observed in performing the Sacrifice of the Mass and in distributing and reserving the Sacrament of the Eucharist.

Ius. Pont.—Ius Pontificium de Propaganda Fide.

Mansi—*Sacrorum Conciliorum Nova et Amplissima Collectio.*

MGH—Monumenta Germaniae Historica.

MPG—Migne, *Patrologia Graeca.*

MPL—Migne, *Patrologia Latina.*

Mühlbauer—*Decreta Authentica Congregationis Sacrorum Rituum*, ed. Mühlbauer.

Potthast—*Regesta Pontificum Romanorum inde ad anno post Christum natum MCXCVIII ad annum MCCCIV.*

Rituale Rom.—Rituale Romanum.

S.C.C.—Sacra Congregatio Concilii.

S.C.Consist.—Sacra Congregatio Consistorialis.

S.C. de Prop. Fide—Sacra Congregatio de Propaganda Fide.

S.C. de Sacramentis—Sacra Congregatio de Sacramentis.

S.C. Ep. et Reg.—Sacra Congregatio Episcoporum et Regularium.

S.R.C.—Sacrorum Rituum Congregatio.

BIOGRAPHICAL NOTE

Daniel Raymond Cahill was born on October 23, 1918, in San Francisco, Calif. He attended St. Peter's and St. Anne's Schools in that city. In 1932 he entered St. Joseph's College, Mountain View, Calif., the preparatory seminary for the Archdiocese of San Francisco. In 1938 he entered St. Patrick's Seminary, Menlo Park, Calif., and with the completion of his philosophy course received the degree of Bachelor of Arts. He was ordained to the Holy Priesthood at St. Mary's Cathedral, San Francisco, on December 18, 1943. After three years of parochial work in Oakland, Calif., he was assigned to the Catholic University of America to pursue a course of studies in Canon Law. He received the degree of Bachelor of Canon Law in June, 1947, and the degree of Licentiate in Canon Law in June, 1948.

ALPHABETICAL INDEX

CANON LAW STUDIES*

1. Freriks, Rev. Celestine A., C.PP.S., J.C.D., Religious Congregations in Their External Relations, 121 pp., 1916.
2. Galliher, Rev. Daniel M., O.P., J.C.D., Canonical Elections, 117 pp., 1917.
3. Borkowski, Rev. Aurelius L., O.F.M., J.C.D., De Confraternitatibus Ecclesiasticis, 136 pp., 1918.
4. Castillo, Rev. Cayo, J.C.D., Disertacion Historico-Canonica sobre la Potestad del Cabildo en Sede Vacante o Impedida del Vicario Capitular, 99 pp., 1919 (1918).
5. Kubelbeck, Rev. William J., S.T.B., J.C.D., The Sacred Penitentiaria and Its Relation to Faculties of Ordinaries and Priests, 129 pp., 1918.
6. Petrovits, Rev. Joseph J. C., S.T.D., J.C.D., The New Church Law on Matrimony, X-461 pp., 1919.
7. Hickey, Rev. John J., S.T.B., J.C.D., Irregularities and Simple Impediments in the New Code of Canon Law, 100 pp., 1920.
8. Klekotka, Rev. Peter J., S.T.B., J.C.D., Diocesan Consultors, 179 pp., 1920.
9. Wanenmacher, Rev. Francis, J.C.D., The Evidence in Ecclesiastical Procedure Affecting the Marriage Bond, 1920 (Printed 1935).
10. Golden, Rev. Henry Francis, J.C.D., Parochial Benefices in the New Code, IV-119 pp., 1921 (Printed 1925).
11. Koudelka, Rev. Charles J., J.C.D., Pastors, Their Rights and Duties According to the New Code of Canon Law, 211 pp., 1921.
12. Melo, Rev. Antonius, O.F.M., J.C.D., De Exemptione Regularium, X-188 pp., 1921.
13. Schaaf, Rev. Valentine Theodore, O.F.M., S.T.B., J.C.D., The Cloister, X-180 pp., 1921.
14. Burke, Rev. Thomas Joseph, S.T.D., J.C.D., Competence in Ecclesiastical Tribunals, IV-117 pp., 1922.
15. Leech, Rev. George Leo, J.C.D., A Comparative Study of the Constitution "Apostolicae Sedis" and the "Codex Juris Canonici," 179 pp., 1922.
16. Motry, Rev. Hubert Louis, S.T.D., J.C.D., Diocesan Faculties According to the Code of Canon Law, II-167 pp., 1922.

*All published numbers are available from the Catholic University of America Press, 620 Michigan Ave., N.E., Washington 17, D. C., except the following: Nos. 1-114 inclusive, 116, 118, 120, 121, 122, 123, 136, 153, 162, 182 and 198. But the following numbers, now reissued, are obtainable from *The Jurist,* The Catholic University of America, Washington 17, D. C., namely: Nos. 5, 7, 11, 17, 18, 19, 26, 28, 30, 31, 34, 42, 44, 51, 52 and 61.

17. Murphy, Rev. George Lawrence, J.C.D., Delinquencies and Penalties in the Administration and the Reception of the Sacraments, IV-121 pp., 1923.
18. O'Reilly, Rev. John Anthony, S.T.B., J.C.D., Ecclesiastical Sepulture in the New Code of Canon Law, II-129 pp., 1923.
19. Michalicka, Rev. Wenceslas Cyril, O.S.B., J.C.D., Judicial Procedure in Dismissal of Clerical Exempt Religious, 107 pp., 1923.
20. Dargin, Rev. Edward Vincent, S.T.B., J.C.D., Reserved Cases According to the Code of Canon Law, IV-103 pp., 1924.
21. Godfrey, Rev. John A., S.T.B., J.C.D., The Right of Patronage According to the Code of Canon Law, 153 pp., 1924.
22. Hagedorn, Rev. Francis Edward, J.C.D., General Legislation on Indulgences, II-154 pp., 1924.
23. King, Rev. James Ignatius, J.C.D., The Administration of the Sacraments to Dying Non-Catholics, V-141 pp., 1924.
24. Winslow, Rev. Francis Joseph, M.M., J.C.D., Vicars and Prefects Apostolic, IV-149 pp., 1924.
25. Correa, Rev. Jose Servelion, S.T.L., J.C.D., La Potestad Legislativa de la Iglesia Catolica, IV-127 pp., 1925.
26. Dugan, Rev. Henry Francis, A.M., J.C.D., The Judiciary Department of the Diocesan Curia, 87 pp., 1925.
27. Keller, Rev. Charles Frederick, S.T.B., J.C.D., Mass Stipends, 167 pp., 1925.
238. Paschang, Rev. John Linus, J.C.D., The Sacramentals According to the Code of Canon Law, 129 pp., 1925.
29. Piontek, Rev. Cyrillus, O.F.M., S.T.B., J.C.D., De Indulto Exclaustrationis necnon Saecularizationis, XIII-289 pp., 1925.
30. Kearney, Rev. Richard Joseph, S.T.B., J.C.D., Sponsors at Baptism According to the Code of Canon Law, IV-127 pp. 1925.
31. Bartlett, Rev. Chester Joseph, A.M., LL.B., J.C.D., The Tenure of Parochial Property in the United States of America, V-108 pp., 1926.
32. Kilker, Rev. Adrian Jerome, J.C.D., Extreme Unction, V-425 pp., 1926.
33. McCormick, Rev. Robert Emmett, J.C.D., Confessors of Religious, VIII-266 pp., 1926.
34. Miller, Rev. Newton Thomas, J.C.D., Founded Masses According to the Code of Canon Law, VII-93 pp., 1926.
35. Roelker, Rev. Edward G., S.T.D., J.C.D., Principles of Privilege According to the Code of Canon Law, XI-166 pp., 1926.
36. Bakalarczyk, Rev. Richardus, M.I.C., J.U.D., De Novitiatu, VIII-208 pp., 1927.
37. Pizzuti, Rev. Lawrence, O.F.M., J.U.L., De Parochis Religiosis, 1927. (Not Printed.)
38. Bliley, Rev. Nicholas Martin, O.S.B., J.C.D., Altars According to the Code of Canon Law, XIX-132 pp., 1927.

39. Brown, Mr. Brendan Francis, A.B., LL.M., J.U.D., The Canonical Juristic Personality with Special Reference to its Status in the United States of America, V-212 pp., 1927.
40. Cavanaugh, Rev. William Thomas, C.P., J.U.D., The Reservation of the Blessed Sacrament, VIII-101 pp., 1927.
41. Doheny, Rev. William J., C.S.C., A.B., J.U.D., Church Property: Modes of Acquisition, X-118 pp., 1927.
42. Feldhaus, Rev. Aloysius H., C.PP.S., J.C.D., Oratories, IX-141 pp., 1927.
43. Kelly, Rev. James Patrick, A.B., J.C.D., The Jurisdiction of the Simple Confessor, X-208 pp., 1927.
44. Neuberger, Rev. Nicholas J., J.C.D., Canon 6 or the Relation of the Codex Juris Canonici to the Preceding Legislation, V-95 pp., 1927.
45. O'Keefe, Rev. Gerald Michael, J.C.D., Matrimonial Dispensations, Powers of Bishops, Priests, and Confessors, VIII-232 pp., 1927.
46. Quigley, Rev. Joseph, A.M., A.B., J.C.D., Condemned Societies, 139 pp., 1927.
47. Zaplotnik, Rev. Johannes Leo, J.C.D., De Vicariis Foraneis, X-142 pp., 1927.
48. Duskie, Rev. John Aloysius, A.B., J.C.D., The Canonical Status of the Orientals in the United States, VIII-196 pp., 1928.
49. Hyland, Rev. Francis Edward, J.C.D., Excommunication, Its Nature, Historical Development and Effects, VIII-181 pp., 1928.
50. Reinmann, Rev. Gerald Joseph, O.M.C., J.C.D., The Third Order Secular of Saint Francis, 201 pp., 1928.
51. Schenk, Rev. Francis J., J.C.D., The Matrimonial Impediments of Mixed Religion and Disparity of Cult, XVI-318 pp., 1929.
52. Coady, Rev. John Joseph, S.T.D., J.U.D., A.M., The Appointment of Pastors, VIII-150 pp., 1929.
53. Kay, Rev. Thomas Henry, J.C.D., Competence in Matrimonial Procedure, VIII-164 pp., 1929.
54. Turner, Rev. Sidney Joseph, C.P., J.U.D., The Vow of Poverty, XLIX-217 pp., 1929.
55. Kearney, Rev. Raymond A., A.B., S.T.D., J.C.D., The Principles of Delegation, VII-149 pp., 1929.
56. Conran, Rev. Edward James, A.B., J.C.D., The Interdict, V-163 pp., 1930.
57. O'Neill, Rev. William H., J.C.D., Papal Rescripts of Favor, VII-218 pp., 1930.
58. Bastnagel, Rev. Clement Vincent, J.U.D., The Appointment of Parochial Adjutants and Assistants, XV-257 pp., 1930.
59. Ferry, Rev. William A., A.B., J.C.D., Stole Fees, V-136 pp., 1930.
60. Costello, Rev. John Michael, A.B., J.C.D., Domicile and Quasi-Domicile, VII-201 pp., 1930.
61. Kremer, Rev. Michael Nicholas, A.B., S.T.B., J.C.D., Church Support in the United States, VI-136 pp., 1930.

o

62. ANGULO, REV. LUIS, C.M., J.C.D., Legislation de la Iglesia sobre la intencion en la application de la Santa Misa, VII-104 pp., 1931.
63. FREY, REV. WOLFGANG NORBERT, O.S.B., A.B., J.C.D., The Act of Religious Profession, VIII-174 pp., 1931.
64. ROBERTS, REV. JAMES BRENDAN, A.B., J.C.D., The Banns of Marriage, XIV-140 pp., 1931.
65. RYDER, REV. RAYMOND ALOYSIUS, A.B., J.C.D., Simony, IX-151 pp., 1931.
66. CAMPAGNA, REV. ANGELO, Ph.D., J.U.D., Il Vicario Generale del Vescovo, VII-205 pp., 1931.
67. COX, REV. JOSEPH GODFREY, A.B., J.C.D., The Administration of Seminaries, VI-124 pp., 1931.
68. GREGORY, REV. DONALD J., J.U.D., The Pauline Privilege, XV-165 pp., 1931.
69. DONOHUE, REV. JOHN F., J.C.D., The Impediment of Crime, VII-110 pp., 1931.
70. DOOLEY, REV. EUGENE A., O.M.I., J.C.D., Church Law on Sacred Relics, IX-143 pp., 1931.
71. ORTH, REV. CLEMENT RAYMOND, O.M.C., J.C.D., The Approbation of Religious Institutes, 171 pp., 1931.
72. PERNICONE, REV. JOSEPH M., A.B., J.C.D., The Ecclesiastical Prohibition of Books, XII-267 pp., 1932.
73. CLINTON, REV. CONNELL, A.B., J.C.D., The Paschal Precept, IX-108 pp., 1932.
74. DONNELLY, REV. FRANCIS B., A.M., S.T.L., J.C.D., The Diocesan Synod, VIII-125 pp., 1932.
75. TORRENTE, REV. CAMILO, C.M.F., J.C.D., Las Procesiones Sagradas, V-145 pp., 1932.
76. MURPHY, REV. EDWIN J., C.PP.S., J.C.D., Suspension Ex Informata Conscientia, XI-122 pp., 1932.
77. MACKENZIE, REV. ERIC F., A.M., S.T.L., J.C.D., The Delict of Heresy in its Commission, Penalization, Absolution, VII-124 pp., 1932.
78. LYONS, REV. AVITUS E., S.T.B., J.C.D., The Collegiate Tribunal of First Instance, XI-147 pp., 1932.
79. CONNOLLY, REV. THOMAS A., J.C.D., Appeals, XI-195 pp., 1932.
80. SANGMEISTER, REV. JOSEPH V., A.B., J.C.D., Force and Fear as Precluding Matrimonial Consent, V-211 pp., 1932.
81. JAEGER, REV. LEO A., A.B., J.C.D., The Administration of Vacant and Quasi-Vacant Episcopal Sees in the United States, IX-229 pp., 1932.
82. RIMLINGER, REV. HERBERT T., J.C.D., Error Invalidating Matrimonial Consent, VII-79 pp., 1932.
83. BARRETT, REV. JOHN D. M., S.S., J.C.D., A Comparative Study of the Plenary Councils of Baltimore and the Code of Canon Law, IX-221 pp., 1932.
84. CARBERRY, REV. JOHN J., Ph.D., S.T.D., J.C.D., The Juridical Form of Marriage, X-177 pp., 1934.

o

85. DOLAN, REV. JOHN L., A.B., J.C.D., The Defensor Vinculi, XII-157 pp., 1934.
86. HANNAN, REV. JEROME D., A.M., S.T.D., LL.B., J.C.D., The Canon Law of Wills, IX-517 pp., 1934.
87. LEMIEUX, REV. DELISE A., A.M., J.C.D., The Sentence in Ecclesiastical Procedure, IX-131 pp., 1934.
88. O'ROURKE, REV. JAMES J., A.B., J.C.D., Parish Registers, VII-109 pp., 1934.
89. TIMLIN, REV. BARTHOLOMEW, O.F.M., A.M., J.C.D., Conditional Matrimonial Consent, X-381 pp., 1934.
90. WAHL, REV. FRANCIS X., A.B., J.C.D., The Matrimonial Impediments of Consanguinity and Affinity, VI-125 pp., 1934.
91. WHITE, REV. ROBERT J., A.B., LL.B., S.T.B., J.C.D., Canonical Ante-Nuptial Promises and the Civil Law, VI-152 pp., 1934.
92. HERRERA, REV. ANTONIO PARRA, O.C.D., J.C.D., Legislacion Ecclesiastica sobra el Ayuno y la Abstinencia, XI-191 pp., 1935.
93. KENNEDY, REV. EDWIN J., J.C.D., The Special Matrimonial Process in Cases of Evident Nullity, X-165 pp., 1935.
94. MANNING, REV. JOHN J., A.B., J.C.D., Presumption of Law in Matrimonial Procedure, XI-111 pp., 1935.
95. MOEDER, REV. JOHN M., J.C.D., The Proper Bishop for Ordination and Dimissorial Letters, VII-135 pp., 1935.
96. O'MARA, REV. WILLIAM A., A.B., J.C.D., Canonical Causes for Matrimonial Dispensations, IX-155 pp., 1935.
97. REILLY, REV. PETER, J.C.D., Residence of Pastors, IX-81 pp., 1935.
98. SMITH, REV. MARINER T., O.P., S.T.Lr., J.C.D., The Penal Law for Religious, VII-169 pp., 1935.
99. WHALEN, REV. DONALD W., A.M., J.C.D., The Value of Testimonial Evidence in Matrimonial Procedure, XIII-297 pp., 1935.
100. CLEARY, REV. JOSEPH F., J.C.D., Canonical Limitations on the Alienation of Church Property, VIII-141 pp., 1936.
101. GLYNN, REV. JOHN C., J.C.D., The Promoter of Justice, XX-337 pp., 1936.
102. BRENNAN, REV. JAMES H., S.S., M.A., S.T.B., J.C.D., The Simple Convalidation of Marriage, VI-135 pp., 1937.
103. BRUNINI, REV. JOSEPH BERNARD, J.C.D., The Clerical Obligations of Canons 139 and 142, X-121 pp., 1937.
104. CONNOR, REV. MAURICE, A.B., J.C.D., The Administrative Removal of Pastors, VIII-159 pp., 1937.
105. GUILFOYLE, REV. MERLIN JOSEPH, J.C.D., Custom, XI-144 pp., 1937.
106. HUGHES, REV. JAMES AUSTIN, A.B., A.M., J.C.D., Witnesses in Criminal Trials of Clerics, IX-140 pp., 1937.
107. JANSEN, REV. RAYMOND J., A.B., S.T.L., J.C.D., Canonical Provisions for Catechetical Instruction, VII-153 pp., 1937.
108. KEALY, REV. JOHN JAMES, A.B., J.C.D., The Introductory Libellus in Church Court Procedure, XI-131 pp., 1937.

109. McManus, Rev. James Edward, C.Ss.R., J.C.D., The Administration of Temporal Goods in Religious Institutes, XVI-196 pp., 1937.
110. Moriarty, Rev. Eugene James, J.C.D., Oaths in Ecclesiastical Courts, X-115 pp., 1937.
111. Rainer, Rev. Eligius George, C.Ss.R., J.C.D., Suspension of Clerics, XVII-249 pp., 1937.
112. Reilly, Rev. Thomas F., C.Ss.R., J.C.D., Visitation of Religious, VI-195 pp., 1938.
113. Moriarity, Rev. Francis E., C.Ss.R., J.C.D., The Extraordinary Absolution from Censures, XV-334 pp., 1938.
114. Connolly, Rev. Nicholas P., J.C.D., The Canonical Erection of Parishes, X-132 pp., 1938.
115. Donovan, Rev. James Joseph, J.C.D., The Pastor's Obligation in Prenuptial Investigation, XII-322 pp., 1938.
116. Harrigan, Rev. Robert J., M.A., S.T.B., J.C.D., The Radical Sanation of Invalid Marriages, VIII-208 pp., 1938.
117. Boffa, Rev. Conrad Humbert, J.C.D., Canonical Provisions for Catholic Schools, VII-211 pp., 1939.
118. Parsons, Rev. Anscar John, O.M.Cap., J.C.D., Canonical Elections, XII-236 pp., 1939.
119. Reilly, Rev. Edward Michael, A.B., J.C.D., The General Norms of Dispensation, XII-156 pp., 1939.
120. Ryan, Rev. Gerald Aloysius, A.B., J.C.D., Principles of Episcopal Jurisdiction, XIII-172 pp., 1939.
121. Burton, Rev. Francis James, C.S.C., A.B., J.C.D., A Commentary on Canon 1125, X-222 pp., 1940.
122. Miaskiewicz, Rev. Francis Sigismund, J.C.D., Supplied Jurisdiction According to Canon 209, XII-340 pp., 1940.
123. Rice, Rev. Patrick William, A.B., J.C.D., Proof of Death in Prenuptial Investigation, VIII-156 pp., 1940.
124. Anglin, Rev. Thomas Francis, M.S., J.C.D., The Eucharistic Fast, VIII-183 pp., 1941.
125. Coleman, Rev. John Jerome, J.C.D., The Minister of Confirmation, VI-153 pp., 1941.
126. Downs, Rev. Joseph Emmanuel, A.B., J.C.D., The Concept of Clerical Immunity, XI-163 pp., 1941.
127. Esswein, Rev. Anthony Albert, J.C.D., Extrajudicial Penal Powers of Ecclesiastical Superiors, X-144 pp., 1941.
128. Farrell, Rev. Benjamin Francis, M.A., S.T.L., J.C.D., The Rights and Duties of the Local Ordinary Regarding Congregations of Women Religious of Pontifical Approval, V-195 pp., 1941.
129. Feeney, Rev. Thomas John, A.B., S.T.L., J.C.D., Restitutio in Integrum, VI-169 pp., 1941.
130. Findlay, Rev. Stephen William, O.S.B., A.B., J.C.D., Canonical Norms Governing the Deposition and Degradation of Clerics, XVII-279 pp., 1941.

131. GOODWINE, REV. JOHN, A.B., S.T.L., J.C.D., The Right of the Church to Acquire Property, VIII-119 pp., 1941.
132. HESTON, REV. EDWARD LOUIS, C.S.C., PH.D., S.T.D., J.C.D., The Alienation of Church Property in the United States, XII-222 pp., 1941.
133. HOGAN, REV. JAMES JOHN, A.B., S.T.L., J.C.D., Judicial Advocates and Procurators, XIII-200 pp., 1941.
134. KEALY, REV. THOMAS M., A.B., LITT.D., J.C.D., Dowry of Women Religious, IX-152 pp., 1941.
135. KEENE, REV. MICHAEL JAMES, O.S.B., J.C.D., Religious Ordinaries and Canon 198, V-164 pp., 1941 (Printed 1942).
136. KERIN, REV. CHARLES A., S.S., M.A., S.T.B., J.C.D., The Privation of Christian Burial, XVI-279 pp., 1941.
137. LOUIS, REV. WILLIAM FRANCIS, M.A., J.C.D., Diocesan Archives, X-101 pp., 1941.
138. MCDEVITT, REV. GILBERT JOSEPH, A.B., J.C.D., Legitimacy and Legitimation, X-247 pp., 1941.
139. MCDONOUGH, REV. THOMAS JOSEPH, A.B., J.C.D., Apostolic Administrators, X-217 pp., 1941.
140. MEIER, REV. CARL ANTHONY, A.B., J.C.D., Penal Administrative Procedure Against Negligent Pastors, XI-240 pp., 1941.
141. SCHMIDT, REV. JOHN ROGG, A.B., J.C.D., The Principles of Authentic Interpretation in Canon 17 of the Code of Canon Law, XII-331 pp., 1941.
142. SLAFKOSKY, REV. ANDREW LEONARD, A.B., J.C.D., The Canonical Episcopal Visitation of the Diocese, X-197 pp., 1941.
143. SWOBODA, REV. INNOCENT ROBERT, O.F.M., J.C.D., Ignorance in Relation to the Imputability of Delicts, IX-271 pp., 1941.
144. DUBE, REV. ARTHUR JOSEPH, A.B., J.C.D., The General Principles for the Reckoning of Time in Canon Law, VIII-299 pp., 1941.
145. MCBRIDE, REV. JAMES T., A.B., J.C.D., Incardination and Excardination of Seculars, XX-585 pp., 1941.
146. KROL, REV. JOHN T., J.C.D., The Defendant in Ecclesiastical Trials, XII-207 pp., 1942.
147. COMYNS, REV. JOSEPH J., C.Ss.R., A.B., J.C.D., Papal and Episcopal Administration of Church Property, XIV-155 pp., 1942.
148. BARRY, REV. GARRETT FRANCIS, O.M.I., J.C.D., Violation of the Cloister, XII-260 pp., 1942.
149. BOLDUC, REV. GATIEN, C.S.V., A.B., S.T.L., J.C.D., Les Etudes dans les Religions Clericales, VIII-155 pp., 1942.
150. BOYLES, REV. DAVID JOHN, M.A., J.C.D., The Juridic Effects of Moral Certitude on Pre-Nuptial Guarantees, XII-188 pp., 1942.
151. CANAVAN, REV. WALTER JOSEPH, M.A., LITT.D., J.C.D., The Profession of Faith, XII-143 pp., 1942.
152. DESROCHERS, REV. BRUNO, A.B., PH.L., S.T.B., J.C.D., Le Premier Concile Plenier de Quebec et le Code de Droit Canonique, XIV-186 pp., 1942.

153. DILLON, REV. ROBERT EDWARD, A.B., J.C.D., Common Law Marriage, X-148 pp., 1942.
154. DODWELL, REV. EDWARD JOHN, PH.D., S.T.B., J.C.D., The Time and Place for the Celebration of Marriage, X-156 pp., 1942.
155. DONNELLAN, REV. THOMAS ANDREW, A.B., J.C.D., The Obligation of the Missa pro Populo, VII-131 pp., 1942.
156. ELTZ, REV. LOUIS ANTHONY, A.B., J.C.D., Cooperation in Crime, XII-208 pp., 1942.
157. GASS, REV. SYLVESTER FRANCIS, M.A., J.C.D., Ecclesiastical Pensions, XI-206 pp., 1942.
158. GUINIVEN, REV. JOHN JOSEPH, C.Ss.R., J.C.D., The Precept of Hearing Mass, XIV-188 pp., 1942.
159. GULCZYNSKI, REV. JOHN THEOPHILUS, J.C.D., The Desecration and Violation of Churches, X-126 pp., 1942.
160. HAMMILL, REV. JOHN LEO, M.A., J.C.D., The Obligations of the Traveler According to Canon 14, VIII-204 pp., 1942.
161. HAYDT, REV. JOHN JOSEPH, A.B., J.C.D., Reserved Benefices, XI-148 pp., 1942.
162. HUSER, REV. ROGER JOHN, O.F.M., A.B., J.C.D., The Crime of Abortion in Canon Law, XII-187 pp., 1942.
163. KEARNEY, REV. FRANCIS PATRICK, A.B., S.T.L., J.C.D., The Principles of Canon 1127, X-162 pp., 1942.
164. LINAHEN, REV. LEO JAMES, S.T.L., J.C.D., De Absolutione Complicis in Peccato Turpi, 114 pp., 1942.
165. MCCLOSKEY, REV. JOSEPH ALOYSIUS, A.B., J.C.D., The Subject of Ecclesiastical Law According to Canon 12, XVII-246 pp., 1942 (Printed 1943).
166. O'NEILL, REV. FRANCIS JOSEPH, C.Ss.R., J.C.D., The Dismissal of Religious in Temporary Vows, XIII-220 pp., 1942.
167. PRINCE, REV. JOHN EDWARD, A.B., S.T.D., J.C.D., The Diocesan Chancellor, X-136 pp., 1942.
168. RIESNER, REV. ALBERT JOSEPH, C.Ss.R., J.C.D., Apostates and Fugitives from Religious Institutes, IX-168 pp., 1942.
169. STENGER, REV. JOSEPH BERNARD, J.C.D., The Mortgaging of Church Property, 186 pp., 1942.
170. WALDRON, REV. JOSEPH FRANCIS, A.B., J.C.D., The Minister of Baptism, XII-197 pp., 1942.
171. WILLETT, REV. ROBERT ALBERT, J.C.D., The Probative Value of Documents in Ecclesiastical Trials, X-124 pp., 1942.
172. WOEBER, REV. EDWARD MARTIN, M.A., J.C.D., The Interpellations, XII-161 pp., 1942.
173. BENKO, REV. MATTHEW ALOYSIUS, O.S.B., M.A., J.C.D., The Abbot Nullius, XIV-148 pp., 1943.
174. CHRIST, REV. JOSEPH JAMES, M.A., S.T.L., J.C.D., Dispensation from Vindicative Penalties, XIV-285 pp., 1943.

175. Clancy, Rev. Patrick M. J., O.P., A.B., S.T.Lr., J.C.D., The Local Religious Superior, X-299 pp., 1943.
176. Clarke, Rev. Thomas James, J.C.D., Parish Societies, XII-147 pp., 1943.
177. Connolly, Rev. John Patrick, S.T.L., J.C.D., Synodal Examiners and Parish Priest Consultors, X-223 pp., 1943.
178. Drumm, Rev. William Martin, A.B., J.C.D., Hospital Chaplains, XII-175 pp., 1943.
179. Flanagan, Rev. Bernard Joseph, A.B., S.T.L., J.C.D., The Canonical Erection of Religious Houses, X-147 pp., 1943.
180. Kelleher, Rev. Stephen Joseph, A.B., S.T.B., J.C.D., Discussions with non-Catholics; Canonical Legislation, X-93 pp., 1943.
181. Lewis, Rev. Gordian, C.P., J.C.D., Chapters in Religious Institutes, XII-169 pp., 1943.
182. Marx, Rev. Adolph, J.C.D., The Declaration of Nullity of Marriages Contracted Outside the Church, X-151 pp., 1943.
183. Matulenas, Rev. Raymond Anthony, O.S.B., A.B., J.C.D., Communication a Source of Privileges, XII-225 pp., 1943.
184. O'Leary, Rev. Charles Gerard, C.Ss.R., J.C.D., Religious Dismissed After Perpetual Profession, X-213 pp., 1943.
185. Power, Rev. Cornelius Michael, J.C.D., The Blessing of Cemeteries. XII-231 pp., 1943.
186. Shuhler, Rev. Ralph Vincent, O.S.A., J.C.D., Privileges of Regulars to Absolve and Dispense, XII-195 pp., 1943.
187. Ziolkowski, Rev. Thaddeus Stanislaus, A.B., J.C.D., The Consecration and Blessing of Churches, XII-151 pp., 1943.
188. Heneghan, Rev. John Joseph, S.T.D., J.C.D., The Marriages of Unworthy Catholics: Canons 1065 and 1066, XVI-213 pp., 1944.
189. Carroll, Rev. Coleman Francis, M.C., S.T.L., J.C.L., Charitable Institutions.
190. Ciesluk, Rev. Joseph Edward, Ph.B., S.T.L., J.C.D., National Parishes in the United States, VI-178 pp., 1944.
191. Coburn, Rev. Vincent Paul, A.B., J.C.D., Marriages of Conscience, XII-172 pp., 1944.
192. Connors, Rev. Charles Paul, C.S.Sp., A.B., J.C.D., Extra-Judicial Procurators in the Code of Canon Law, X-94 pp., 1944.
193. Coyle, Rev. Paul Raymond, A.B., J.C.D., Judicial Exceptions, X-142 pp., 1944.
194. Fair, Rev. Bartholomew Francis, A.B., S.T.L., J.C.D., The Impediment of Abduction, XII-122 pp., 1944.
195. Gallagher, Rev. Thomas Raphael, O.P., A.B., S.T.Lr., J.C.D., The Examination of the Qualities of the Ordinand, X-166 pp., 1944.
196. Gannon, Rev. John Mark, S.T.L., J.C.D., The Interstices Required for the Promotion to Orders, XII-100 pp., 1944.

197. Goldsmith, Rev. J. William, B.C.S., S.T.L., J.C.D., The Competence of Church and State over Marriage—Disputed Points, X-128 pp., 1944.
198. Goodwine, Rev. Joseph Gerard, A.B., S.T.B., J.C.D., The Reception of Converts, XIV-326 pp., 1944.
199. Kowalski, Rev. Romuald Eugene, O.F.M., A.B., J.C.D., Sustenance of Religious Houses of Regulars, X-174 pp., 1944.
200. McCoy, Rev. Alan Edward, O.F.M., J.C.D., Force and Fear in Relation to Delictual Imputability and Penal Responsibility, XII-160 pp., 1944.
201. McDevitt, Rev. Vincent John, Ph.B., S.T.L., J.C.L., Perjury.
202. Martin, Rev. Thomas Owen, Ph.D., S.T.D., J.C.D., Adverse possession, Prescription and Limitation of Actions; The Canonical "Praescriptio," XX-208 pp., 1944.
203. Miklosovic, Rev Paul John, A.B., J.C.L., Attempted Marriages and Their Consequent Juridic Effects.
204. Mundy, Rev. Thomas Maurice, A.B., S.T.L., J.C.D., The Union of Parishes, X-164 pp., 1944.
205. O'Dea, Rev. John Coyle, A.B., J.C.D., The Matrimonial Impediment of Nonage, VIII-126 pp., 1944.
206. Olalia, Rev. Alexander Ayson, S.T.L., J.C.D., A Comparative Study of the Christian Constitution of States and the Constitution of the Philippine Commonwealth, XII-136 pp., 1944.
207. Poisson, Rev. Pierre-Marie, C.S.C., A.B., Ph.L., Th.L., J.C.L., Droits Patrimoniaux des Maisons et des Eglises Religieuses.
208. Stadalnikas, Rev. Casimir Joseph, M.I.C., J.C.D., Reservation of Censures, X-141 pp., 1944.
209. Sullivan, Rev. Eugene Henry, S.T.L., J.C.D., Proof of the Reception of the Sacraments, X-165 pp., 1944.
210. Vaughan, Rev. William Edward, J.C.D., Constitutions for Diocesan Courts, X-210 pp., 1944.
211. Paro, Rev. Gino, S.T.D., J.C.D., The Right of Papal Legation, X-221 pp., 1944 (Printed 1947).
212. Balzer, Rev. Ralph Francis, C.P., J.C.D., The Computation of Time in a Canonical Novitiate, X-227 pp., 1945.
213. Dougherty, Rev. John Whelan, A.B., S.T.L., J.C.D., De Inquisitione Speciali, XII-195 pp., 1945.
214. Dziob, Rev. Michael Walter, J.C.D., The Sacred Congregation for the Oriental Church, XII-181 pp., 1945.
215. Eidenschink, Rev. John Albert, O.S.B., B.A., J.C.D., The Election of Bishops in the Letters of Pope Gregory the Great, VIII-200 pp., 1945.
216. Gill, Rev. Nicholas, C.P., J.C.D., The Spiritual Prefect in Clerical Religious Houses of Study, X-140 pp., 1945.
217. Hynes, Rev. Harry Gerard, S.T.L., J.C.D., The Privileges of Cardinals, XII-183 pp., 1945.

218. McDevitt, Rev. Gerald Vincent, S.T.L., J.C.D., The Renunciation of an Ecclesiastical Office, XIV-179 pp., 1946.
219. Manning, Rev. Joseph Leroy, J.C.D., The Free Conferral of Offices. VII-116 pp., 1945.
220. Meyer, Rev. Louis G., O.S.B., A.B., S.T.B., J.C.D., Alms-Gathering by Religious, XII-163 pp., 1946.
221. O'Donnell, Rev. Cletus Francis, M.A., J.C.D., The Marriage of Minors, XII-268 pp., 1945.
222. Prunskis, Rev. Joseph, J.C.D., Comparative Law, Ecclesiastical and Civil in Lithuanian Concordat, X-161 pp., 1945.
223. Sweeney, Rev. Francis Patrick, C.Ss.R., J.C.D., The Reduction of Clerics to the Lay State, X-199 pp., 1945.
224. Vogelpohl, Rev. Henry John, J.C.D., The Simple Impediments to Holy Orders, XVI-190 pp., 1945.
225. Brockhaus, Rev. Thomas Aquinas, O.S.B., A.B., J.C.D., Religious who Are Known as Conversi, X-127 pp., 1945.
226. Griese, Rev. Nicholas Orville, S.T.D., J.C.D., Marriage and The Procreation of Offspring, XVI-224 pp., 1945.
227. Boudreaux, Rev. Warren Louis, J.C.D., The "ab acatholicis nati" of Canon 1099, § 2, XII-110 pp., 1946.
228. Bowe, Rev. Thomas Joseph, A.B., J.C.D., Religious Superioresses, VIII-206 pp., 1946.
229. Diederichs, Rev. Michael Ferdinand, S.C.J., J.C.D., The Jurisdiction of the Latin Ordinaries over their Oriental Subjects, XIV-153 pp., 1946.
230. Dingman, Rev. Maurice John, A.B., S.T.L., J.C.L., The Plaintiff in Contentious Trials.
231. Frison, Rev. Basil, C.M.F., M.Mus., J.C.D., The Retroactivity of Law, X-221 pp., 1946.
232. Galvin, Rev. William Anthony, M.A., J.C.D., The Administrative Transfer of Pastors, XII-288 pp., 1946.
233. Goracy, Rev. Joseph C., J.C.L., The Diriment Impediment of Major Orders.
234. Hale, Rev. Joseph Francis, M.A., S.T.L., J.C.D., The Pastor of Burial, X-247 pp., 1946 (Printed 1949).
235. Henry, Rev. Joseph Arthur, A.B., J.C.D., The Mass and Holy Communion: Inter-Ritual Law, XII-138 pp., 1946.
236. Linenberger, Rev. Herbert, C.PP.S., J.C.D., The False Denunciation of an Innocent Confession, VIII-205 pp., 1946 (Printed 1949).
237. Lowry, Rev. James Martin, A.B., J.C.D., Dispensation from Private Vows, XII-266 pp., 1946.
238. Lynch, Rev. George Edward, A.B., S.T.L., J.C.D., Coadjutors and Auxiliaries of Bishops, X-107 pp., 1946 (Printed 1947).
239. Lynch, Rev. Timothy, M.S.SS.T., J.C.D., Contracts between Bishops and Religious Congregations, XIV-232 pp., 1946.

240. McClunn, Rev. Justin David, A.B., S.T.L., J.C.D., Administrative Recourse, VII-142 pp., 1946.
241. Lohmuller, Rev. Martin M., A.B., J.C.D., The Promulgation of Law, XII-140 pp., 1947.
242. McGrath, Rev. James, A.B., J.C.D., The Privilege of the Canon, XII-156 pp., 1946.
243. Marbach, Rev. Joseph Francis, A.B., J.C.D., Marriage Legislation for the Catholics of the Oriental Rites in the United States and Canada, XIV-314 pp., 1946.
244. Shimkus, Rev. Bernard Aloysius, A.B., J.C.L., The Determination and Transfer of Rite.
245. Smith, Rev. Vincent Michael, A.B., S.T.L., J.C.L., Ignorance Affecting Matrimonial Consent.
246. Wachtrle, Rev. Paul Anthony, A.B., J.C.L., The Baptism of the Children of Non-Catholics.
247. Crotty, Rev. Matthew M., J.C.D., The Recipient of First Holy Communion, X-142 pp., 1947.
248. Eagleton, Rev. George, J.C.D., The Quinquennial Faculties, Formula IV, XIV-199 pp., 1947 (Printed 1948).
249. Gibbons, Rev. Marion L., C.M., LL.B., J.C.D., Domicile of The Wife Unlawfully Separated from Her Husband, XIV-171 pp., 1947.
250. Kelly, Rev. Bernard M., S.T.L., J.C.D., The Functions Reserved to Pastors, XII-141 pp., 1947.
251. Kilcullen, Rev. Thomas J., LL.M., J.C.D., The Collegiate Moral Person as Party Litigant, X-150 pp., 1947.
252. Lafontaine, Rev. Germain J., W.F., J.C.D., Relations Canoniques entre Le Missionnaire et Ses Superieurs, X-117 pp., 1947.
253. Lane, Rev. Loras T., A.B., S.T.L., J.C.L., Matrimonial Procedure in the Ordinary Court of Second Instance.
254. Lover, Rev. James F., C.Ss.R., J.C.D., The Master of Novices, X-168 pp., 1947.
255. McNicholas, Rev. Timothy J., J.C.L., The Septimae Manus Witness.
256. Marositz, Rev. Joseph J., M.S.C., J.C.D., Obligations and Privileges of Religious Promoted to the Episcopal or Cardinalitial Dignities, XII-180 pp., 1947.
257. Murphy, Rev. Francis J., A.B., J.C.D., Legislative Powers of the Provincial Council, XII-158 pp., 1947.
258. O'Brien, Rev. Romaeus W., O.Carm., J.C.D., The Provincial Superior in Religious Orders of Men, X-294 pp., 1947.
259. Pfaller, Rev. Benedict A., O.S.B., J.C.L., The Ipso Facto Effected Dismissal of Religious.
260. Popek, Rev. Alphonse S., M.A., J.C.D., The Rights and Obligations of Metropolitans, XVIII-460 pp., 1947.
261. Ristuccia, Rev. Bernard J., C.M., J.C.D., Quasi-Religious, XVI-318 pp., 1947 (Printed 1949).

262. SONNTAG, REV. NATHANIEL L., O.F.M.CAP., J.C.D., Censorship of Special Classes of Books, XII-147 pp., 1947.
263. STADLER, REV. JOSEPH N., J.C.L., Frequent Holy Communion.
264. SZAL, REV. IGNATIUS J., J.C.L., The Communication of Catholics with Schismatics.
265. WAGNER, REV. URBAN S., O.F.M. CONV., J.C.D., Parochial Substitute Vicars and Supplying Priests, IX-126 pp., 1947.
266. QUINN, REV. JOSEPH, M.A., J.C.L., Documents Required for the Reception of Orders.
267. BENNINGTON, REV. JAMES CLEMENT, A.B., J.C.L., The Recipient of Confirmation.
268. BLAHER, REV. DAMIAN JOSEPH, O.F.M., A.B., J.C.L., The Ordinary Processes in Causes of Beatification and Canonization.
269. CLUNE, REV. ROBERT BELL, A.B., J.C.L., The Judicial Interrogation of the Parties.
270. COURTMANCHE, REV. BASIL F., A.B., J.C.L., The Total Simulation of Matrimonial Consent.
271. DLOUHY, REV. MAUR JOHN, O.S.B., A.B., J.C.L., The Ordination of Exempt Religious.
272. DONOVAN, REV. JOHN THOMAS, PH.B., S.T.L., J.C.D., The Clerical Obligations of Canons 138 and 140, XII-209 pp., 1948.
273. FREKING REV. FREDERICK W., A.B., S.T.B., J.C.L., The Canonical Installation of Pastors.
274. FULTON, REV. THOMAS B., J.C.L., Prenuptial Investigation.
275. GODLEY, REV. JAMES P., J.C.L., The Time and the Place for the Celebration of Mass.
276. KANE, REV. THOMAS A., A.B., B.S., J.C.D., The Jurisdiction of the Patriarchs of the Major Sees in Antiquity and in the Middle Ages, XII-111 pp., 1948 (Printed 1949).
277. KENNEDY, REV. ANDREW A., J.C.L., The Annual Pastoral Report to the Local Ordinary.
278. KONRAD, REV. JOSEPH GEORGE, J.C.L., Transfer of Religious.
279. KRESS, REV. ALPHONSE, J.C.L., Contumacy in Ecclesiastical Trials.
280. MCCARTNEY, REV. MARCELLUS ANTHONY, O.F.M., M.A., J.C.L., Faculties of Regular Confessors.
281. MCCASLIN, REV. EDWARD PATRICK, M.A., S.T.L., J.C.L., The Division of Parishes.
282. MCELROY, REV. FRANCIS J., A.B., J.C.L., The Privileges of Bishops.
283. QUINN, REV. STEPHEN, M.S.SS.T., J.C.D., Relation between the Local Ordinary and Religious of Diocesan Approval, XII-158 pp., 1948 (Printed 1949).
284. SCHNEIDER, REV. EDELHARD LOUIS, A.D.S., M.A., J.C.D., The Status of Secularized ex-Religious Clerics, X-155 pp., 1948.
285. THOMPSON, REV. CHESTER J., A.B., J.C.L., The Simple Removal from Office.

286. O'Brien, Rev. Kenneth R., A.B., J.C.D., The Nature of Support of Diocesan Priests in the United States, XVI-162 pp., 1949.
287. Metz, Rev. John E., S.T.L., J.C.D., The Recording Judge in the Ecclesiastical Collegiate Tribunal, X-130 pp., 1949.
288. Reinhardt, Rev. Marion J., S.T.L., J.C.L., The Rogatory Commission.
289. Ortega Uhink, Rev. Juan, S.J., J.C.L., *De Delicto Sollicitationis.*
290. Casey, Rev. James V., J.C.L., A Study of Canon 2222, § 1.
291. Allgeier, Rev. Joseph L., J.C.L., The Canonical Obligations of Preaching in Parish Churches.
292. Cahill, Rev. Daniel R., J.C.L., The Custody of the Holy Eucharist.
293. Carr, Rev. Aidan, O.F.M., Conv., S.T.D., J.C.L., Vocation to the Priesthood: Its Canonical Concept.
294. Knopke, Rev. Roch F., O.F.M., J.C.L., Reverential Fear in Matrimonial Cases in Asiatic Countries: Rota Cases.
295. Lavelle, Rev. Howard D., J.C.L., The Obligation of Holding Sacred Missions in Parishes.
296. Michells, Rev. Anthony B., J.C.L., The Constitutive Elements of Parishes.
297. Noone, Rev. John J., J.C.L., Nullity in Judicial Acts.
298. Sheehan, Rev. Daniel E., J.C.L., The Minister of Holy Communion.
299. Statkus, Rev. Francis J., J.C.L., The Minister of the Last Sacraments.
300. Cook, Rev. John P., J.C.L., Ecclesiastical Communities and Their Ability to Induce Legal Customs.
301. Fazzalaro, Rev. Francis J., J.C.L., The Place for the Hearing of Confessions.
302. Hannan, Rev. Philip M., J.C.L., The Canonical Concept of *Congrua Sustentatio* for the Secular Clergy.
303. Quinn, Rev. Hugh G., S.T.L., J.C.L., The Particular Penal Precept.
304. Gallagher, Rev. John F., J.C.L., The Matrimonial Impediment of Public Propriety.
305. Welsh, Rev. Thomas J., J.C.L., The Use of the Portable Altar.

www.ingramcontent.com/pod-product-compliance
Lightning Source LLC
LaVergne TN
LVHW050235080826
844660LV00012B/536
* 9 7 8 0 8 1 3 2 2 4 6 8 8 *